D0498237

Battlegrounds of Memory

Clay Lewis

BATTLE-
GROUNDS
OF
MEMORY

The University of Georgia Press

ATHENS & LONDON

✻

All rights reserved
Designed by Erin Kirk New
Set in 11 on 13 Centaur
Printed and bound by Maple-Vail Book Manufacturing Group
The paper in this book meets the guidelines for
permanence and durability of the Committee on
Production Guidelines for Book Longevity of the
Council on Library Resources.

Printed in the United States of America

02 01 00 99 98   c   5 4 3 2 1

Library of Congress Cataloging in Publication Data
Lewis, Clay.
Battlegrounds of memory / Clay Lewis.
p. cm.
ISBN 0-8203-2009-9 (alk. paper)
1. Lewis, Clay.   2. Lewis family.   3. Southern States—Biography.
4. Family violence—Southern States.   5. Intergenerational
relations—Southern States.   I. Title.
CT275.L3834A3   1998
975.04'092'2—dc21
[B]   98-4906

British Library Cataloging in Publication Data available

Several chapters of *Battlegrounds of Memory* were published in an
earlier form in the *Southern Review* and *Texas Quarterly*.

For my children

Contents

Ruxton Station

1

Manassas

6

Bearing Witness

20

Battles Without Names

33

Casualty

66

Old Wars

81

If You Don't Weaken

104

Anna's Tombstone

134

Killing Absences

151

Abiding Figures

194

Last Glimpses

220

Battlegrounds of Memory

Ruxton Station

As he left for work on Christmas Eve morning, Dad promised us he would return early from his office party. Sure he wanted to go to the carol-sing and tree lighting down at Ruxton Station with me, Mother, and my sister, Ellen. After he went out to the garage, Mother said, "I'll believe it when I see it." Ellen, who was ten, stepped closer to Mother. I was home from college; this was my last Christmas before graduating.

For years Dad had come home drunk from his office Christmas party. He started, I remember, when I was in junior high school and he was promoted to manager of a three-state region of his company. That year he had the party at our house. He got drunk, and after everybody left, Mother screamed, out of control. The next year he had the party at his office, out of Mother's sight. He told us he would be home "at the latest" by six; at ten Mother was frantic. Tight-lipped, she paced the floor. Then she beckoned me over to a front window. Under the dim street light was my father's Pontiac all right, and inside he was a shadow slumped over the wheel.

"There's your father," she told me angrily. "There he is."

"Maybe he's taking a nap."

Her voice crackled. "He's drunk. Your father is an old drunk who doesn't give a hoot in hell about us or our Christmas."

I did not answer.

When the following Christmas Eve was the same, Mother directed me to speak to Dad. He might listen to me, she said. As Christmas approached, I worked up my courage enough to blurt out to him some words I had overrehearsed. But he was his old self: "Your mother's exaggerating. You understand that as well as I do. But if it concerns you, son, okay. That's a promise." We were turning off Charles Street onto Malvern, our lane.

But that promise he did not keep, nor the following year's. Mother said I was not being forceful enough. She said if I were, I would be getting results.

Then it was Christmas Eve 1957. Dreary afternoon had slid into twilight. He was only a little late, I told myself. When it got to be time to leave, I announced to Mother and Ellen that for certain he would meet up with us down at Ruxton Station.

"Clay, your father isn't going to any old carol sing. He's going to get falling-down drunk at his office Christmas party like he always does."

"He promised."

Mother laughed.

Near dark, kids darting around, families in heavy coats clumped together, voices timid in the chill, and the big spruce hung bravely with red and green Christmas lights. In damp cold air, I smelled bourbon, sherry. Hearing a car thump over the old wooden, humpback bridge behind us, I was certain it was Dad; yes, he had promised me. Here he was. But my heart was sinking. When we walked back to our car, we did not say a word.

He was not at home, smiling, welcoming us. The house was empty—forlorn yellow-light candles in our front windows. As Mother put a special supper on the table, we did not say much. I said grace, and we started eating. When the garage door went up, we looked at each other. I bit my lip. He would be fine; he just had to work late. But my father was staggering, thick-tongued. He had trouble with his overcoat. He nearly missed getting himself into his chair at the head of the table.

"You old drunk," mother said, eyes popping with anger in the candlelight.

"So what?" he managed to say.

Forkfuls were falling in his lap, and Mother turned from him to me: "What are you going to do about this, Clay? You're the man of the house, *what are you going to do about this?*"

Vision stained red, I was up. I had him under his arms, kicked his chair away, my strength frightening me. I dragged him through the house, down the hall to their bedroom. I threw him hard on his bed. It might have stopped there, but he bounced—slid off between bed and wall. As if he had disobeyed me, a deeper fury took hold. After yanking him back up on his bed, I slammed my fist hard into his face. And again. And again. He was too drunk to defend himself. Through the crying of my little sister I heard Mother screaming: "My lord, Clay, quit! *Quit it!*"

This family violence was not mentioned the next morning as, emotions exhausted, we opened our gifts. Silently we went down to the Church of the Good Shepherd for the Christmas Day service. We did not say a word driving home, the world quiet, passing Ruxton Station, Harrington's, which was the village store, and coming up Malvern Avenue along the frozen-over creek. Among the four of us in the Dodge, silence, as guilt and rage knotted tightly with love in the dark of our minds.

✡

In the decades after World War II, Baltimore gentry lived in Ruxton in old Victorian houses. The bootstrapping middle class lived in new ramblers and ranch houses built on lots carved out of broken-up estates. Here were the smart vets rising quickly and others doing well in the postwar boom. My folks were the latter. Both of them were from the small-town South, both with no college education, both with more grit, nerve, and intelligence than was good for them. Although we lived with the Baltimore gentry, shopped with them at Harrington's, belonged with them to the Church of the Good Shepherd, and did many charitable and civic deeds with them, we would never be *of* them. They treated us nicely, of course, but we *were* johnny-come-latelies. Mother's father did not know what a cotillion was and certainly had not attended Princeton. He was born and brought up on a North Carolina tenant farm. Dad's father grew up on a Mississippi hill farm. Our money, clothes, new houses, and excellent automobiles definitely did not gentry make.

Ruxton Station was the village's heart. Shingled, with ornate barge-board eaves and a big bowed window, the once-elegant station had in a half century become shabby. It needed paint, replacement of rotted shingles and busted gutters, and serious attention devoted to overgrown shrubbery that was overwhelming this Queen Anne gem. Just south of the station, that narrow humpbacked bridge crossed the main B&O line. On the other side was Harrington's. The bridge was not only blind (too steep for cars to see head-on traffic coming in the opposite direction) but wood-planked and rickety. Crossing it or otherwise coming within sight of old Ruxton Station, Mother always exclaimed: "That's what I call beautiful! Isn't it beautiful, Clay?" If I did not want to argue, I did not answer. She enjoyed saying this to get my goat. Perhaps she did love Ruxton Station; I am not sure. But I do know that I loved standing on that trembling bridge, wood planks bouncing, blamming with passing cars, while three-engine freights slammed by on the tracks beneath my feet.

✡

The spring that followed my beating of my father, I graduated from college, and late in September I left Ruxton for Marine Corps training at Quantico, Virginia. Early that foggy morning, Dad drove me down to Ruxton Station to catch the commuter train into Baltimore. As I hauled my suitcase out of the back seat, I glanced up—noticed the big, scraggly spruce still hung with Christmas lights. Dad had come around to my side of the car.

"Good luck, son," he said, heartily shaking my hand.

"Thanks," I said, glad for his plain-speak.

Hefting my suitcase up to the train platform, I felt a cold scald in my belly—incision of a recent appendectomy almost healed. In the pearly fog commuters had spread themselves out along the platform. Behind me the Dodge's door opened, closed, and tires crunched in the gravel drive. All of a sudden I thought: Hey, my life begins right here. Since childhood in World War II, I had wanted to be a marine. Anxiety humming, I was ready to prove myself.

Ten years later, 1968, I was in Iowa City with my wife and two children. Struggling with depression, I happened on to a TV rerun of *Rebel Without a Cause*. In our upstairs apartment in an old house, lights off; outside in summer dusk children called to one another.

James Dean was halfway up the stairs. Above him, his bullying mother; below, his weak father sat on the floor. His mother wanted Dean to cover up his involvement in a death. Dean wanted to tell the truth to the police. His mother told him, "In ten years you'll never know what happened."

Still confronting her, Dean said, "Dad, stand up for me."

Dad buried his face in his hands.

Dean turned, rushed down several steps, grabbed his father, and with rage stood him up, then threw him to the floor, started choking him.

Mother screamed: "You want to kill your own father!"

Again it is Christmas 1957, and I am weeping, an old scream of rage and despair caught in my throat.

✡

This book, which I have labored on for more than twenty years, attempts to understand the causes and consequences of that Christmas Eve forty years ago. That few minutes, so distinctly American, has opened like Proust's madeleine. I have found roots in the generations of my family, which is southern. I have seen the ugly scars of history that in hundreds of ways mark us all—the depression, the Civil War, the busted dreams of frontier America, the great shift from country to city, the surge of World War II, and the cold war. Absolution for my sins, which I have fervently sought (and continue to seek), I have not found. Instead, I have discovered life-deep complicity in a heritage of loss, violence, and passion. And with these, heart-filling Grace. In the awful persistence of deep patterns of inter-generational violence, I have found amazing sensitivity and what I believe to be the strongest possible testament to the force of love in human affairs.

Obviously, the simple story of Christmas Eve 1957 has expanded to include not only my life, in greatest extent and depth, but what I hope is a large portion of the life you and I share together in this great nation. I have looked back, not out of virtue, or even curiosity, but because I could not do otherwise. My mother and father fled their small-town southern pasts in the 1920s and 1930s for the bright promise of the federal city, Washington. In much of my life, and certainly in this book, I have strived to return to, and understand, what they with such vigor attempted to leave behind. And of course could not.

Ruxton Station was torn down fifteen years ago, the property sold so that little town houses could be built. Absent now, lost, but I remember. In memory its presence remains.

Manassas

The nighttime was cold, I remember. As my father parked the Plymouth, I looked out the back side window at the house where we once had lived. Lights were on but the shades were drawn down; now another family lived there. Across the street was Aunt Dessie's. Her porch light was on to welcome us, and her living room was lighted up. Aunt Dessie's boys, Bill and Jim, stepped out onto the porch. They were both in high school. Hands in pockets, they grinned, talked fast. They were eager to join up, to fight in the war.

As we went up the steps, Dad said, "Well, I guess this war'll have enough fighting to go around."

Mother teased, "How could you boys be old enough to fight in a war?"

Bill and Jim hopped with the cold.

It was the night President Roosevelt declared war, December 8, 1941. We had driven from our house in a new subdivision called Hillwood back to old Takoma Park. Aunt Dessie was Mother's aunt, my great-aunt. Her sister was Mother's mother, who had died long before I was born. Aunt Dessie had taken care of me when Mother worked downtown. You could tell she loved you.

In her living room radiators sang and the big Philco was on. A kind-hearted person, tonight Aunt Dessie was peeved, mouth drawn tight, brown eyes gleaming behind her glasses. Once she had told me about her father, who fought with General Lee in many great battles of the Civil War. Paying attention to her, I was on the hardwood floor next to the living-room rug with my lead soldiers. Her father had been wounded, captured by Yankees, and sent to a Yankee prison where hundreds died of cold. "You boys all think war is the be-all-and-end-all," Aunt Dessie had said. "You won't listen to anything else!" When she had discovered me looking at *Life* pictures of soldiers, tanks, and diving airplanes, she had scolded me for being like all men and boys. Tonight, though, she said just a brisk hello.

Of Roosevelt's great speech declaring war I remember nothing. As we sat around their Philco, Aunt Dessie's eyes burned, Uncle Walter was, as usual, cheerful, Dad looked a little serious, Mother was enjoying herself, and Jim and Bill fidgeted, grinned.

Driving home later Dad said, laughing, that if the U.S. Army wanted him, they could come and get him. I knew he was not kidding. He had spent many years in the army. His uniforms, sergeant stripes on the sleeves, were in a trunk in our basement. He was a little old, thirty-five, but as I later told him, lots of men his age got into the war. He also had a job vital to the war effort—sending combat X-ray machines to the military. I labored throughout the war not to hold against him his lack of enthusiasm for fighting Nazis and Japs.

We played war in Sligo Creek woods ("I got you! You're dead! *You're dead!*"), and in my street we learned marching and the manual of arms with our almost exact Springfield rifles (no toy M1s yet). We practiced identifying friendly and enemy planes, and with lightning speed named planes entering our little patch of sky. When Mr. Denison, our neighbor-hood air raid warden, came to our front door in his World War I helmet, I saw to it that we were totally blacked out—no light escaping to tell German bombardiers where we were. At school, at least once a month, we spent a morning of air raid drill sitting in the halls—away from shattering glass windows—and singing patriotic songs. We watched for signs of hoarders in our neighborhood. We were alert for spies.

But we knew then it was all play, and we yearned for the fire of World War II to touch our neighborhood. Fathers served in the army, Air Corps, and Coast Guard, and Jimmy and Johnny Hill's big brother was a navy carrier pilot. Dad's Oklahoma cousin, Homer, spent a weekend with us on his way to Patton's Third Army; we wrote him V-mail letters, but his rare letters back just told of being scared. Mother's old boss, a captain who had lived in Takoma Park also, got his leg torn up by strafing Stukkas in North Africa; his letters from hospitals were very short. And there was my fourth-grade teacher, Mrs. Schmidt, who while I was in her class learned a third son had been killed in combat. When for as long as half an hour she stared blankly out windows rattling in winter wind, her eyes red-swollen but dry of tears, the class sat quietly waiting for her attention to return to us. (Once in the supply room I heard her sighing under her breath, "My babies, my babies.") My friends and I knew where all the gold stars were hung in front windows in Takoma Park; riding our bikes, we searched them out. While we watched *Movietone News* and listened to 6 P.M. radio news about our triumphant forces around the world, we were stuck with collecting tinfoil and scrap metal, ration stamps, and three nights a week of Spam for supper.

When Mother took me sightseeing in downtown Washington, which was once a week in wartime summers, she said it was so that I would "know what we're fighting for." This meant that we wanted to keep the Germans and Japs away from our monuments and museums, I guessed. I kept quiet about not exactly understanding. Downtown on bustling streets, at government buildings with uniforms everywhere, even at museums, real war was much closer.

We left early, summer dew still on lawns. The little shuttle bus got us inside the District of Columbia, where we transferred to a big downtown bus. Bus almost empty, Mother sat next to me with her purse on her knees, quiet with her thoughts. Overarching elms along New Hampshire Avenue hung limp in morning humidity, but when our bus sped by, its air-swash wildly stirred them. We passed blocks of row houses with faded green-and-white-striped awnings, edges scalloped, and on porches under them kids lazed on gliders and on porch chairs bulky mothers talked. At the Soldiers' Home cemetery a spiked black-iron fence rushed past; behind it military rows of white tombstones raced past too. (My father and my uncles, Mother's brothers, once dared run a midnight footrace through that cemetery. On those same spikes I was seeing, they had ripped pant legs. This high-old-time family story happened before I was born, but I loved remembering it as we rode past.) Then Griffith Stadium, where the Senators played and where I had seen the one-armed Saint Louis Browns outfielder. From a nearby bakery, came the sweet smell of baking bread. Then into downtown with hustling-and-bustling military and cheerful hurry-hurry of everybody. Never did I fail to notice on top of several department stores sandbagged antiaircraft batteries to protect us from Nazi bombers. Here was some real wartime danger.

Mother loved the National Gallery of Art (she called it the Mellon), but I could not get enough of the Smithsonian Castle. In a hut out back there was a Spad, from World War I, and in the main building hung high in steel girders was the sleek *Winnie Mae*, which had flown around the world. And there was a huge, black-gleaming firearm collection. And exhibits of old army uniforms from every U.S. war. It was not the things that pulled me; it was what they connected me to—great deeds, fire, terrible battle. On every visit to the Smithsonian, I climbed a back balcony to see Traveler, Robert E. Lee's actual horse in a glass case. He was dapple gray, his big, shiny eyes almost alive. What raging battles and exploits had he actually been in? Mother followed me, ambling along without much interest, searching for benches on which to rest her weary bones.

After a couple of weeks of having things my way, I got nervous. The National Gallery, glossy marble, pictures and statues, I did not like. But to please Mother I told her the Mellon was where I wanted to go that week. As I sped by Fra Angelicos, Vermeers, Cézannes, Van Goghs, Mother chose a single painting, usually Rembrandt's darks and lights, sat down, and looked beamingly at it. When my circling routes brought me back to her, she still was content, happy in her heart with her picture. I did not try to understand. In the gallery's rotunda, with its round of black marble columns and circular splashing fountain, speedy bronze Mercury atop it, she did the same—content just to be there inside the splashing music.

Our lunch we had packed, the usual Spam and peanut-butter-and-jelly sandwiches. In elm shade on the Mall we spread our picnic. We talked little—gazing idly out into blazing summer sunlight. After lunch mother got livelier. Walking up to F Street, we went to the Capitol Theater for an afternoon movie and live stage show—comics or jugglers and always a beautiful singing lady and a sing-a-long organ. This part of our excursions was not my favorite. Movies, sure—but hot afternoons spent in dark, air-cooled theaters touched off sure-fire headaches when we stepped from that dim, heavily decorated lobby (modeled after some French palace) onto afternoon sidewalks blazing with sun. And stage shows upset me as much as nightmares; I still can't say why. (The same was true of cartoon movies: *Bre'r Rabbit*, even *Snow White*, especially *Fantasia*.) But, as we said then, I just had to grin and bear it. Her pleasure was the movie and stage show.

✿

Every summer during World War II, Mother had us escape Washington's heat and humidity for a week at old Orkney Springs Hotel down in the Shenandoah. (With our A gas-rationing sticker, we could not go much farther.) On the way down old Route 29, she worked on Dad to stop at the Manassas battlefields, which we passed right through. But always racing the clock, he would not do it. At fifty-five miles per hour, Mother did her best to read clusters of historical markers. "Grandpa fought here," she exclaimed with some exasperation. Dad had a Mississippi grandfather who also fought in the Civil War, but that was Out West, and even if it had been Manassas, I doubt he would have touched the Plymouth's brake pedal.

Our room at Orkney was in the annex, which had been a hospital for Confederate soldiers during the Civil War. The main hotel building, put up in the 1870s, was huge, a wooden, porch-circled, gingerbreaded, four-story Victorian affair that Mother loved (as much as, later, Ruxton Station). On its oak-shaded porches, she played bridge all afternoon with the ladies of Richmond and Norfolk. Twice a day Dad went off to play the hilly nine-hole golf course. At meals he told us about seeing deer, raccoons, and rabbits on the fairways. And about the latest funny incident on a clifflike par-three that was dangerous to life and limb. I played tag with kids on the porches—scowls, finger wagging, rattly old voices calling after us and disappearing into the thunder of our running feet. And rode Orkney horses hard at full gallop up and down mountain valleys. And studied soldiers. One was young, with a chest full of ribbons, a lieutenant colonel in the Air Corps who had just completed twenty-five bombing missions in England. He was here on his honeymoon but would soon return to his squadron in England. He did not look heroic; his gray eyes constantly moved. Passing on the porches one morning, he nodded hello and stopped.

"Saw you yesterday. You looked like you belonged on that horse," he said.

"Thanks," I got out. "My dad's a better rider than I am."

He laughed. "Your name's Clay?" He stuck out his hand and I shook it. "Mine's Bob."

"Nice to meet you." Tell me what it is like in the Flying Fortresses. Are you afraid you'll be killed? But I didn't get out a word. I didn't wash my hand for several days.

Although sheets were starched and ironed, mattresses smelled of mildew. After I had gone to bed, Mother and Dad went over to the main hotel, up to the fourth floor ballroom, where there was a nightly dance with a little orchestra. From up there I heard peppy clarinet and saxophone music. Along the porch outside our room, footsteps thunked hollowly. Shadows suddenly slid over the wall of our room. I heard snatches of conversation, mixed with music, leaves breeze-chattering, that I did not understand. Pulling blankets up close to my ears, I rolled toward the wall. I thought my mattress might have blood stains from wounded Confederates. A man lying exactly where I was lying might have yelled out in pain. Or if he was brave, bit his lip, suffered in silence.

✫

I got to Manassas before Mother did. My best friend in our Takoma Park neighborhood was named Byrd, and his family, both sides, were from the town of Manassas. (Like my folks, his had moved out of small southern towns to Washington's bright promise.) With World War II going hard, we could not go "down home" to North Carolina where mother's father, my grandfather, lived. Only twenty-five miles away, Manassas was a short trip, so my friend often visited his grandparents there. When he returned, he had good stories about the place his father had grown up in—about the fun he had there. And about the stuff from the Civil War you could just pick up out in the woods of the battlefield: canteens, rifles, belt buckles, hundreds of minié balls. He had shown some to me.

In Manassas I spent my first night away from home.

It was the middle of winter. His grandfather's house was at one end of Main Street, big and with wide porches, but inside, chilly and full of shadows and smelling of musty rugs. In the high-ceilinged rooms voices had shadow-echoes; I couldn't quite understand what was being said to me.

My friend had told me about train tracks that ran along the bottom of his grandfather's backyard. Along there huge locomotives pulled hundred-car freights at full speed. Sometimes the engineers waved. Other times he sat real close to the tracks when the locomotives went by. Almost sick in the old house, I wanted to test my courage with the locomotives.

The backyard was charcoal twilight; I half thought I was dreaming. At the bottom of the railroad cut, we went up to the track and—figuring closely—sat down on crushed rocks into which railroad ties had been sunk. It was chilly; my heart beat fast; we didn't talk. There was a clear picture in my mind of how the locomotive would appear coming around the bend. The actual locomotive blew that picture into a thousand pieces when it was suddenly there, completely enormous, its dark rushing iron filling the air. I was gathered into it and a moment later was surprised to find myself still sitting by the tracks with my friend, freight cars going clickety-clack, clickety-clack as they went by. We did not move until all had passed, and then, still quiet, we got up to go up the embankment. The cold was blue-gray; the kudzu leaves, as we passed through them, shivered and trembled like snake scales. The stories my friend had told me about the trains, about how much fun it was, were untrue. He had done it (I did not doubt that), but it was not fun—had not been the way he told it.

We were going up the slope of the backyard, and his grandfather's house was eaves, gables, shadows, roof lines cutting up into twilight sky. Ahead of me my friend's shoulders rolled familiarly, but he was a flat shadow, a darkness in the twilight, and this mixture of familiarity and strangeness made chills in a million pinpricks leap up my back. In the house, in the kitchen full of people talking happily, their voices lost in high-ceiling echoes, my chills continued and I clinched my jaws tight and I tried to fix my attention on a pot on the stove. But a little vapor was boiling off it, and when I noticed this the nightmare sensations rushed. I fixed my attention on a doorknob, but immediately it looked exactly like an egg.

At some point we were taken out to my friend's aunt's house where we would spend the night. The aunt lived in the country, a few miles out from Manassas. In flat fields her farmhouse sat by itself at the bottom of a huge dark ocean. Where the Manassas battlefields were I did not know. The aunt's bright, musical voice was nice. In the farmhouse kitchen she fussed over me, asked if I was hungry, asked if I missed my folks. No, no. The kitchen heat was fierce and touched my face. We were taken upstairs to an ice-cold bedroom. A single bulb, dangling from the ceiling, fizzed in the hollow room. My clothes I did not want to take off. My friend, who had been unusually quiet, began to undress and talk about what we would do the next day. I wanted to go home. Taking off my clothes, my underwear, chilly air rushed into my body's warm places. My goose bumps made me ashamed. When my friend stood up on the bed to turn off the light, the bed tossed and pitched with him, with me. The dark was immediate, complete—darker than I had ever seen. The old iron bed smelled of rust. It screeched as I squirmed for a warm hollow. The dark roared like wind. My friend's breathing slowed.

I woke to grey dawn and saw my breath. Moving slowly not to jounce the bed and wake my friend, I got up—floor planks a cold shock. At the window I looked down on a yard that was a mess of frozen mud ruts, wheel rims, junked cars; violence, this its consequence. Frost silvered everything. The house was silent, no noise at all, and out beyond the yard the fields of stubble corn glimmered with frost, too, and still farther out, the crowns of distant trees glittered. My forehead was pressed against the windowpane, its cold half-moon. Nothing would be the same—this calm and sorrowful. My home, too, would not be the same.

On the way back to Washington, my friend's father drove us through the Manassas battlefields. He told of finding in a half-washed-out grave in a tree line a boy's skeleton, some Confederate buttons, a Confederate belt buckle. I was quiet, and so was my friend. When he stopped the car to ask if we wanted to get out, see what we could find, we both shook our heads no. We weren't enthusiastic. My friend's father drove us home to Takoma Park.

✡

Mother considered herself a rebel in her family, but she loved to go home to North Carolina. We could not go during most of World War II, with trains crowded and gas rationed. But in 1945 Mother decided to chance the train with me. Out front of Union Station on the plaza, fountains splashed cool in the hot evening. Inside the station's high vaults, train announcements reverberated, echoed, but Mother said she understood every word and laughed at my worrying. On high-backed benches soldiers and marines, ribbons above their pockets, waited for their trains. They had all just returned from heroic battles, I was sure. Everybody stepped quickly, some half running, and soon we were hurrying along with them to our train, going someplace, too. The trains smelled of hot, steam-wet iron. My father shook my hand, as if I were a man, and told me to take care of Mother. I helped her up the thunking metal steps.

Coming down those steps the next morning, I was on hot, sun-dazzled rock at trackside. Instead of a bustling platform, a grand station, there were weeds, a scrubby field, forlornly screeching crickets, and the backyards of old-looking houses. We had made a terrible mistake, I was sure. But Mother told me the conductor had stopped the train here in the East Spencer railroad yards so we could walk to her father's house instead of going into Salisbury and paying for a taxi. Laughing with her success, she told me to pick up the suitcase as she took off at a good clip toward the old houses. I was sure everybody on the train was laughing at us. Sun was hot on my head, my shirt, burned the back of my neck, and crossing the field I remembered the splashing music of the fountains at Union Station.

In a happy, excited voice Mother pointed to the house, my grandfather's, where she was born and grew up. We came around the back of a small barn. A pale-eyed goat glared at us and a rooster squawked, flapped his wings, stirred dust up in the wired-in chicken coop. The hens went on pecking. Mother called the outhouse a chicksales. We plunged through a gap in bushes taller than she was (lilacs, blossoms already gone) and into a nice grassy backyard. My grandfather was out of the kitchen, across the back porch, down the steps, before I got a good look at him. Wiry, a quick man with a lopsided grin. His pug face was a few inches from my face. In his glinting wire-rim glasses I saw myself, murky, and his sharp, grinning blue eyes. On his forehead was an ugly black scar. He smelled of lye soap, of coffee, of bleach. His hands strong, he tossed me in the air, hugged me hard, and bouncing around the yard with me, said: "Well hey-here! Hey-here! Betty's boy come all the way down from Washington to see me!" The back porch smelled of rotted wood from the sloshing-over of wash pans. Soapy water was on the ground where, I figured later, the wash pans had been tossed. My grandfather's strangeness frightened me, and while he was holding me tightly, singsong voice going on, I missed my father.

My grandfather made me eat a big bowl of homemade peach ice cream that did not taste at all like the ice cream we bought at Highs in Takoma Park. He teased Mother, spanked her on the backside; when he got rough she ran like a child. When he noticed me being quiet, he called me to him, stood me between his knees, and demanded to know the reason for my silence. I could not tell him; I did not know.

On tracks back of his house trains chugged, whistled, banged with the coupling of cars, all night too, and this commotion boiled into my dreams in the high-ceilinged bedroom I shared with Mother. The ringing noise of the chamber pot I hated as much as wet speargrass along the path to the outhouse's ultimate dark. On Saturdays in the sunny backyard I had to take baths naked in a galvanized tub. The yard was screened with lilacs, but that was not good enough. Running full speed out the kitchen screen door, I plunged into the soapy tub—mortified, publicly shamed—and my grandfather, laughing hard, set to work scrubbing me with a brush, laughing at my ouches and cries.

Up the street were kids I played with. (Mother had grown up with their mother and father.) In the scrubby field back of the houses we raced soapbox scooters on narrow paths. Mine turned over; I wasn't expert. I thought of the creek at home—around rocks, its arrows and ripples; water sliding coolly, easily, under dappled shade; playing down there, losing ourselves, on hot afternoons like these.

My grandfather got me interested in his goats. One evening before supper he asked if I wanted to ride one. "Yes sir," I said, but then I noticed the twinkle in his eyes. He put me up on a big white billy goat, and almost before he had let go, it tossed me hard up against the shed. My head and my pride were hurt, but he laughed all the way back to the house, and then had a high time telling Mother. She laughed and said of the knot on the side of my head, "Well, if that's the worst thing that happens to you, you'll have a fortunate life." How different she was here opened a nightmare I fought to keep away.

One cool, cloudy afternoon she took me about a mile down the road from her house to show me a huge old oak tree. In a solemn voice she told me of being brought here when she was about my age. She was told that a black man had raped a white woman. The men of East Spencer had got their shotguns and found the man. Then they found his wife and three children. Black people must be taught a lesson they would not forget. The black man and his wife and children were forced to climb up into this oak tree. The men tied ropes around all of their necks—other ends knotted to thick branches. Beginning with the children, the men fired shotguns at the heels of the black people, made them jump, ropes snapping tight. Flashing of the muzzle blast up in the limbs of this dark tree, the kid stung, leaping, soon jerking and snapping at rope's end among thrashing limbs, until, neck stretched and crooked, the kid hung there quietly. The man and his wife crying, pleading. And then it was her turn. And then only he was left and the men with the shotguns climbed up to where they would shoot his heels. Dying for him now better than going on living. This story Mother told me took hold of my mind. It was there with railroad-yard crash at night and my grandfather's ornery country humor and the close-up sight of his ugly black scars, and there, too, awake or dreaming, was the ache of missing my own father. The bedroom I shared with Mother smelled old.

✻

Back home I told and retold the story of that lynching. The kids got tired of it, but I kept on because I believed that telling would keep this nightmare inside my story. And if it did break out into daylight, my being the teller would mean that such things did not happen to me or my mother and dad. Night lynchings in old oaks happened only to other people, not us. Mother assured me this terrible thing never happened to decent families, but with a nine-year-old's clearer logic, I knew that decent had nothing to do with it. If it happened, it could happen to anybody, to my family, me included.

Granddaddy Kenerly's laugh sounded like a knife on whetstone. Once he got me between his knees, holding my shoulders, looked hard into my eyes and said: "You ain't goin' to be a Yankee, are you, Clay? *No grandson of mine is goin' to be a damn Yankee, is he?*"

"No, sir," I said.

"They ain't whipped us long as we don't yell 'Uncle!,' ain't that the truth?" His lips were skinned back from his teeth. His mouth was lopsided, and his eyes gleamed.

"Yes, sir."

✻

The next summer, June 1946, my father went with us to North Carolina. Granddaddy Kenerly had retired from the Southern Shops to a farm not far from the tenant farm where he grew up. He had an old plow horse that I could gallop.

One lavender evening my grandfather plowed a little field with a mule, Dad and I watching. Dad called, asked if he could try plowing for old times' sake. (I guessed he meant he had plowed as a kid in Oklahoma.) My grandfather said sure; Dad put the plow line over one shoulder, under the other arm, and called softly to the horse. He came up, and as well as my grandfather Dad ran a straight row down the field, the plow blade singing in the dry dirt, chinking rocks, Dad walking the furrows almost as loose-hipped. It was getting dark. I begged them both to let me try, and when there were only a few rows left, my grandfather gave in. I got behind the tall plow, arms up and spread to reach work-smooth handles. They fixed the plow line for me. My grandfather started the horse, but I could not keep the plow blade in the dry earth. It kept coming up, bouncing along the ground, would not scour. One of them (I did not know which) came in behind me, and halfway up the unplowed row, hands came over my hands on the plow handles, pushed down hard, mine aching, until the plow blade—a sliver cutting phantom in the dirt in front of me—disappeared into earth and began its deep song again. When the pressure of the hands lifted, the plow blade came up, began to bounce again. My lack of strength made me ashamed. When the rows were finished the sky was deep violet and the earth was dark. Mother, I now recall, had gone into town with her stepmother. With no lamps lighted, the house was as dark as the earth.

✿

One morning a few days later my grandfather lent Dad an old pair of bleached overalls. In them Dad did not look like Dad. They went down to the barn, to the pen where my grandfather kept his little shoat. I had been carrying panfuls of scraps and garbage ("slops") to the shoat every evening after supper; I usually tarried to watch it root its nose around in the mess I had dumped into the pen—this at the same time awful and funny.

My grandfather had carried his old .22 rifle down from the house, but he propped it against the pen, and grinning in a funny way, climbed over the side of the pen, eased himself inside with the shoat. I did not know what was going to happen. The shoat rooted around in some corn. Dad, grinning himself a little oddly, climbed into the pen with my grandfather and the shoat. Then my grandfather pulled something out of the hammer pocket on the leg of his overalls. He opened a big-bladed knife. He gave the knife to my father, said something I didn't catch. I remember the planks of the pen, how worn-smooth they were, how they gleamed in the sun. My grandfather straddled the shoat, scissored it with his legs, then lifted it—now terrific squealing, twisting—held it between his knees, while he grabbed up the front quarters with the crook of his arm. His face I could not see. My father stepped beside him, spread his left hand, lifted the jaw of the shoat, exposing bristled pale tight skin. I saw Dad's face for a second: he was grinning. He laid the sharp tip end of the blade into the tight throat skin, sank it deep, then raced the blade to open a quick deep smile all the way across the shoat's tight-stretched throat. For a second the grin did not fill with blood. I prayed it wouldn't. Then blood welled up, filled the slash—shocked me with its beautiful blue-red same as mine. Squealing went down into a gurgle as my grandfather dropped his grip and the shoat started to kick and thrash away its life in the dirt of the pen, spilling and throwing blood everywhere. At last he went on his side, gurgling dropped to a bubbling wheeze. Then his side caked with dirt and blood did not rise, did not fall.

Both of them—their legs, arms, hands, their bellies, groins splashed, stuttered with blood. They stared down at the shoat they had killed. It did not breathe, but still they looked. Then my grandfather took the knife, toed the shoat onto its back, and kneeling, quickly slashed out the shoat's testicles—lifted them to show Dad.

I was running up the lane to the house. I knocked through the kitchen screen door and went right by Mother and her stepmother, who were rolling out pale dough for biscuits, cutting it with overturned glasses. I did not stop until I was upstairs, the bedroom door closed (there was no lock), the green shade drawn. Pinpricks of sunlight came through the old shade, shimmered on the floor. The bedroom smelled of the slop jar, which I had forgotten to empty. When I lay down on the bed, the springs cried out, and no matter how fast or hard I breathed, I could not catch my breath, get enough air, stop panting in that hot room without a bit of breeze.

First Mother and then Dad (washed, changed out of his bloody overalls) came up to ask what was wrong. Nothing, I told them. They asked if I planned to help get ready for the big family reunion barbecue that night.

My grandfather wanted me to set up the sawhorses, put planks on them to be used as tables.

Hating my weakness, I told them I wanted to go home. They smiled, said I had to get myself out of the dumps to enjoy the barbecue and visit with fifty relations who were coming this evening. I said I would be down to help in a little bit. It was Dad who told me I should not let the slaughter of that little shoat get me down. It happened all the time, he said. I told him yes, I understood. He left, softly closing the door behind him.

I was alone in the green, underwater light, and again having trouble breathing. I think I eventually fell asleep and took a sweaty nap.

I did set up the sawhorse tables in the yard. That evening, under the oaks—roots making the sawhorse tables wobble, making it hard for old people to walk—I ate a little barbecue. Everybody said it was some of the best they had ever eaten.

✡

That reunion was the last time I saw my grandfather alive. A year or two later, he was driving his horse and wagon for fun through a rocky pasture, got bounced out, broke his hip. A week later he died of complications. For the funeral he was laid out in the parlor of the farmhouse. He and the coffin and the sick-sweet flowers did not look as if they belonged there. In his Sunday suit, down in all that white satin, my grandfather didn't look like himself. He was so quiet and still, so pleasant looking. On his forehead I found the black scar, and I made out the pug face, which did seem different, I realized, because he did not need his glasses anymore. The thick veins in the backs of his hands were his.

As the coffin was closed, I was on the front porch with neighbor men who had an all-night wake. My grandfather's second wife wailed. I hear the sound still, rising high and falling and then lifting high again. Shivers rippled up my backbone. I saw the giant oak in the side yard, its huge gnarled limbs and mottles of shimmering green shade and sunlight.

Bearing Witness

After our 1945 trip to North Carolina, we took a second trip home. This time it was way out to Oklahoma, where Dad grew up. When we heard of the Lewis family reunion, he right away told us he just could not spare the time off from work. Then he told us we could not afford it. Then that our old 1939 Plymouth would never make it. Although Mother had been out to Oklahoma and had been treated badly by Dad's family ("They put on airs and lorded it over me"), she argued down each of Dad's objections. She said that a Lewis family reunion gave the boy a chance to meet, in one fell swoop, his grandparents, uncles and aunts, great-uncles and -aunts, and cousins. Even as a nine-year-old, I knew Mother was drawn to what resisted her most.

The prospect of seeing *actual places* from Dad's stories, which I had to beg him for, trembled in my chest. A creek pool where he saved a friend from drowning. The prairies where he rode bareback with his friend Sam, a Choctaw, sometimes taking shotguns and shooting huge jackrabbits flushed from under horses' galloping hooves and running away in arcs. Killing a good many, he said, leaving them where they dropped. The exact ground where his house stood when he was born. (A sepia picture showed him on the front porch, age four, grinning shyly, squinting in bright sunlight. Long ago the house burned to the ground.) And the storefront of his father's grocery, where he had swiped candy. And his grandfather's bank.

Dad himself had watched this tough-as-nails grandfather blaze away with his rifle at men robbing his bank, horses milling around, they firing back, then mounting, still firing, riding off down the street at a gallop, just as in western movies. His Oklahoma stories I told and retold to kids in our neighborhood. Down in our basement in a trunk I had seen his birth certificate, 1906, saying INDIAN TERRITORY.

As the day to leave drew nearer, I was beside myself with excitement. Dad got solemn.

He drove the Plymouth hard. He did not want to get to Oklahoma as much as he plain wanted to drive hard and fast. He squinted into bright hazy sunlight. Nothing was funny. Mother told him he was crazy for trying to drive so far in a single day. He pushed harder, passed a lot, had close calls—Mother gasping, Dad jerking the wheel. The back seat was my nest.

Next day in Tennessee we hit detours that sent us on gravel roads winding up and down mountains. Dad's lips tightened. Mother wanted to stop, look at the views, but Dad told her heck no and that we were making up for lost time. Mottles of shade and sunlight skimmed up the hood and fenders, filled the interior, racing over us all, then were out in swirling gray dust that went as fast as we did. When we passed cars going the other way, dusty green leaves switched by our car windows. I forgot where we were, where we were going. In rushing leafy green sunlight, drowning. I slept. When we thumped back up on the main highway, Dad drove faster. He passed so close I saw the chrome teeth of oncoming grills before he snatched us, horns blowing, back into our lane. Mother chewed the inside of her cheek. Dad cocked his head to listen to a new clinking rattle in the Plymouth's engine. Mother looked at Dad. Hot wind roared in the car.

The old Plymouth started losing power on hills, even little ones, and Dad repeated that he was sure we could make Memphis. He was real sure of that. The sky turned slate gray. Going up a hill, rattles changed to car-shaking knocks. In Dad's hands the steering wheel shook. He clicked off the ignition, but our Plymouth still shook as it coasted over the hill's crest, smoke streaming out from under the hood, by windows. The shaking got worse. We coasted into a crossroads country store. When Dad braked, the hood blew off, its great black wings flapping and clattering as it tumbled over the fender.

When Dad began to laugh, so did Mother. Out the windshield I saw, coming off the engine, thick grey boiling smoke. Now they were both laughing hard, throwing open doors, tumbling out. Tears boiled in my chest. Throwing myself down on the back seat, I buried my face.

Mother yelled, "Get out, Clay! Get out of there!"

Dad's hand grabbed my leg, pulled me, and he picked me up and carried me at a half run away from the smoking car. He was still laughing; Dad had stopped being Dad. Then he was back at the car, the trunk open, pitching boxes, suitcases, golf clubs out as fast and as far as he could. He had packed and repacked the trunk four times before we left the curb in front of our house in Takoma Park. Now it was all being pitched in every direction, landing in the dirt driveway of the crossroads store. The smoke still roiled out of the engine, rose up into the twilight sky, disappeared. I did not want to cry. Mother put her arm around me, but I angrily shrugged it off.

The man who ran the store had thick suspenders. He helped Dad collect stuff from the trunk and put it into a pile out in the driveway. The man's wife took Mother and me inside the little store, which was a cave of thick, warm, unfamiliar smells. Mother talked easily with the lady, just as Dad talked with the man outside. Their voices were different, slower. My stomach felt sick. The lady pulled a dripping cold Nehi out of the soft-drink cooler. Handing me the cold bottle, she said I was their guest until the Greyhound bus arrived. The wet, icy bottle in my hand, sick chills went up my spine, prickled in my scalp.

Mother and the lady went out front, talking happily. The screen door tapped closed. Light in the store was shellac colored, and hanging down from the ceiling dark were flypaper snake-curls. Shelves packed with everything went up, disappeared into the same dark. I was still holding the unopened Nehi. I slid it, *chinking*, back into the cooler's icy black water.

Out front in the dark, the four of them were sitting. The cane-bottom chairs creaked. Their voices murmured, and sometimes I could not tell whose was whose. I slipped out the wide screen door, not letting it slap-tap. I saw four silhouettes, light coming through the window behind them, over their shoulders, around their heads, and after a couple of moments, I figured out who was who. The air was cooler, not as strange and close as inside. The silhouette of the dead Plymouth at the edge of the driveway was falling into the dark. I felt some tears, but now there was anger too.

The lady went into the store, turned off the light, returned. She said the dark would not attract bugs. I sat off to myself on an upended soft-drink case. Voices were just there in the dark, coming from nowhere, and when I recognized Mother's or Dad's, it was slow, lolling softly on the words, barely theirs. I heard cars on the highway before the side-cast of their headlights picked out of the dark the store, gas pumps, the four of them, me, rolling past and returning us to dark.

What was happening should not be happening. Mother and Dad were not acting like themselves. We had missed some good living by being up north in a city, he said. Any day the country was better than the city rat race. He said he was from the country and so was Betty (Mother), and that they were taking the boy over there out to see his family in Oklahoma now that the war was over and they could travel again.

When the Greyhound came, Mother and Dad said they were real sorry to leave, that we would try to stop by on the way home. They thanked the Tennessee people for their hospitality. When I asked Dad if we would see our car again, he laughed. He said no, he hoped not. Leaving our old Plymouth at the crossroads store seemed wrong. Why was Dad laughing? As the Greyhound pulled away with us, I looked back for our Plymouth. It was too dark, and my reflection in the bus window got in the way.

Years ago, but really just that morning in Knoxville, Dad told me of the beautiful lobby fountain at the Peabody Hotel in Memphis. Seeing it now for myself, I thought it was okay, but not as spectacular as I had imagined. Not by a long shot as mighty as the fountains at Union Station. Not the Mellon's sweet music. This late at night, the only guest in the Peabody lobby was a heavy, waddling lady who carried a Pekingese dog. When she put her ugly dog down over by the elevator, he yipped—shrill, splatter-echoing off the lobby's marble. When she picked him up, he instantly stopped, began happily panting. I wanted to run and punch her in her big stomach. I wanted to seize the Pekingese, push its head under the water of the fountain, drown him, watch his life thrash away. These wild urges frightened me.

Our hot room did not bother Mother and Dad. The bellman put up my cot under the window. After he left, Mother went into the bathroom.

Facing into the corner, I took off my shorts, dropped my underwear, pulled on my pajamas. As Dad undressed too, he told me we would try to buy another car in the morning, and if we could not, we would just take the train on out to Oklahoma. He was watching me as he talked and undressed. He was naked over by the double bed, but I did not look up. He stepped around the end of the bed, rooted in the suitcase. He was not rushing. He found his pajamas and stepped into them, not turning away at all. My cheeks and ears burned with embarrassment. While I folded my clothes on a chair, he just left his in a stomped-down pile by the bed. When Mother came out, she looked right at Dad's pile on the floor, did not say a word. Talking happily about meeting life's little adversities, she got into bed. As Dad got into the other side of the double bed, she said I should wash off with a cool washrag. I told her I did not want to. Dad told me to do what Mother had told me to do. I did.

The room was dark when I came out. Up in the ceiling shadows, an overhead fan clicked slowly but stirred little air. Mother and Dad were quiet. Damp cool on my face and arms was soon dry. Air heavy, close, sheets soon warm. Out the window and across the street, about as high as we were, was a giant illuminated clock face. Reading its Roman numerals— wasn't sure. Keep looking at the clock, I told myself, until it was morning, time to get up. Do not fall asleep, *just don't*. The snarling, needle-toothed dogs of nightmares will tear you to pieces. I wished the lighted clock did not look, to me, like a beautiful and new-risen moon.

I woke with a jolt, only then knowing I had been asleep. Light from the bathroom cut across my legs, and inside in eye-achy light was Mother, the shoulder of her peach nightgown. The door closed, room dark again, but under it a slit of light. No breeze from the turning ceiling fan. The water tap in the bathroom was running, a snap popped. Something chinked against the sink, then drain's cool whisper-song. Hearing these, I remembered bed sounds boiling with my dream's snapping dogs, gray smoke rising, road signs I could not read, terrible sensations of falling when there is no bottom. My skin was either too hot or too cold, I could not tell which. Crying welled up. Under the bathroom door the light went off. Mother's nightgown whispered by my cot; some air stirred against my skin. She and Dad kissed, they whispered, and they rolled apart. My mind I fixed on being still. Their tossing in the double bed slowed, their breathing too, both inside the steady clicking of the ceiling fan that stirred not a breath of cool air.

Quietly I rolled toward the window, again looked out at the clock in its tower. How long, I do not know. My eyes ached, felt dry, and my body I did not feel. The clock would be telling time—1:22, I seem to remember—and then it would be the moon, the horrible moon of a summer night.

✡

In the train window, prairies flatten out in dawn's blue-gray light. Cattle, tree-protected ranch buildings, low houses, and dark clusters of towns rushed by, water towers up in paler sky, gone quickly. It was pretty much what I had imagined while listening to Dad's stories, what I had seen in western movies, but I understood it would not be like that. Nothing was. Mother and Dad were asleep, heads rolled back on their seats, as out the window I watched dawn open on the place of the stories I loved most.

The coach was already hot when we arrived, about nine, in Durant. Through the train window I saw shimmering heat waves rising from the station platform, from the depot's roof, from street pavement. There were cowboy hats, boots, Levis, but with these old bib overalls like my grandfather in North Carolina wore, business suits, white shirts, ties, exactly like my father wore every day to work.

When we walked out of the depot, sun immediately was hot on my head, my neck, across my shoulders. Even in the car heat roared in at me, and I squinted in eye-achy glare. Up an alley there was a mule-drawn wagon and a saddled horse, but in the streets plain old Chevies, Fords, and Plymouths. The school Dad had attended was a block of red brick set in a cinder field, as prisonlike as my school back in Washington.

I was losing my bearings. Here Dad had grown up. Here I had yearned to visit all of my life. But there was an Indian wearing a pineapple sport shirt. And cowboys in boots and hats ambled in to see a Bette Davis movie my folks had dragged me along to see back in Washington. And my grandfather's and grandmother's bungalow was an exact copy of hundreds in Takoma Park: same porch, same dormer window, same snowball and wisteria bushes in the yard. Inside it was not cooler—furnacelike heat roaring in through windows and doors. I stayed close to Mother and

Dad. They said I could take a nap in the back bedroom, where there was a little breeze. Seeing the stir of chintz curtains, soft billowing, I said I was not tired. If I gave in to heat and confusion, I did not know what would happen to me.

Lives that had come from my grandmother and grandfather were, for a few days, coming back to them. Up from Uvalde, Texas, came Uncle Wilson. He was huge, weighed over three hundred pounds, and when he walked the floors of the house shook, knickknacks chattered. He had brought Aunt Vivian, his half-Choctaw wife, and his three sons (my cousins): Gene Ray, the oldest, who was big like his father and always hung around where the men were talking; Hardy, the youngest, younger than I, who always stayed around the kitchen where the women spent the days cooking; and Bobby, my age, whom I liked immediately and completely.

And Aunt Mary E. arrived from Hugo, Oklahoma, with Uncle Floyd. Before the car was parked, Aunt Mary E. was calling out to us on the porch—how wasn't it just *too hot* and the drive up had ruined and wilted her dress and she just had to change before she could hug anybody and she hoped we had not waited supper on them. With Uncle Floyd (a full Choctaw) helping, she eased herself out of the car. Like all the rest of the family except Dad and my grandfather, she was big and overweight. She smoothed her dress, tugged at it, adjusted herself. She was a schoolteacher. Stepping as if her ankles were sore, she came up the walk—tiny white shoes under her swaying bulk. Dusk, cement step still warm with the sun.

And Aunt Martha arrived from Dallas, Texas, on the bus. She was not big as much as she was overweight. Her powdered face showed runnels of perspiration. She talked as much as Aunt Mary E. but was a little faster. She told us her fiancé, Scott, had *wanted* to drive her up from Dallas, he was *sooo* sweet, but at the very last minute he had been called away on family business and did we know his family had some oil wells west of Fort Worth. She told everybody she was now an executive secretary.

Like all the women, Mother included, Aunt Martha disappeared into the kitchen, and except for meals, I rarely saw her elsewhere. Aunt Mary E. took over the kitchen from her mother, and from very early in the morning until late at night her bossy loud voice—a terrible musical singsong to it—came out of there. Bobby and I could hear her in the backyard under the chinaberry tree, where there was a little coolness. We talked, about what I don't remember, only its slow decorum, the long, sweet rhythms. From the kitchen came Aunt Mary E.'s voice; I don't believe I ever heard Mother's.

Once in their bedroom, which was an enclosed porch, Mother talked solemnly to Dad. The door to the kitchen was closed. Why I was in their room I do not know. Chintz curtains stirred with breeze, but heat was still fierce. Hushing her voice, Mother told Dad that being in the kitchen morning, noon, and night was driving her to distraction, food food food, that was all they talked about, all they did, fix it, eat it. And Mary E. bossed all the time, insulted Grandmother Lewis, insulted everybody including Mother, and she (Mother) was not sure how much longer she could hold her temper.

Dad sat on the side of the bed, a hand on each knee, his head down. He studied the veins in the backs of his hands. Her back to the dresser, Mother folded her arms. In the dresser mirror was her back and Dad's bowed head, his knees, his hands. Out the windows was the chinaberry tree where Bobby and I talked. Beyond that was a chicken-wire pen where my grandfather kept his hot, miserable-looking hunting dogs. (He still kept his dogs, though he was too sick to hunt with them.) Those pitiable dogs I was looking at when Dad broke his silence.

Not looking up, he told Mother he knew it was hard on her, but to please try to bear up under it a few more days. Still looking at his hands spread on his knees, he shrugged, then just sat there.

"Answer me this. Why are they so durn hateful to me and each other?"

"They've had hard times. Their lives aren't what they thought they'd get. They expected more."

Mother stood still. She looked at Dad sitting on the edge of the bed. "I've never seen such unhappy people."

I felt nothing. Since the night we left the Plymouth and stayed in Memphis, I had seen Mother and Dad as just part of *out there*. I watched them, paid attention, but they were not me anymore.

But here memory stirs. And I recall that being alone and different from our folks and our families, that profound ache and painful exhilaration, was what Bobby and I talked about under the chinaberry tree.

✿

We all ate together in the dining room that was built for a family of four and a couple of guests, not for a three-generation family of thirteen. We squeezed around the big table. (It had come out from Mississippi, been in the banker's family since the 1840s, and now filled up the too-little dining room.) That dining room was close with smells of ham and fried chicken and a steaming bowl of navy beans (Uncle Wilson's favorite, I recall, and he liked them fixed a particular way which Aunt Mary E. worried over constantly, though I never heard Uncle Wilson complain about any food. Both are dead now.) And on the table was a huge bowl of mashed potatoes, mounded up with butter gobs sliding down, and corn bread hot out of the oven and buttermilk biscuits stacked in a steaming pyramid, their sour and sweet smell there with thick pungency of cream chicken gravy and high nice whine of red-eye gravy, of vinegar in the tomato and cabbage slaw. All of it impossible confusion in the small dining room at the outsized table packed with thirteen people, temperature about ninety degrees. I was not a bit hungry as I shoved into the table beside Bobby. Uncle Wilson settled himself, forearms bigger than my thighs, at the head of the table and I saw how Dad did not take up as much table room as Aunt Mary E. Mother looked down at her shiny clean plate, the perspiration from the kitchen beaded on her lip, at her temples. I was half sick with the thick heavy warm smell and sight of it, the closeness. You couldn't get away. Somebody big—Aunt Martha, I think it was— sitting on the other side of me, spooned huge helpings of everything onto my plate, until it was mounded up, only the rim of the plate visible, and then splashed gravy over everything—getting some in the slaw. I could not eat it, not even half, but I had to. I was getting bites chewed and swallowed, but then Aunt Mary E. scrutinized my plate. She reported to the table what I had not eaten. Dad kept looking at his plate, and the kids glanced at me with genuine pity. Aunt Mary E. then sang her insult at whoever had fixed whatever it was that I could not fork down: "Didn't I tell you there was too much salt in it? Didn't I? See, Albert's boy *can't even eat it!*" And hot sick built in me, perspiration now, wishing I could crawl under the table, into the darkness of chair and table legs, knees, shoes. But I ate. I stuck my fork again into that huge mountain of food, got some of it into my mouth, choke-swallowed it, the milk I tried to wash it down with warm.

They are eating and eating and eating. Uncle Wilson hulked over his small plate, and Dad looked as if he were eating alone, and Mother, when she glanced up, stared past me into the empty space of the living room, and Aunt Martha and Aunt Mary E. took mincing, ladylike bites, but forked it in, forked it into their mouths already full of food, their jaws working, and I was seeing the action of the bones in their chewing, hearing the smacking of lips, of saliva, feeling sicker all the time. (In the hot nights I dreamed of their teeth full of food.) And in their blue eyes fierce light was almost savage as they grabbed for food and talked, still chewing, still swallowing, still swigging tea. But there would be other moments when they weren't grabbing or getting or talking, when they were just eating, just chewing and swallowing, and then that fierce light would be out of their eyes and I would see a self-absorbed, sweet, clear innocence in the blue eyes that were like mine. It lasted as long as they did not need to do or get anything else.

✡

On that 1945 visit to Oklahoma, I avoided my grandmother and grandfather. My unspoken fear was that at any moment she would have one of her "fits" or my grandfather would have one of his strokes, and that in front of my eyes one of them would die. This got mixed up with huge quantities of strange rich food, that packed dining room, the close thick motionless air.

My grandfather did have a stroke the second day. In the living room his head began to roll on the chair back. His hands clutched hard at the carved wood of the chair arms, white moons in his knuckles, his eyes rolling back in his head, only white showing, and his jaw was working sideways and chewing air. Then he toppled sideways, the chair turning over, a crash, he lying on the floor on his side like a baby. His cheek was against the red imitation Oriental rug, and his eyes finally steadied—exact color of mine, my daughter's—and focused peacefully on something in the air. Uncle Wilson's huge body was bent over him, and he was slipping little white tablets under Granddaddy Lewis's tongue, and Dad was on his knees beside his father, his hand on the old man's shoulder, as if that could do some good. I knew this would happen again, only then it would be at the table and my grandfather would die.

Grandmother Lewis was in the living room, too, when her words slurred and then became crazy snapping strings of sound like words. Always vigilant, Aunt Mary E. bustled in from the kitchen to take charge, and the first thing she did was to order the children out of the house. From the dining room I watched as my grandmother's head started to jerk and snap, then her body, and she slid out of her chair onto the floor. While she grinned, huge snaplike convulsions went through her and her eyes had a crazy light in them. She grunted and moaned, teeth gnashing, and her face twisted and jerked now, snap-like jolts still going through her, a mixture of bubbly spit and blood on her lips. Aunt Mary E. and Aunt Martha kneeled by her, did not do much, just let the convulsions slowly diminish—a spirit leaving her body—until she too lay like a baby on her side, and her eyes had a similar innocent haze in them.

And the fear of Granddaddy and Grandmother Lewis dying at the dining-room table was as thick as the still hot air close to my face, the thick unaccustomed smells, my full stomach—plate not half empty—and Aunt Mary E. and Aunt Martha watching me, and Mother and Dad just trying not to be conspicuous, not even looking at me, and I feeling sicker and sicker. And when I knew no exertion of will whatsoever could empty my plate, that I would be defeated, surrender, suffer humiliation, I got self-pitying. And into my mind came Dad's Oklahoma boyhood, which in Washington I had imagined so often, and the stories I told to kids back in Takoma Park and to myself in bed as dusky summer twilight became dark in my room.

✿

On the next to last day Dad borrowed Uncle Wilson's car to drive the two of us to Bokchito, to the actual places of his boyhood stories. I think he was eager to get away from his family for a while.

The Bokchito bank his grandfather had established was now owned by another family, the same one that owned the DX station, the feed store, and a great deal of land in this end of Bryan County. When Dad was still a boy they had moved from here to the county seat, Durant. The bank building, where there had been gunfights with mounted bandits, was now empty, windows boarded up. Where his house had been was now a weedy vacant lot. Dad tried but he could not find where exactly the storm cellar had been. He took me up to a weedy, overgrown cemetery to show me two small tombstones. One said BILLY, the other JIMMY, and the graves were for Dad's brothers, twins who had died within a few days of their birth. He had been about ten years old, but he told me he remembered nothing, not even their funeral or the graveside ceremony. When I asked where the nickel movie theater was, he remembered only that it was on the south side of Main Street in a block of brick stores which were now mostly vacant. This bothered him. I said it was not important.

Dad did go right to the store his father had before they moved to Durant. Cupping my hands to the dirty glass to see from street sunlight into the dim interior, I made out a few shelves along the walls where gunnysacks full of something were stored with some old tires. When I stepped back, perspiration-smeared dirt was on the heels of my hands. I wiped them off on my Levis. I was now as quiet as Dad.

The last thing we did was go down to Bokchito Creek. Dad wanted to show me the swimming hole, and I remembered his story about saving a boy's life there. About a half mile from town we parked the car and then walked down through some brush to cottonwoods along the creek. The heat and sunlight were terrific. The shade under the cottonwoods, which hardly stirred, was hotter. I felt dizzy. Something was wrong, and then I realized it was the absence of the music of living water. Dad's creek was bone-dry, dusty. Not even stagnant pools. We climbed down into the dry creek bed. Dad looked up the creek bed as if he expected the water's return. He kicked a couple of stones, which clattered away. His hands were in his pockets. Standing twenty feet from me, he looked small. The roots of a huge cottonwood had been exposed by the eroding action of the water which was now dried up. Dad did not say anything. He wandered around.

I said, "Dad, I can see how it must've been deep."

He glanced over at me, perspiration dripping off his nose, his shirt sopped. Then he quickly looked away without answering.

He was looking again up the dry creek bed. My chest tightened, and then I knew he had lost something too. He was hurt, confused, and did not know what to think either. This was why he had not wanted to come out here to Oklahoma and be reminded. This was why he acted so quiet with his folks. He was still looking away, up the creek bed, toward its dried-up source.

"Let's go, Dad," I said quietly in that close, terrifically hot shade.

He turned, walked past me down the creek bed, pointed further downstream, and said, "I think that's where it was—the swimming hole—down there by that willow with the roots cut away."

I looked at the dusty place he pointed to. It was a little lower than where we stood, maybe deep enough to drown in, I thought. I said, "Sure, I can see it."

Then Dad said, "Let's go." I followed him out of the creek bed, using the water-eroded roots of the cottonwood as places to put our feet.

After we had been back in Takoma Park a while, I started telling the old stories about Oklahoma and acted as if what had happened had not happened.

Battles Without Names

During World War II we quit going regularly to Petworth Baptist Church. Dad wanted golf on Sunday morning and Mother said church services and cooking a good Sunday dinner could not both be done. That we went at all was for me. They believed I ought to be brought up a Christian, but on the Sundays we did attend Petworth, I was regarded as a noisy heathen, a child who for his own good ought to be marched down to the church basement for a good old-fashioned thrashing. Then one spring Sunday the sermon was terribly long (even by Southern Baptist standards) with not a little heel banging and squirming by me. When we got home, Dad announced that Baptist sermons were too durn long, and anyway he was sick to death of having a preacher rant and rave about how sinful he was. "I've had it. No more."

And Mother shot back: "And besides, you'd rather play golf!"

They both laughed.

Then he said: "Well, take the boy to church yourself then."

Without answering, Mother returned to the kitchen. From in there came the soft splattering and popping of frying chicken.

We never went back to Petworth, even though one of Mother's brothers, Ray, was a deacon there, and he, Aunt Bid, and my cousins went without fail every Sunday. (Uncle Ray liked me because I was trouble, he said. On the church steps after services, he did quick skin-the-cats with me and followed them with a stick of Doublemint gum. When we quit going I missed seeing him as much as I was glad to be free of the jaw-aching frustration and boredom.)

It was now a Sunday, early August 1945: the Germans had surrendered, grown-ups smiled more easily, atomic bombs had not yet fallen on Japan. We had been home from our big trip out to Oklahoma for a couple of weeks. For some reason, Dad had skipped his golf. He was sunk in his mohair easy chair perusing the Sunday *Star*. Mother was out in the kitchen. On the scratchy summer rug I was finishing Buzz Sawyer, when somebody came up on the stoop. Charles from down the street pressed his forehead against the screen. He stared in at us, not saying a word. Beyond him I saw a pleasant, not-too-hot Sunday morning.

Did I want to cool off under the hose with him and his brother Jimmy; his folks had said okay. They had just gotten home from church.

In our living room I was already cool. Charles, a bully with a mean streak, was two years older. I always felt sorry for him. I said yeah.

While I was upstairs getting on my bathing suit, a car slowly came up the street, parked. The Laytons, returning from church; he was a D.C. policeman.

Down at the Dennys, we took turns shooting the hose—two running through the gleaming rainbow spray. The grass got sopped, we slipped, fell, got coolly soaked, and then Charles had me from behind in a headlock. I cracked him an elbow in the ribs; he yelped, let go. We were still messing around, I thought, in that bright splash and sunshine, but Charles, who was pretty big, got me from behind again—tight bear hug pinning my arms—and yelled to his brother Jimmy, "Hit him! Hit him with the hose nozzle!"

At the crown of my head, a wet thump, then another. At the rim of my consciousness darkness rose quickly like dusk into an unlighted room, and (as though thinking of someone else) I wondered how long Charles would keep yelling, "Hit him! Hit him!" Then he wasn't bear hugging me any-more and I wobbled up onto my feet, started up the street to my house.

Neighbor ladies—Mrs. Hill, Mrs. Carter—rushed out of their houses. "Oh lord, Clay!"

"Betty, Betty Lewis, it's Clay!" One took me by the arm, steered me up the street toward home. I wondered what was wrong.

Mother appeared in our screen door, saw me, and laughed. "Take him around back."

In the backyard Mrs. Hill told me to lie down. On my hose-wet body the sun was warm. Mother bustled out, carrying something, turned on our hose. And then, from the gathering crowd of adults, kids, I heard Mrs. Layton say, "Look at all that blood!" And Mrs. Hill: "Where's he hurt?!"

The hose's gentle splash came onto my back, along with the touch of Mother's hand. "His back is okay," she said. And the soft cool splash moved up on my shoulders, down my arms, as I lay quiet and Mother washed off the blood covering me. The cool hose stream chilled, sweetened. Then it touched tenderness at the crown of my head. "There it is!" Mother declared. The crowd, which had come in tight, eased when they saw with their own eyes the blood's source.

I was numb. The swiftness that had turned a Sunday summer morning from quiet ease into blood and neighborhood alarm and attention was too much.

As we drove to Cheverly Hospital, my head began to throb. Dad told me to lie down, be quiet. He didn't like this interruption in his Sunday morning. Mother was still in high spirits. Into the emergency room, which was quiet, cool, bustled Georgia, the nurse on duty that day and Mother and Dad's longtime bridge-playing friend (with her husband, Vince). They had taken me to Cheverly Hospital because they knew she was on duty. Her brisk, good-spirited manner I always liked. She had been at lunch, and, hearing it was me, she had knocked over a chair running to the emergency room.

She shaved the gashes in my scalp that were too deep to butterfly, too jagged to stitch. She pushed in metal clamps. Stung, but okay. As Georgia's hands ripped adhesive tape, laid on bandage, I sat still. Where the nozzle had struck, I now had ragged-edged aches. Georgia said if I felt faint, if I threw up, I should come back to the hospital right away.

"You'll be fine, Clay," she said, her smile lighting up my heart.

Sliding off the stool, I felt wobbly. While they talked, I stood still and gazed at the instrument tray under the pulled-down light, the strewn-out forceps, scissors, razor, thick strips of rubbery adhesive tape (delicious smell), stubble of my hair, and bloody gauze. In the cool shadow of the room, blinds pulled, I understood how easily I could be hurt.

We did not go right home. Since we were near Greenbelt, Dad wanted to go over to a sandlot baseball game. He had pitched for the Greenbelt ball team in 1938–40, when we lived there. He said he might still know players.

Mother said I should not be out in the sun. That I should rest. (But I knew she just did not like baseball.)

Blob of white bandage warm with sun, I sat with them on the grassy hillside. I did not say my head hurt worse. I watched the casualness of the ball players, their showy confidence when catching a fly, the puff of dust from the catcher's mitt when pitches came in hard. My head hurt. Other spectators, noticing my bandage, turned and stared, and I wished that they could not see that I was hurt. I was woozy in the hot sun. If I said anything they'd fight about whether to go home. On the grassy hillside the three of us sat together while the ball game in its old rhythms went on, and the sun on the bandage on top of my head announced my wound to the world.

✡

Around that bloody Sunday other memories are collected.

In early September of that year, 1945, one evening after supper, Mother wanted us to run down to the Smithsonian to see a special exhibit mentioned in the *Star*. Spur-of-the-moment trips I loved. Dad said, "Why not?" When we parked on the Mall, the sky was lemon and tree shadows, deep lavender. Some of the rooms at the Smithsonian I loved most had been stripped of what I remembered. In them now were huge wall-size photographs of the death camps. Dead stacked like cordwood, their shoes tied in bows like mine. Skeletons with open eyes, alive, laid out on stretchers. A dug-out pit like a building excavation filled with shambles of bodies. My eyes sought for elbows, hands, ears. Then I got even closer and the pictures were gigantic: in the black and white dots I couldn't tell what things were anymore. Spotlights sizzled. Standing too close was my only escape. Icy sensations rippled up my back. Some guilty nightmare of mine had escaped into the world. Mother said we had to leave right away.

We were not there five minutes. For days burning sorrow would not leave me. The war that had been glorious, heroic, was also this. What had been grand was now horror beyond worst nightmare, kids slaughtered as well as adults. And I understood, because Sandy Brockman and other kids in my class went to Hebrew lessons, that if Jews could be killed wholesale, so could we. Several days later the exhibit was removed, the *Star* reported. The Lindbergh and firearms collections were put back.

✡

And on the side-porch glider, reading the *Star*, I figured out what atomic bombs had done to Hiroshima and Nagasaki. The pictures of rubble, nothing recognizable; people (not soldiers) deformed, puffily burned. There was a blast diagram that superimposed what happened at Hiroshima on a map of Washington, D.C. The Washington Monument was ground zero. Dad, downtown at I Street and Pennsylvania Avenue, would be killed instantly. The blast would burn Mother and me. We would suffer those puffy burns, radiation sickness, and die in a month's time. I was just being a worry wart, Mother said. Dad told me to forget it. The United States was the only country on earth with an atomic bomb. But I understood that nothing was safe, including us. The only world I had known was dead.

I began to pray, to a faintly distinct but uninvolved god, that we would not be incinerated, killed. Forgetting my prayers (and some nights I did fall asleep in the words), I might be guilty of causing a catastrophe.

And this too.

It was autumn. I walked in leafy chatter, slightly embarrassed by my heart's thrill at the leaf-stripped limbs overhead, cathedral tossing with gusty hymn. Paul, two years older, had coaxed me into going with him after school to meet two girls in farmer Powell's hayfield, which was on the other side of the woods behind my house. His interest in girls bothered me. The ones he knew lived in the new houses built after the war in bulldozed-down woods where once we played, rode horses, chopped down trees for the fun of it.

Until we walked right into their beaten-down patch of hayfield we hadn't seen them. They smiled up at us, giggling. We checked across the hayfield toward the farmhouse but saw no one. At the edge of the hayfield was an old apple orchard, where on a Sunday morning I had killed with my BB gun a robin for no good reason at all. We sat down in the intimacy of their little stomped-down room. Paul kidded, then kissed the dark-haired girl, who laughed loudly. My eyes didn't know where to go. My insides were thick and hot. "He's never even kissed a girl," Paul said. I argued hard, but the loud girl laughed and pointed at me, and if I had not taken pride in *never* having fights with Paul, I would have beaten him to a pulp.

When they kissed again, I slid over and somehow (roaring emotions confuse my memory) kissed the other girl, who, anyway, was prettier. On her coat was scarlet red piping. Her eyelids floated closed. Her light brown hair smelled of cold. We sat there, she up close to me, wind talking with the hayfield, and clouds blew fast in autumn sky. I kissed her again and it was even nicer.

At school the next day, big windows thumped, rattled in gusts, and gray autumn sky had fast-running clouds. We had planned to meet again in the hayfield that afternoon. Happiness was filling me up.

Paul and I got to the hayfield first. They might not show up, I worried. At first sight of her, her welcoming smile, my heart leaped. Her hand was warm. We beat down a path away from Paul and his girl, then our own little space. We kissed more. Wind tossed in the tops of the hay.

It was Farmer Powell, right up in the sky above us: "What are you kids doing!?" Paul and his girl jumped up, flushed like quail, ran. I told Farmer Powell I was sorry for beating down his hayfield. He said if he saw us again in his hayfield, he would tell our families what we were doing. "Now get! Get on out of here!"

I ran flat-out for my house; she headed for the new housing development.

My school was in the District of Columbia, and she, like most of the kids and Paul, went to Maryland schools. I got home later, and for a few days I didn't see her. Then, on yet another cold, blustering autumn day, I saw her—that beautiful coat—and her friend walking with schoolbooks up the street toward their houses. Maybe they had stayed late at school. I called, but they kept walking. I ran up to them.

"Go away," Paul's loud friend said as they stopped, turned. The girl in the coat with scarlet piping—her blue eyes met mine, just for a second, and my heart slushed. Quietly she said, looking away, "My parents said I can't play with you anymore."

"Yeah," her friend said, "she has to come straight home from school for a month. A month! Just because of you."

My heart hurt.

They walked on, slowly, up toward their houses. I watched until they turned a corner, went out of sight.

For weeks I walked by her house at least a couple of times every afternoon. It was small, brick, identical to others in that neighborhood of lawnless, muddy clay yards, except it was on a corner and at the top of a steeply terraced yard. The windows had pulled-close curtains. Her bedroom would be the small one? Would she peek out, see me, put on her coat, come out?

Her wirehaired terrier sometimes was sitting on the front stoop. Other times he'd be trotting down the street or up the hill to her house. After another vigil, twilight almost full dark, I forced my legs to walk up the steps, one after another, up on the stoop to her front door. I politely knocked. A mother wearing an apron opened the door, saw me, then softly closed the door—didn't slam it. In a few moments, the father, newspaper in one hand, opened the door. His lips were tight; his eyes looked black: "Don't bother us. Don't come around here anymore." Then he banged the door closed, knocker tapping twice in the dark. I hurried down the steps. I ran home.

A few days later I spotted her terrier trotting along. When I whistled, he stopped, looked at me, sat down to wait. But when I got close, he trotted off. Maybe I was going to scratch his ears, maybe punt him like a football. I was not sure. But as he trotted away, I knew I had wanted to hurt him.

Carrying dog biscuits and hamburger in waxed paper, I became obsessed in my hunt for that terrier. In the dusky streets I shot at him with my BB gun, but never did he yelp. Going to sleep, I planned my next trick. I puzzled how, with fresh raw hamburger in my hand, this dumb dog knew I wanted to hurt him. For all my hard figuring on his routes and habits, not once did I hurt him as my heart was hurt. Almost in the Snavelys' yard by the garbage cans which he usually sniffed. Once after stooping down between parked cars waiting for an hour. Easily he escaped both times. In backyards and at dark street corners, I got bone cold waiting with diminishing hopes. Then I quit.

I never saw her again. She moved away and took her happy-faced terrier. In Farmer Powell's hayfield now stand two ten-story apartment buildings.

✡

Other losses are related to that bloody Sunday.

As a kid I understood that my birth set off an Rh-factor difference that caused Mother to lose the babies she wanted. With each miscarriage her bed sheets were stained brown red—big ragged-edged splotches of blood. After World War II doctors got a cure, and my sister was born in 1948.

Returning from a West Virginia camp, stepping into our living room, I saw Mother with baby Ellen in the flooding afternoon sunlight. Mother glowed, she was so happy; clammy loss filled my insides. Nothing would be the same again. I told Mother Ellen was pretty (but she looked blotchy, ugly). Upstairs, my door shut, I looked out and saw Dad's black Buick Special. I hated being so weak.

Changes rushed.

Dad was promoted to district manager, so he drove to his Baltimore office every day and ten days a month traveled his territory in Maryland, Virginia, and West Virginia. He said he was too busy to send back hotel postcards. Besides, he would get back home ahead of the postcards. When Dad was not home, Mother called me the man of the house and insisted I sit in Dad's chair at the head of the dinner table. The seat was crushed down, made me too low. I worried that Dad's airline flights would crash, that he'd have a terrible wreck on U.S. 1, "the nation's most dangerous highway." With good money coming in, Mother bought an Estey spinet piano. While we waited, with dinner ready, table set, candles lit, for Dad to come home from Baltimore, Mother played sad songs and hymns. The melancholy of these years rises the moment I hear unaccompanied piano.

The old Hillwood neighborhood in Takoma Park, where I knew everybody (and was known by everybody), was lost when we moved to Bethesda, off Bradley Boulevard. There the houses were big and the furniture rich looking, and neighbors talked about congressmen and senators and the importance of going to Dartmouth or Princeton. Our house was big, too, a brick colonial and brand new with white plaster walls not dry enough to paint. Where I belonged was *someplace else*—in cool woods hearing Sligo Creek's quiet song. And home would be with stories I had been part of: where I had this fight or that; the telephone pole where

I almost cut off my thumb; the steep hillsides and boulders along the creek where we played war. And with adults I knew about: Mr. Byrd, Paul's father, had been in the field artillery; Mrs. Denny, the mother of Charles and Jimmy, had grown up in a Christian mission in China; Mr. Carter, who was from South Carolina, ran the presses down at the *Star*; the lady across the street was a widow because one day in March her husband, a house painter who (the adults whispered) drank too much, fell drunk off a scaffold to his death hitting a downtown sidewalk; Mr. Miller was a White House reporter for the *Chicago Tribune*.

My moping over what I had lost got worse. One Saturday night I went back to Hillwood for a party at a friend's house. He and most of my other friends were older. They had invited girls and they danced with them on the screened-in side porch to scratchy 45 RPMs. My collar was sweaty, and the chocolate cake, which was delicious, was hard to choke down. The boys off to one side talked fast about what girls they liked and did not like. My old friends told me to ask girls to dance. I said no, I did not know how. When they said I was chicken, I got angry. They said the girls in the new houses were easy. (I thought of the girl from the hayfield but kept quiet.) They bragged about what they had done with them, some of which I did not understand. Paul Byrd bragged too. There was no going back to the boys I had known all my life. That had all been swept away too. I just had memories now. I was glad to leave the party.

In the car with Mother driving home on East-West Highway, I watched old Takoma Park pass by. Through here we had ridden our bikes to the movies, to the swimming pool. I saw all the old bungalows. In one along here Mother's former boss lived, still, with his World War II shattered leg. Like a huge memory long forgotten but now for its own reasons returning, melancholy filled me. Its intensity was almost sufficient consolation.

Thirteen and fourteen years old, I was changing too. Dad told me his great ambition had been to be a medical doctor. He had failed, he told me, and selling X-ray machines to doctors was the best he could do. (It was plenty good enough for me.) He told me that if *I* wanted to be a doctor, I could do it. Up to then indifferent to grades, I became overnight a tight, compulsive student. I flew into rages at math problems I could not solve and at ink blots on compositions that had to be perfect. (Although Dad showed me how to razor off mistakes, my clumsiness always scraped holes in the paper.) They told me not to stay up so late with homework. Unable to do some school task, I called myself stupid, a failure: "You'll never be a doctor." My fighting and hot temper vanished. Walking home from school (preferring this to the bus), I sang "Streets of Laredo"—a lively cowboy now as "cold as the clay."

Worst of all was how Dad changed. Christmas of 1948, his first as a manager, he invited his Baltimore office to our new Bethesda house for a party. Mother, talking fast, cheeks splotchy, was dizzy with anxiety. I wished I had not seen Dad out in the kitchen guzzling vodka straight out of a bottle. He slurred and in the living room staggered like Red Skelton. Men talking to me were gentle: "Al's had a few too many." But after everybody left, Mother screamed, out of control: "I'll kill you if you ever humiliate me again. So help me, I'll kill you."

"Aw Betty, come on now," Dad slurred, going up the tight, closed staircase.

"I will," she screamed. "So help me God, I will." For several weeks she did not utter a word to Dad or me.

Arrowsmith and biographies of famous physicians I read. Down in the basement I worked hours to develop photographs with the set Dad gave me for Christmas. The images were lost in dark or milkily washed out. After school I hurried next door to see Mrs. Parker, whose younger boys I baby-sat. She baked delicious things and, while I ate them at her kitchen table, she told me how important college was. Often she asked me to stay for dinner, really wanted me to. When Mr. Parker got home, he was interested in his martini, and at the dinner table he grumbled at the boys or criticized the wonderful dishes. The boys, Roger and Walter, kept quiet. So did I. Mrs. Parker did not defend herself. Late one winter afternoon, dark out the windows, I was in her happily clattering kitchen when she asked me again to stay for dinner. Not bothering with my coat, I ran home to ask. Mother was fixing dinner, Ellen in her high chair. Mother's face got splotchy, and her speech became the rapid southern singsong of her anger. She told me no, and furthermore I could never again eat dinner with the Parkers, because they did not respect her and she would have no more of this. No, not now, not ever; I belonged at home. I did not argue.

And not long after that, a snowy Saturday night in February, I baby-sat Ellen while Mother and Dad went down to the Aikens for a party. When they got home, their storming woke me up. I heard Mother tell Dad she was shamed, humiliated. That Dad was an old goat for making a pass at Imogene Aiken. That they would never be able to hold their heads up in the neighborhood again. Then I heard her say she was bleeding. And, with a rustling of newspaper, I heard him say, slurring, "Here, bleed through these and then I'll take you to the damn hospital." After a long silence, Dad rumbled with snores. I tiptoed back to bed.

Light, the color of gruely oatmeal, was in the house when I next heard them. Dressed, they were passing my room, no lights on, Dad helping Mother and carrying Ellen. I watched from the window as he helped her down the trampled-snow walk and into the Dodge. Light came up from the snow; the sky, dawn barely visible, was tangled with trees. Ten days she was at the hospital. When I came home from school, I went to Mrs. Parker's, where I ate dinner. (Although she was attentive and kind, as always, I tried not to like her.) At 9 P.M., when Dad returned from the hospital, I went home. In the morning when I got up, he had already left for Baltimore.

Mother almost died of a miscarriage, Mrs. Parker told me. She said it was okay to be worried. When Mother returned from the hospital, I didn't want to leave Mrs. Parker and, catching myself in this desire, was scalded with guilt. No word was ever said of their fight, of Imogene Aiken, of what exactly was wrong with Mother, of what happened at the hospital. They told me not to look sad: "Buck up, Clay," Mother said, "everything is fine!" The scar of this only I knew about.

✿

These changes, which I now see were my fall into the human condition, began on that bloody Sunday with a mortal wound and came to rest in an unqualified moral defeat. When I was not mowing lawns or going to Washington Senators ball games that sticky summer of 1950, I read Ernie Pyle and sportswriters' books all morning on the side-porch glider. My T-shirt stuck to the glider cushions; sweat on my neck cooled, and in the big poplar by the porch, soft breeze-chattering song. The couch cushions squawked, almost with my breathing, and the glider itself creaked side to side, and, in the humid, leafy shadow, among the words of my reading, was the mulchy woods-earth smell and the tang of new bricks and mortar, and I was aware, almost painfully so, of this river of new sensations.

After lunch I slowly pedaled my bike two miles out Bradley Boulevard to the country club Dad had joined so that he could play golf. The forlorn silence of midday summer was broken by the screek-screek and rubber hush of my bike. I turned into the lane, bordered with scraggly trees, and pumped the last little hill, dropping my bike against the bike rack. I smelled hot tar and the sweet of golf greens (good enough to eat), and from around the corner of the old bathhouse, heard the kathump-thump of the diving board, a clean splash, and caught a whiff of chlorine in the air. I had to go down basement steps to the men's locker room, which smelled of mold, of painted-over wood rot, of rusty lockers and cheesy towels. It was usually just me, no pink-bodied men, no clattering lockers. When I stepped out of my sneakers, my underwear, cool rushed into my body's private places. Even alone, being naked embarrassed me. At the pool, only a dozen scattered around on a weekday summer afternoon, I plunged into the cool sensation, thinking, Oh what pleasure, what pleasure, while knowing that the other overintense sensations of the glider, the bike ride, the locker room, were sweet pleasures too.

When, after diving deep, grazing my hands along the bottom, I broke through the sun-lobed pool surface, I allowed myself to look to see if she was there, the pretty, lithe girl in a black swimming suit. She was about my age, dark hair, sun-browned, and her smile, which was sweet, welcoming, melted my heart. She usually lay out with her sister, who was two years older, and her mother, who had the same welcoming, pleasant disposition, on deck chairs over on the grass strip by the tall bushes that bordered the pool. She would not call hello when she saw me, but within a few minutes she came to the pool, put her beautiful tanned legs in the water, lightly shushing them back and forth, and scooped palmfuls of water to splash dazzlingly over her shoulders. I swam over underwater, in the mute of pleasant blue green, and surfaced a few feet from her. For a moment we pretended to be unaware of the other's presence, but then she said, "Did you like the end of your book?" I told her what I had figured I would tell her, but often with more rush and enthusiasm than I had intended. On the crown of my head, across my shoulders, was the warm sun.

Then we swam underwater laps. I usually went farthest, stayed down longest by overcoming my appetite for air until my vision started to darken.

And, resting at the side of the pool, holding the drain gutter, not looking but feeling her clear presence, we talked more. "Do you watch the stars at night?" "Do you like thunderstorms?" "What do you want to be?" And then we went to the diving board. I see, with perfect clarity, the way she glided down the board, seemed to rise high without effort, jackknifed, then pffut entered the pool. Her figure rose to the lapping, sun-lobed surface, and her face—grinning broadly if it was a good dive—exploded through the bubble of air that slicked her black hair perfectly. I learned that beautiful was heartbreaking. She could do, too, with equal precision, back flips and front flips and swans and one-and-a-halfs. She was a wonder. And patiently, with her gentle manner, she taught me to do back flips and front flips—mine, of course, gawkinesses of thrown arms and legs. And when the sun got out in the western sky, hedge shadows lengthening blue, her sister would tease her about having a boyfriend, and her mother, squinting up at me, hand trying to shade her eyes, would ask me about my family and what I liked at school.

The long shadows on Bradley were sweet, riding my bike home, ears full of water, and most of it was downhill. As I turned into our street, I saw our brick colonial, dropped down the driveway, dumped my bike, went in the kitchen, said hello to Mother, tickled Ellen under her chin to make her giggle, my heart held tight to my afternoon's treasure.

I trusted her, but I cannot now remember her name.

She and her mother invited me to come over to their house one evening after supper for ice cream. They drew me a map, and, although I said not a word, I was worried about whether I could find their house. I remember, with great clarity, the long August evening shadows when I came down her street, saw her sitting on the front step waiting for me. She waved, glad to see me, and my heart, turning into her drive, was filled. She wore a dress, yellow I believe, the full skirt just ironed, and I saw the dark of her tanned arms and legs in the dusky street.

Her father came out, said hello, good to see you, and her sister, and her nice mother, and we sat on the porch having ice cream while I talked about the Senators with her father—she chipping in her good opinions, too—as the summer dark came down, with chirping crickets, silvery dew on lawns. I was astonished how easily happiness had filled me up. This is what it is like to be happy, I thought, and I got here by myself. I thanked everybody, said I had enjoyed myself, said I would see them at the pool, and full of my own independence, hopped on my bike in the twilight and rode home.

The moment I walked into the house (Dad was away on a trip, Ellen in bed) Mother was angry. She asked me who these people were and where exactly they lived. She said that neighborhood was not as good as ours. Then when she understood that it was the girl, not her family, that I was so interested in, she did not tease me. She became crazy. I was letting a girl get her hooks in me. Her family was throwing her at me because we lived in a better part of Bethesda. If they had real manners, they never would do such a thing. Besides, it was dangerous to ride my bike to her house. Then she said she would never permit me to go to their house again. No, never. And she said for two weeks I could not go to the pool. Her dark eyes smoldered, her back not touching the Queen Anne chair, the *Star* that she had been reading in her lap. Her voice had become North Carolina upcountry singsong—those rises, snaps. (Only twenty years later, when I read Lawrence's *Sons and Lovers*, did I understand at last Mother's anger that evening.)

I did not tell her that this was crazy. Instead, I accepted what she had said. Even with the happiness of the evening still tingling, I could not risk losing her love. A lifetime later, I see that I was blind to the huge, time-deep story, with its burdens of grief, loss, that was being enacted here and given to me as legacy.

That summer of 1950 the Korean War began, and I became a close student of the tighter and tighter North Korean encirclement of patched-together U.S. forces around Pusan. The U.S. forces were being driven into the sea. Not going to the pool, I read hard, was almost never without a book, but sometimes caught myself preparing what I would tell the girl at the pool about my reading. The worst pain, worse than her absence, was the knowledge of how welcoming she and her family had been and how hurt they would be that I had dropped out of sight.

When I went back to the pool, after a little awkwardness, she and I were at the side of the pool, and I wanted to say that my Mother had told me I could not see her again, never visit her family again, and that Mother was crazy like this sometimes. But I would hurt her more, hurt me too, by saying that Mother bossed my life. I swam away, breaking the dance of our etiquette. Although her liveliness and warm grace remained, it was only what I watched in stolen glances from a distance. That simple heart-filling beauty was woven, now, with cowardly surrender, anger (if not rage) at my own weakness, and desperate (secret) yearning.

✡

To spare Dad his terrible drive, we moved in November 1950 to Baltimore. Our apartment's back windows looked out on a walled family cemetery remaining from the estate that once occupied these fields along York Road. Often I visited the cemetery, where there were tombstones for babies that had hardly lived at all, children, boys my age. Mother and Dad had a terrible time finding a house they both liked, so Dad got a contractor to build a fieldstone ranch for us over in Ruxton. Behind our new house was a hill whereon was the grand manor house of the estate that had been subdivided. Our house again smelled of new plaster: Bethesda was gone, so was Takoma Park, so was our apartment. Now all were just what I remembered. From my new room's window, I could see Sheppard Pratt on a hilltop a half mile away. It was a private asylum for the insane. (Zelda had been a patient there while Scott lived nearby, I now know.) On Sheppard Pratt's ball field my team played home games. Clumps of inmates, supervised by a nurse, came out sometimes to watch us. They usually had broad, empty smiles. A heavyset woman once tried to rip off her dress. The men wore baggy pants, no belts, and shuffled along in a daze.

When there was no teacher to visit, I made a point of missing the school bus so that I would have an excuse to walk home through the grounds of Sheppard Pratt. Almost a square mile, it had been a rich man's estate and continued to be a working farm. Its pastures were hilly, steep, and I made a game out of not stepping in the good-smelling cowpies. As I passed by, Holsteins, drooling and chomping, lifted their heads and their dark sweet eyes. The pastures reminded me of my grandfather's farm in North Carolina, which by then had been sold by my step-grandmother and was a country trailer court. (But the big oak that had sheltered the porch still stood.) In sight of the asylum buildings, I wondered if the mentally sick people inside noticed me passing by. I wondered how their thoughts got crazy. I never told a soul about walking home through Sheppard Pratt.

If people knew I did, that I actually *wanted to*, they might think *I* was crazy, that I belonged inside.

When my high school science club visited a state mental asylum, I saw inside. In a room smelling of urine, schizophrenics spoke their unworldly and overwhelming misery. In a huge ward of senile old ladies, one took my hand: "You're like my grandson," she said, along with other chat, none crazy in the least. The hospital director explained that crowded wards were the result of penicillin, which saved the old who otherwise would have died quietly of pneumonia. He showed us a basement autopsy room and a person's brain in formaldehyde; rarely were there any family objections to autopsies of dead inmates. For his cold authority over their lives, I wanted to punch his face; I wanted to throw myself through a window. Later, it was how abandoned the old and mentally ill were that sat like a huge weight on my heart. Through the Christmas season that followed our visit, I could not stop thinking of them. Mother said I was being too sensitive: "Of course conditions in mental hospitals are bad. What on earth did you expect? Is this news to you?" That Christmas Eve Dad came home drunk, and, also as usual, Mother cussed him out for an hour.

Fierce ambition to be an M.D. drove me. Dad asked me to stop bearing down so hard on my schoolwork. Mother said it was my own business if I wanted to be an old stick-in-the-mud: "He's only harming himself." To be out of the house more, I worked Saturdays for a winery and vineyard, bottling in the winter, making vine cuttings in the spring. About midafternoon on Saturdays, with wages in my pocket, I went to a second job cleaning my father's office building down on Greenmont Avenue. This busy, my mind dwelled less on insane asylums, girls I had crushes on, and other difficult matters. My microscope, an old brass one I had bought with my wages, showed me the invisible, squirming life in a drop of lake water. In my closet I had my grandfather's single-shot .22, a Winchester 12-gauge pump, and an old .44 caliber rolling-block military rifle. These I kept in first-rate condition.

✪

At the winery job, I had a friend who liked to argue about *Macbeth*. His sister was dark-haired, lively, and a tease. They lived in Riderwood, the next village up the track from Ruxton, and I went over to Dick's whenever

I could, enjoying his tough, enthusiastic company, praying I would see Barbara. Usually I saw instead their grandfather, a spry, randy old fellow who Dick had discovered in *flagrante delicto* in his living-room recliner with a neighbor lady. Barbara and Dick's folks were divorced, and they lived with their mother, who was a good-looking, *more* coquettish version of Barbara, and their stepfather, who drank too much. The mother flirted with Dick, embarrassed him. While he was in the tub, she entered the bathroom to smoke and chat. She insisted he do the same when she was in the tub, but Dick refused. I think I had a Galahad idea of saving Barbara from the throes of her folks. My own family I then considered ideal, except at Christmas.

In the back seat of their family's Plymouth convertible (top up on that cold November night), Dick with a girlfriend in the front, I amazingly put my arm around Barbara, pulled her close, and kissed her on the mouth three or four times. She kissed back. *Rapture!* The dark and cold of that back seat, her toothpasty breath, the brush of her hair, the fill of her actual presence, the exact curve on Malvern Avenue—all remembered with happiness's sudden bloom.

It was also the last time I kissed Barbara Stephenson. Although she was polite, smiled, lightly flirted when I saw her in the hall at school, or at the church young people's group on Sunday nights, she said no to dates. Dick said he did not understand either. My huge, heart-clogging crush on her lasted through other girl friends, some serious, and three years of high school. I doubt I spoke five hundred words with her. Although Mother, who knew her from church, told me she was a cheap flirt from a broken family, my passion could not be extinguished. Her simple presence in the turmoil of a church bazaar immediately transmogrified that occasion; to have lived to this moment was proof that my life was blessed. In a crowded, locker-banging hallway at school, her sauntering coolly along, a slight smile, reminded me of the distance between my miserable existence and my yearnings. A constriction in my chest; a crashing of organ notes; a pain so sharp it was almost sweet.

This hard knot of yearning and anguish accounted for another bloody incident. On a Friday night snow was falling heavily. Dick called to ask me over for chili and to study *Hamlet*. He said his folks were out. When he did not say where Barbara was, I figured that she had to be there on a bad, snowy night. Since hope blooms eternal, I was excited by romantically charged fantasies of being in the same house, on a snowy night, with the longtime center of my passions. Mother said no to the car, the roads were too slick. My protest did not mention that she just wanted to keep me away from what she thought were bad influences at that house and, worse, from seeing that Barbara girl. "Okay, I won't use the car." She looked up from the mangle where she was ironing my shirts and Dad's. "I'll walk."

"You'll do no such thing!"

"Yes, I will," I said, getting my coat and setting out.

The snow was already six inches deep, the roads unplowed, and I had to cover two miles each way. Barely twilight, soon it would be dark. But overcoming these difficulties would lift me in Barbara's eyes to heroic heights as I trudged in, snow-covered. She would fix me hot chocolate. We would sit at the kitchen table, snow falling thickly, thickly falling, outside, and the universe would contract to her Riderwood kitchen, just the two of us (where was Dick?), and we would share at last our innermost longings and fears, as happiness bloomed like wild dogwood in winter-dark woods. About a mile from home, trudging up a shortcut lane, I slipped, cracked down on my knee. It hurt, but I was numb from cold. Shoving away the snow, I saw a big round rock that marked a driveway entrance. My knee ached when I walked. Barbara would be even more impressed if I came in limping, hurt in this manly walk through a snowstorm. (How much history and culture is bound-up in teenage fantasies?)

By the time I swung into their driveway, my knee was aching badly, but that was good, for it left me with no quandary over faking or not faking a limp. Their Plymouth was buried, their bushes too, all in hushed quiet. Dick, opening the door, laughed at the sight of me. His folks were next door, he said, "lifting a few with the neighbors." "Where's Barbara?" I asked, as innocently as I could. "She's up in her room." I could not ask more, because Dick and I were friends.

The chili was ready, big, steaming bowls we ate at the dining-room table. We drank cokes and argued good-naturedly about Ophelia ("She goes insane? How come? I don't get it," I said) and about Hamlet's worrying himself so sick he cannot do anything ("My old lady would call him a worry wart," I said). Overhead, when Barbara occasionally creaked the floor or otherwise stirred, my heart tightened. The muffled song of her talking on the phone went on at least an hour. Then the stairs creaked and, trying to keep my eyes on my *Hamlet*, all scribbled over, I felt her passage by the archway to the dining room. She banged around in the kitchen, then swooshed through the swinging door behind me, said, with perfect ease, "Hi, Clay. You guys sure get excited about dumb old homework," and then as I turned, looked, she passed the back of my chair. "Hi," I said. I saw only her backside: tight jeans, father's white shirt with the tail out, her butt ticking back and forth. Carrying a Coke, she passed into the front hall, started up the staircase. She saw me watching her, smiled big, made a finger-wiggling and intentionally silly wave, then disappeared from view. My heart slushed; how the hell could she *always* do exactly what ripped like an explosion through my nerves and obsessed me for months. "My old man would say," I said, my mouth dry, "that Hamlet has to get off dead center. He has to do something."

Dick said, "Barbara's a cock-tease," and laughed.

When I got up from the table, my knee hurt: sharp pain, big ache. Dick said he would drive me home, but, wanting the clarity of pain, I insisted on walking. Swinging my stiff knee as if it were wooden, I took longer to walk home. The snowfall had stopped; on dark back lanes, a night sky spread full of stars. At home taking off my wet Levis, a torn hole at the knee, dark blood. Bare white legs, ragged wound at knee cap; at glisten of bone, stomach queasy. I went to bed.

Next morning, ache was sharper. Mother harped on my bad judgment in going over to that Stephenson house. If I had listened to her, I would be fine; since I had chosen not to, I would just have to take my punishment. She would drive me to Dr. Harvath's office. I insisted, angrily, that I could drive myself. We stormed and shouted, but I prevailed. (Actually, driving was hard; my right leg hurt so much I had to use my left for accelerator and brake.) Harvath was tough, if not a bit cruel. He had patched up marines in World War II. He got a kick out of being able to see my knee bone, the patella. Kneading what hurt like fire, he called in his nurse and showed off his prize. "If you hadn't waited so long, there wouldn't be this much pain. Why the hell didn't you get it sewn last night?" I knew what was coming. "I'm not going to numb it," Harvath said. "Hell, you can handle a little pain, can't you?" "Yeah," I said. But sweat broke out immediately. I gripped hard the table edges while he pulled five crooked-needle stitches through my knee. The SOB was *not* going to hear me yell.

Recalling that pain, I remember—yes, the girl at the pool, 1950, her name was Joann! *Joann!*

✡

The scar of that romantic night remains, but its story is completed by two additional injuries from that year, 1953–54, my last in high school.

My romantic life was arranged so that serious girlfriends could be kept at least three hundred miles from Baltimore. (This was my first imaginative construction, but it was not put in place until *after* Barbara became part of my heart's mysteries.) During high school and college I worked as a life guard at a resort near Asheville, North Carolina. (The city was another of Scott Fitzgerald's haunts, although again I did not then know this. There Zelda was burned to death in a mental asylum fire. Also there Thomas Wolfe played out his oedipal-fired epic. In high school I was too serious to read nonrequired novels. Even so, in my bones was— and is—the romantic upon which Wolfe and Fitzgerald drew. Simple loss lifted to the tragic beauty of the doomed.)

The resort's mountain lake was a jewel. In the roped-off swimming area was a lifeguard's raft, a chair atop it, and from that bobbing and tipping throne, in the melted-gold squint of sunlight, I behind my dark sunglasses observed waitresses' walks. Each had her own orchestrated procession beautiful to me. The sweet grace of their dives, pffut!, I also studied. And their slow, balletic swimming strokes. Daily these pleasures.

Mountain evenings I paired off with one from Asheville or Aiken or Charleston. We went down to the pavilion for the night's entertainment. All of them were beautiful with their sunburns and starched cotton dresses smelling sweet and tart. After a little-theater production (once I was forced to be Shadrach in the fiery furnace), or music, or skit, or group singing, she and I walked slowly around the lake's edge to a bench. Kissing—how fierily passionate was our innocent courting! On the dark lake, moonlight shimmered and above us in the pines, night breezes sighed. Life was sweet. One of these summers I read Eisenhower's *Crusade in Europe* and Liddle Hart's biography of Sherman, the latter delicious with the pleasure of betraying Mother's Lost Cause hatred of him! Reading of war kept in check the courting. There was a retired marine master sergeant who was married to the tight-lipped lady who supervised staff. He had made four Pacific landings, fought out of Chosin Reservoir, been wounded three times, and twice received a Silver Star for bravery. When I pressed him to tell me about combat, he mumbled, talked in fits and starts while looking at the far shore of the lake. At summer's end I pledged to my girlfriend of the moment that I would write, visit when I could, and see her back here next summer. Thus did I make a distant anchor in my relations with Mother and a perfectly good reason not to risk asking out girls back in Baltimore who might say no (or if yes, whom Mother might criticize). I could then throw myself into schoolwork and earning independence with Saturday money.

And, from the first raw, sun-scattered day in March until my departure for North Carolina, I took baseball as seriously as science classes. It had been my father's sport. He had pitched in Washington sandlot leagues and had been scouted by the Boston Red Sox. I was a pitcher, too. Playing catch in the Ruxton yard was all we did together. By the eleventh grade, my pitches had pop enough to sting Dad. His grimace registered my speed, but he never complained. That year I pitched some one-hit shutouts and made the county all-star team.

In March of the next year when baseball practice started, I threw hard, worked on control. A good strong rhythm was returning. To complicate my life to the point of choking it, I swore not to miss a single daily Lenten service at Good Shepherd. From practice I rushed every day to the little church where a half dozen of us (I the only one under forty) crouched mumbling in the shadowy pews. And, finally, yet another complication had arrived in the mail. My resort girlfriend and her folks had invited me down to Charleston for the June debutante parties. The high-and-mighty of such affairs made me wince, but also the exotic of it aroused my curiosity. And the prospect of my going got Mother's goat. She said debutante parties were an affront to southern working people, most particularly her father, who had been proud all his life to belong to the railroad workers' union.

That morning I woke up to the clinging cobwebs of an upsetting dream I could not remember. It angered me that I was forgetting it so quickly. Because of ball practice and the daily 5:30 Lenten services, I had to stay up later than usual to finish my homework. "If you got to bed at a decent hour," Mother called, "you wouldn't be so out of sorts in the morning."

I was missing things I needed for school, stewing around. Asking Mother if she had seen my ball glove, she called back: "Well, I'll bet it's exactly where you left it!" Then she laughed.

My starched shirt already blotched with sweat at the arm pits, I stormed into the kitchen, with books, glove. I slammed down in one of the chromium-legged chairs to eat eggs and toast that were cold.

"Your big brother, Ellen, has got himself worked up into a tizzy this morning."

Ellen, then six, twirling an end of her hair, gazing out the open kitchen door into the sunny backyard, managed to laugh with Mother. The food I could not swallow fast enough. Through the eggy mush in my mouth I managed: "It's too late to catch the bus. I've got to have the car or you'll have to drive me both ways. I'm going to church again tonight."

"Tell me one little thing, please? Why should we inconvenience ourselves just because you get a crazy idea in your head about attending all the Lent services?" She paused. "Ride the school bus home, as usual, then take the car from here."

"But I got to go to ball practice!" I said, too loudly, thinking that I had her. "Did you forget that?" Too late I knew I had blundered into another of her ambushes.

"I certainly did not," she said very brightly, not even angry. "It is you, young man, who have forgotten that this family does not exist to satisfy your every whim. You play your old baseball all you want. And go down to Good Shepherd every evening, that's fine. But when you do *both*, and every day *require* either the car or us to drive you, then you are *demanding* we cater to your selfishness and, to boot, inconvenience ourselves."

The last stung. I was choking, gulping swallows of milk. Through the kitchen screen door I felt spring sunlight in our backyard.

As usual, Mother had a final twist: "Go ahead, take the car."

Guilt knotted. I jumped up, grabbed my plate, glass, fork to slide into the sink.

And yet another: "And, young man, while we are on the subject of you and this family . . ."

"I got to go," I said, quickly gathering up my books and stuff.

"Since you're driving our car, you have time to listen to this." There was no more coyness in her voice. Now she closed in for the morning's kill. But she was right: I did not have to hurry. I had picked up everything. I stopped in the doorway to the dining room, turned, faced her. Ellen had gone to the kitchen door; with her nose pressed against the screen, she looked out into the backyard.

"I don't want you going down to that Nina Pinkney's in Charleston. I won't have it. We're proud of our families. We have nothing to be ashamed of. You come from working people and you ought to be proud of it and not be running off to South Carolina for this *deb-u-tante* business where as sure as I am standing here you'll make a fool of yourself and embarrass us all. Just tell them no, no you won't go. In her *set* she'll be able to find plenty of *escorts*. Now that's the last thing I'm going to say about this. That is the final word."

Eggs and milk mush in my stomach were greasy, and anger filled my eyes, my brain. Out the door to the breezeway I blammed, into the garage, where I tossed up the overhead door—it almost bouncing back down. I jerked open the car door. Goddammit, I had forgotten the keys. I wanted to crash through a wall.

Then Mother, smirking, was in the breezeway door, dangling the car keys at me. She was making me come get them.

"Bull in a china shop," she said. "You're just an old bull in a china shop."

When I snatched the keys out of her hand, she laughed, said, "You'd better learn to control that temper, young man."

I backed the car out, holding myself tight, got it turned in the driveway angle, out onto the street. From the garage, door still open, Mother was watching. She looked solemn. I drove up the hill at a normal rate of speed, sweating bad, rolling down the windows, and the knots of it all were pulled so damn tight I concentrated on watching for kids, on not exceeding the speed limit. With one minute to spare before the tardy bell, I pulled into the school parking lot. There was one very tight place left. I jockeyed the Mercury back and forth, sweating again, anger crackling. It was not parked well, but it was parked. My door opened about two inches. Pushing across the front seat, I gathered up my pile, got the other door open, squeezed out, and, starting to slide between cars, flicked closed the car door with my right hand. My skin was on fire; I jerked, shit, shit, dropped everything, ripped open the door with my left hand, got out my right index finger. Oh god, oh god damn! It burned; it was bloody. I gathered up my books, my ball glove, and headed for school, hearing late bells ringing. My right index finger was bad.

The school nurse was Miss Payne. My voice too tight to speak, I showed her the bloody, swollen finger. Her cold blue eyes, behind tortoiseshell glasses, registered nothing. Then her voice asked what had happened, whether it was on school property. My jaws ached from holding down pain. She nodded me into the medical room. She put my finger in warm water, and I needed to pee, and I thought, shouldn't it be cold water? Shouldn't you put injuries in cold water to stop the pain?

As the day went on, the pain in my finger burned hotter. Could not think—just burning. Miss Payne had said I'd be fine, should stay in school. I had to wait out the day. I told Mr. Reber, the ball coach, that I had stupidly slammed my finger in a car door. "Which finger?" he asked, and I showed him my pitching hand, the bandaged index finger oozed with dried blood. The look in his eyes changed. "Okay," he said quietly. "Take care of that now. We'll see how it is in a couple of days." As I drove home, very deliberately, I noticed that the burning was surrounded by aching that included my whole body, my neck, my elbows and knees, my head.

"Well for goodness sakes," Mother said when I walked into the house. She was cheerful, glad to see me, even when I held up the bandaged finger. "How'd you do it?"

"Slammed it in the car door," I said, heading for my bedroom.

She laughed. My brain was on fire when I dropped onto the bed. She got my shoes off and called Ellen. In a few moments Ellen sidled in beside Mother at the foot of my bed.

"Old Clay slammed his finger in the car door," she said to Ellen. "Now you be careful. That's why I tell you to be careful."

Ellen's big brown eyes stared up at me from the foot of the bed. She did not say a word.

When I told Mother the nurse had put my hand in warm water, she said, "No wonder she's a school nurse!" In a few minutes she was back with a mixing bowl of ice and water. She sat down, carefully unwrapped the bandage on my finger. My god, it looked terrible, awful—swollen blue-red, bloody. Sweat broke out on my forehead. With the ice water the burn eased but not the ache. Mother wiped my face with a cold washcloth, then laid it on my forehead. She gave me two aspirin. She was still brisk, cheerful: "Try to sleep." She took Ellen by the hand, picked up the mixing bowl of ice water, and went out. She nudged closed the door. The pain had backed off, even some aching. Realizing I had missed Lenten services today, I slid into a nightmare of frozen outdoor water spigots, ice spikes hanging out of them, and pink angora sweaters. If I touched them, I would get them muddy.

I woke and every inch of my skin was burning. My mind could not think. I pitched on the bed, bit my lip hard. When Mother came in, I tried not to roll and pitch. She went out, came back with another soppy washcloth and, I registered with shock, one of Dad's bottles of Jack Daniel's bourbon. Telling me to toss them down, she poured me three straight shots. Fire in my throat, but gagging, I got them down. She was laughing: "It's old fashioned, but it'll work." This was the first time I ever had hard liquor in that alcohol-obsessed family. Still rolling and pitching with burning, my mind whirled. Mother said: "Soon you'll be feeling no pain," and laughed. She had another washcloth, this one dry, which she rolled up, put in my mouth. "When the pain gets bad, just bite as hard as you can." I did; it helped, but my loosening mind recalled the boy in "How Green Was My Valley" who is caned by his schoolmaster, supple whirring cutting bleeding welts, and a little girl runs in to give him a handkerchief to bite. I bit down hard. Mother left.

This time when I woke up, the fire was cooler, ache much less.

A week later, I went to ball practice. Gripping the ball hard, my finger burned. My pitching days were over. I did go down to Charleston, South Carolina, for parties with my debutante girlfriend. The expensive and showy clothes, the hysteria of my girlfriend's mother, the sinfulness of wasting so much food, the smug-happy talk—all ate on my nerves. Her father, a stockbroker (who had lost the family fortune in Peru), loved to read and had collector editions all over the house. Whenever I could I went up to the bedroom I shared with Nina's brother and there read Steinbeck's *Grapes of Wrath*. Nina herself, I should mention, was welcoming, and her voice's sweet, calm song filled me up. On Charleston Battery, another bench, we watched, silently, dawn open lavender, then heart-stopping rose, then shimmering gold on the ocean beyond Fort Sumter. That was the last time I saw Nina. (This is one of my life's regrets.) Back in Baltimore, Mother for weeks pumped me for details of my visit. I told her as little as possible.

✡

And another injury from 1954, my last full year at home.

At the winery where I worked with Dick, there was also Lester. He lived out in the country, wore hair slicked back with ducktails, sported a black leather jacket, and aspired to own an over-the-road semi. He was not mean, but he carried a switchblade. He walked with a swagger, affected sneers, but he was okay, I knew. Eating our lunches in winter sunlight, I wanted to show him that he was flat wrong for not wanting to go to college like us. He said staying in school longer than the law required was stupid. He said he wanted real money. When I repeated the litany of reasons why he should go to college, he looked bored. He made me angry.

At Towson High School, where my friends had plans to attend Cornell, Princeton, and Dartmouth, there was another group from along Loch Raven Boulevard who dressed and swaggered like Lester. They took Auto Mechanics and disdained sports. At lunch they hung out on the sidewalk in front of school smoking, talking tough. After school they hung out around their hot rods in the back parking lot. Their girlfriends, with hot lipstick, bleached hair, and too-tight sweaters, clung to them, smoked too.

One lunch hour I sat in the school's front hall. The bank of glass doors had been bucked open, propped. Warm spring air breezed into stale school halls. Sitting in a spare desk, I stood up to stretch, and when I went to sit back down the desk was not there—cracked my head against the wall, fell on the floor.

"That chair was mine!" I yelled at Auto Mechanics now occupying it. He smirked.

"You got up, I took it. You lose, pal."

"I was sitting there." My head stung; air was maroon.

"Oh yeah," he said, standing up too. He was five inches taller.

Maroon darkened. He was sneering. No small Mr. Good Student was a threat. He could take what he wanted.

My punch, short and fast, caught him in the solar plexus, knocked him up against the wall. Gasping for breath, eyes panicky. I should have landed my fist in his face—two, three times. I should have finished it. But he was defenseless. A full minute I stood there. He got his breath back.

"You wanna fight, let's go," he managed.

"What?" I had sat down in the chair.

"Outside."

This was a bad mistake. Out into the warm springtime we went, down the walk to the street where his friends were hanging out.

"Okay, tough guy," he said. Turning, he hit me in the stomach, but missed the solar plexus. I got a hard punch smack into his nose—blood—and another one, then one stung when I cracked his jaw. Fear in his eyes turned to rage.

He hit me hard, a roundhouse punch, right on the jaw; dark came in around the rim of my mind; I saw stars. He hit me again on the jaw, grabbed me in a headlock and whammed my head. He slammed me again into the hood of a parked car. Then he went to work jamming my eye into the Buick's hood ornament, made two or three passes. I couldn't break his headlock. His friends were yelling, and then a couple of them pulled him off.

Miss Payne stitched the eye herself and told me to lie down on one of the beds. I said no. Walking unsteadily down the hall, I told myself that, encountering Auto Mechanics again, I would fight him again. Next day, there he was, but he had a black-and-blue shiner and swollen nose. He pretended he did not recognize me, even with a big bandage riding above my eye.

This sudden reappearance of my childhood temper scared me. Now I had to struggle with it while in middle of social arrangements and a complicating morality. The scar is just above my right eyelid, in that soft skin. An adult, I could hurt and be hurt.

✡

In the pine woods of North Carolina on a rainy Thursday, 1957, the journey I had embarked on on bloody Sunday, 1945, and continued in the at-sea dark of Bethesda, Baltimore, and Ruxton, finally reached landfall, the adult moral universe, life's only true *terra firma*. This event, wherein I receive, like Don Quixote, yet another injury marking my already marked body, occurred a mile from the Bennett Place, where the last major Confederate army surrendered to Sherman.

A friend at college, Bill Bullock, was from Smithfield, North Carolina, where his father was wealthy and politically prominent. Bullock swaggered with brittle confidence, had all the money he needed. I imagined he would marry someone as darkly beautiful as Ava Gardner, who was also from Smithfield. He was finishing premed that year and already was accepted at a medical school.

Two years earlier my long-term dream of becoming an M.D. had crashed. It happened in a window-steamed back seat with a vigorous girl from Cedar Rapids who was wearing a lush cashmere sweater. I told myself I'd somehow, without studying, do well on tomorrow's chem quiz. And that same autumn, a blustery night, pines overhead roughly sighing, I nearly ran away with Alex from Norfolk, the first person I knew who loved literature, writing. No, I was not studying for tomorrow's test. No, that night Alex and I did not catch a Greyhound to Santa Fe. Instead, we went across campus and located the precise center of the football field, stretched out on our backs, and for several hours watched the orderly revolution of the heavens. No studying for chem that night. When I failed the course, a burden lifted. But the crash of the hope and aspiration of all those years left an ache.

My ambitions simply switched from my old man's devastated hopes to his actual successes. I took up a major in economics. I would be a business success as he was, live in an imposing house, drive expensive cars, have a beautiful wife. The honor and respect of being a medical doctor I had lost, but I could still prove myself by climbing the ladder of business success. For Bullock things had been easy. My envy I shouted down, tried to hold at bay.

He had a fire-engine red 1957 Corvette with an extra-hot engine. On a drizzly afternoon I was just back from the melancholic pleasures of library studying. The time had come for me to sample first hand the wonders of his Corvette, he said. He was a little wild, as rich southern males are. I was afraid of riding with him. But given *my* southern heritage, this was exactly why I said sure, sounded good.

The engine had a huge throb. I felt it in my teeth, my spine. We roared the gentle curves out through Duke Forest. Although he was driving, at the slightest touch of the accelerator I felt the Corvette's powerful lunge. Out at the Hillsboro Road he turned hard left, onto an older country road, and in a long straight through wet pines, he easily went up through a hundred, the engine with plenty left. As he touched the brake, a twitch of fishtail, and he popped down a gear for an S-turn left, then right. We slicked, icy cold shot up my spine, and the big car slid into the opposite lane, rear end fishtailing left. Bill tried to flick the car back right, but the fishtail deepened, and ahead rounding the corner I saw a straight-up little Plymouth, blue. And the instant of plowing into them head on, the O-shaped mouths of two gray-haired women in its front seat.

Blind, I'm blind. But getting my door open, Bullock saying, "You okay? Jesus!" I realized blood filled my eyes. Slowly, through it, I saw wet pine trees by the road, shatter of red plexiglass, and the steaming, crumpled mess of the front end of the Plymouth. The ladies moaned, "Oh lord, help me." I got over to them, opened a door. There was blood, and they looked badly hurt. Touching the driver's shoulder, I said, "Don't move. Just be still. I'll get an ambulance."

There was a sandy two-rut lane leading back from the road. I glanced back, saw Bill out of the car now, not hurt but dazed. He was looking at the Corvette's smashed front end. When I started down the lane, dizziness tightened in, then eased. A quarter mile, an old frame house, poor looking, and yard dogs started barking as I went up on the porch, blammed the doorjamb. A knot of people opened the door, then stepped back the instant they saw me. They were startled by the blood all over me, my shirt, my khakis and face.

"There's been an accident," I managed. "Out on the road. I need to call an ambulance."

"We don't have a phone," the man, who was skinny, said, his big dark eyes registering concern and alarm. "There's one next door. I'll go call. You stay here. I'll be back to ride you down to the road."

He rushed by me, out the door. He had nothing for the rain.

"I sure appreciate it," I said to the woman, also drawn looking. "Two ladies hurt bad."

"He'll be right back."

There was a single light bulb hanging from the ceiling, and the kids had poor but clean clothes. Cardboard patched a broken windowpane and batting was coming out of the couch and back in the kitchen a wash pan, plunk, plunk of a roof leak.

"I had better go," I said, as one of the children, barefoot, a sweet little girl, came out of the kitchen with a washcloth, gave it to her mother.

"Here now," she said. "Wait just a little minute. Let me put this on that eye." Although my eye and nose ached bad, I—God help me—wanted to pull back from her because they were poor. Rage at myself for thinking this of these kind people.

"Sit here," the mother said. I sat, cool of washcloth touching my nose, my eye. "You've been hurt bad," she said. The children's eyes showed they understood too.

"That's nice of you," I said. My chest eased—heart swelling with love of them. Why such kindness to a college kid? The little dark-eyed girl who had brought the cloth took my hand, which was on the arm of the chair, and just held it. I wanted to weep.

The man ran back up on the porch.

I stood up—wooziness rose, then subsided. And his strong hand was under my arm, helping me, the wife on the other side, and as I went out, crossed the porch, down to his pickup with the engine running, I was unsteady. They helped me into the truck.

I said thanks, goodbye. The children, all barefoot, were up on the porch under that light-bulb glare looking down at me. With despair I told myself I would remember them all of my life; I would never forget. The pickup door next to me closed, and the man eased the truck down the ruts. Heard ambulance sirens. At the accident, gray, rainy twilight, red flashers sweeping the shattered Corvette, the still-steaming Plymouth, a state police car too, squawking emergency radios, women's moans low.

When Bullock saw me, he hobbled over. He said, "Jesus, you're a mess." He said his knees hurt but aside from that, he was okay. "Those old ladies ain't so good, though." Then, his voice went quiet: "Tell the cop I wasn't in their lane. He's going to charge me. We gotta stick together on this."

"But you were on their side of the road."

He managed a shit-eating grin. The emergency lights were flashing all over us, the jumble of vehicles, the wall of wet pines on both sides of this curve in the road. "That doesn't matter. We stick together on this, you following me. We stick together."

What I told the state police officer was what Bullock told me to say. The ambulance, siren rising, pulled out, and the tow truck arrived to deal with the wrecks. Bullock was going to ride into town in the tow truck. Before they left, the ambulance medics said I needed to go to the emergency room, that my eye and nose were bad and needed attention.

The father in the pickup drove me to the hospital. I ached badly, my face, my head; and as the excitement subsided, dark rushed up into my mind. Sliding out of the truck, I thanked the man. He said he wanted to go with me into the emergency room. I told him I was okay. Their concern for me again almost made me weep. I resolved to thank him and his family properly, to take them a gift. When I pushed through the double doors into the emergency room, a nurse looked up. She started around the desk toward me.

When I came to, I was on the emergency room table with a huge white light a couple of feet from my face. Stinging shot after shot of anesthetic was going into my nose, the tissue around my eye. They shoved my nose around, it clicked, and they sewed it and my eye up. Scars on top of scars.

With my girlfriend later that evening, I drank tomato juice and ate a big onion stuffed hamburger. I insisted on driving my own car, even with one eye bandaged. Appearing tough was important, even if the pain in my face was bad. Later in the toss of sleep, I felt again the urge to weep at the kindness of the poor family.

At the suggestion of his father, Bullock daily sent flowers to the old women, who were in the hospital. He said his old man's lawyer had advised them not to pay medical expenses for the ladies because doing so implied culpability. His father's insurance had paid for a complete repair of his Corvette; it was as good as new. I turned down another ride.

The hearing on reckless driving was in Hillsboro, the county seat and a colonial town where Cornwallis had wintered. Bullock's father, the Smithfield politician, drove over with his lawyer, who was a Chapel Hill law school buddy of the judge who would hear the case. The lawyer had a concerned, quiet way of talking to me in the car. He said having the reckless driving charge dismissed was important because otherwise the Bullock family would be exposed to damage suits from the women. He said the Bullocks had been generous to them. Then he asked me, "You will testify that the car was in the proper lane when the accident occurred?" I said, "Yes," and thought, Bullock is a friend of mine. This is the way you treat friends. He was mostly in the correct lane; I mean, that was almost true.

The courtroom had a high ceiling and tall windows, and although almost empty, it was full of solemn light. The state police officer was there. The Bullocks' attorney went back to chambers to say hey to his buddy the judge. They came out together and the judge went up to the high bench. The officer testified that the Corvette had come to rest on the wrong side of the road, that the glass and debris indicated the collision had occurred in the Plymouth's lane. The Bullocks, sitting beside me, bristled. Their attorney, relaxed and cool, asked the officer a string of questions: Had he actually witnessed the accident? Did debris always indicate where an accident had occurred? Did he discover skid marks to confirm his guess about where the collision had occurred? (He had not; the road was too wet.) Then the attorney put Bullock on the stand. In his best southern-responsible demeanor, Bullock said that the women were on his side of the road. That the collision had occurred in his lane. He said he was very sorry he was unable to evade their car when it came over into his lane.

Then the attorney called me to the stand. And it was a stand; I had to go up six steps to the witness chair where I looked down at the attorney, who remained seated at the table, and out over all the empty benches. The judge, to my left, appeared to be having a pleasant time.

Hand on the Bible, I swore to tell the truth. Sweat started. My voice said my name into the large, empty space of the courtroom.

"Tell us in your own words what happened."

The courtroom's quiet light, my oath, the place's history—these lifted me out of myself: "We were going over a hundred on the straightaway. I saw the speedometer. Bill was showing me what his Corvette would do." Down at the table he was wide-eyed. "As we went into the corner, the car fishtailed into the oncoming lane. He tried to get it back, but the rear end fishtailed more. We were in the other lane when we hit head on with the Plymouth." I had gone back on what I said I would say. I could not lie. I felt alone.

The lawyer prodded at what I had said, but I did not change my testimony. Bill squeezed his hands tightly together on the table.

I stepped down. The Bullocks stiffened when I sat down behind them.

The attorney, unrattled, concluded by telling his pal the judge that people under stress see, as they both know so well, many different things. He recited how I had been injured, the stitches, the broken nose, the loss of blood, my passing out as I entered the hospital. Then he said that, really, this was a civil matter between Mr. Bullock and the ladies and that with no solid evidence the traffic charges should be dropped. The judge gave a little speech in which he repeated what the Bullock's attorney had just said. He dismissed the charges.

We went to a Howard Johnson's for lunch, and Mr. Bullock insisted we all order big steaks. I tried to explain what had happened—that after I swore an oath, I could not say anything that was not true. Bullock, tight as a drum, told me I was flat wrong. That there was no skid; he was entirely on his own side of the road when *they* hit him. Mr. Bullock and the attorney laughed, said that it did not matter. That the judge saw it our way.

Neither Bullock nor I tried again to be friends. He thought I had betrayed him, and I had. But I was most upset about not returning to the ramshackle house in the woods where the people had been so kind to me. Late that spring, as I was preparing to leave college, I drove down the rutted lane through pines to their house. It was abandoned, the door standing wide open. Not saying thanks to them was heavier for my having to confess to myself that I was a snob. The Bullocks were ugly, and I was like them. This thought roared hot as a bonfire. I was afraid to step outside the privileges the Bullocks represented. And the family in the woods was more the North Carolina family I came from, because Mother did, than the one we pretended to come from.

I wanted to plunge my fear, my vulnerability, into the fire of the world. Their names I did not know.

Casualty

My college girlfriend in 1957–58 was from Saint Louis. When we first met on a blind date, I knew she came from a well-to-do Saint Louis family, a "high up" one. Even so, I immediately told her the story of my father's down-and-out weeks in Saint Louis. My gritty account was as interesting to her as the details of her society family were to me. I saw her often, things got serious, and the summer after I graduated, I arranged to live in Saint Louis with a college friend. Continuing to see my girlfriend, I desired that. But another strong attraction, one I kept to myself, was living where Dad's boyhood adventures had taken place more than forty years earlier.

At age sixteen, July 1922, Dad had jumped a KATY freight in Durant. It took him up to Saint Louis, where a railroad cop caught him, beat him hard with a billy club. With no money, he could not go to a hospital. He slept for several days in Forest Park and ate green apples pulled off trees. (Forest Park was the site of the 1904 Saint Louis World's Fair. The movie *Meet Me in St. Louis* looks back from 1944 and World War II to the fair.) Sick from the apples, Dad washed dishes in a greasy spoon, got a bed in a flophouse, and soon had enough money to buy a ticket to Wisconsin, where his job handling horses at a logging camp was still waiting. This story of boyhood adventure he told me during World War II, and it was the first I heard of Saint Louis. About a year later I set foot there. Returning from our 1945 reunion in Oklahoma, we rode the KATY up to Saint Louis, where we had a four-hour layover. It was hot and muggy, the station was grimy, and I remember air so full of soot it stung to breathe.

To be accepted in my girlfriend's family would undo the shame my family, that is, my father, had suffered here. (And his story was about shame: having nothing, taking a beating in the name of authority from a railroad cop.) I enjoyed the fantasy of my girlfriend's folks in their cozy lives in 1922 and my father, dirty, injured, half sick, out in the dark of Forest Park. Now his son was almost inside with them. Although these thoughts concerned my father, I never told him.

The family's residence was in old-money Ladue. It was a big stone neo-Norman beautifully half hidden by apple trees. It occupied a hill top above five acres of rolling lawn scattered with oak trees. When I turned in at the driveway and began my winding ascent, I always was struck by how grand the house was. It had French doors, a terrace (not a patio), an upstairs library, a fireplace in the master bedroom, a baronial fireplace in the living room, and a small, cozy apartment for a live-in maid. Such a house I had seen only in movies I did not like.

I treasured the belief that I might pass into this grand world of *New Yorker* readers, martinis (not beer, bourbon, or white lightning), and conversations that were not blood sport as much as occasions for amused, ironic detachment. Helped by my girlfriend's father, I got a position selling advertising spots on a brand new radio station. It was a tough sell, and I carried a portable radio to prove the station's existence. But I did not mind the difficulties, because in those days media, the ad business, "selling time" were considered sophisticated. My luck was running high.

After a hot summer day calling on car dealers, I eased out to the big house on Ladue Road. This would be my wonderful life, I told myself. Swinging into the drive, I slowed to the rhythm of sunlight and old-tree shadow. On the driveway apron I parked, then sat, engine off, to smell in the warm Saint Louis evening sweet boxwood hedges. Ambling to the front door, I was met by my smiling girlfriend. The house was cool, with the first home air-conditioning I had encountered, and was lightly redolent of lemons and furniture polish. Sweeps of a vacuum cleaner showed how recently the maid had attended to the living room; my footprints tracked the carpet's beautiful expanse. As we sat down for dinner, peach sunsets poured through tall windows into the dining room, ignited dark corners under the sideboard, and, receding, hazed the expanse of lawn and occasional oaks all the way down to tree-lined Price Road. We dined on roast beef and salads (the first I regularly had) and little dinner rolls. Here there was no fried chicken, cream gravy, green beans cooked in fatback, and corn bread. Crystal goblets were used and the talk was full of thatches of names, families, and family generations. It was hard to follow but full of deep belonging. The intense and often brutal emotional warfare of our dinner table at home I did not miss at all.

This summer was my second look at the exotics of debuts. From the pantry phone my girlfriend's mother stage-managed the intricacies of etiquette and debutante protocol. We were sent to an outdoor evening party at the Saint Louis Country Club, where night breezes riffled dark trees and danced dangling strings of pastel Chinese lanterns. The music was wah-wahing saxophones and clear sweet clarinets. And we went to brunches and teas and dinner parties heavy with silver perfectly polished and unctuous butlers in starched white jackets. And with some excitement we attended that summer's most talked about extravaganza, a "Venetian Night" with a made-for-the-occasion lake and gondoliers and an almost-famous band and two circus-size tents, air-conditioned of course, where hundreds of us had an elegant midnight supper. I pretended, fiercely, to belong to all this.

Her mother, who was shrewd, detected that I was not swept away by these doings. Once she tried to deal me out for a home-grown Saint Louis boy, which was actually okay with me, but my girlfriend pitched a fit. I steered clear of the mother and ate plenty of yawns when her stupendous memory for who married whom back three generations, and who was related to whom, and who had taken what glorious vacations, got to be too much. I would not argue nor excuse myself from the table. I kept attention in my gaze, even when I was hopelessly lost. These thorns of irritation, I told myself, were small price to pay for belonging to this tightly woven little universe. Yes, if I was careful, this sow's ear might pass as a silk purse.

That summer, which in memory is luminous, I began to read Sigmund Freud. I'm sure I wanted to appear sophisticated. (And I'm now sure I also wanted to upset my own pretending!) My girlfriend's Ivy League friends, male and female, took offense at my overheated and intentionally provocative comments. An allusion to Freud was quite all right, but plunging in was decidedly a no-no. This impoliteness aside, I otherwise chatted at Medarts, at Shady Grove, in Ladue houses, about the relative merits of the Saint Louis Country Club and Bellreive, the Saint Louis Opera, which neighborhoods were best, and, this most intensely, who was getting married to whom and where the reception was and how much it and the wedding dress would cost. Randolph So-and-So occupied us, how he was "doing just marvelously" in his father's brokerage, and (*sotto voce*) Negroes, how they wanted to be with their own, how they were ruining perfectly wonderful old neighborhoods built at the time of the fair. Once in the late evening and after several nightcaps my girlfriend's father, a gentleman of the old school I admired, told me that the house of his birth near the fairgrounds was now occupied—voice dropping to a whisper—by "coons."

Mere mention of the Saint Louis World's Fair, or more properly, the Louisiana Exposition of 1904, caused eyes to dance and voices to burble. Even those unborn at that time elaborated vivid descriptions of the fair's splendors, its lagoons, its exotic pavilions. That summer Saint Louis was the grand hub of the universe and now, half a century later, memories of that glorious summer puffed up Saint Louisans' smugness, sentimentality, and bigotry. (T. S. Eliot fled; Tennessee Williams understood the confection that was Saint Louis; I had read neither.) Half aware then of these hypocrisies and self-delusions, I no less urgently desired admittance to this closed world. I aimed to rub out every trace of my awkward, rough-edged manners. I aimed to erase the plain fact that Mother spoke with an upcountry North Carolina accent and that her father had repaired locomotives for the Southern Railroad (and, sin of sins, belonged to a union). Erase, too, that my father was a runaway Okie who, hungry, lived for a few days on apples filched on the grounds of their beloved fair, and that his father kept a shirttail store in a little nowhere town in Oklahoma. I wanted to be a 1950s Jay Gatsby before I had ever heard of Jay Gatsby.

On a blustery day in the previous spring, I had signed up for the Marine Corps. I had known all summer that when autumn came, my campaign to belong in Saint Louis society would have to be suspended for three years of military service. When my active duty was completed, my girlfriend and I, by then married, would return. Then, foundations well laid, I would erect the edifice of my life as a well-heeled Saint Louisan. Yes, excellently planned, except that summer I learned that in the ointment was a big, ugly fly. Young men of good Saint Louis families, after

finishing college, were permitted service as officers in the navy. On comple-
tion of active duty, they of course returned to Saint Louis, married
Mary Institute or John Burroughs girls, started families in cute first homes
in Clayton or Webster or even Kirkwood, initiated careers in family busi-
nesses or banks or brokerages, and of course joined the Missouri Athletic
Club and one of several approved country clubs. At dinner parties they
would be permitted amusing and expurgated tales of naval service. But,
unfortunately for me, service in the navy was one thing, and service in the
Marine Corps quite another. Don't poor southern boys and big city Irish
go into the marines? Its bloody history, gaudy uniforms, and reputation
for actually *liking to fight,* made the Marine Corps . . . well, joining such an
organization simply did not reflect good taste. My girlfriend's best friend,
a student at Smith College, exclaimed, "Oh dear, *nobody* joins the marines!"
After that when I spoke at all of military service, I never mentioned the
USMC. I hoped that by keeping quiet my faux pax would go relatively
unnoticed. After all, I would be out of town. My mistake might not be
fatal. Esau still might become Jacob.

This fervent hope sweetened summer evenings with my girlfriend.
After she and I talked, stole extra slices of bakery-bought cake, and necked
on the couch—ears tuned for the creaking of a parental step on the staircase—I left for my college friend's house in the south suburbs. Closing
the heavy door behind me, I luxuriated again in the sweet aroma of
boxwood hedges. After briefly inspecting the canopy of heaven, which in
damp evening air was a bit hazy, I climbed in my car, cranked up, and slowly
descended the drive. I took old Ballas Road, which had been a farm lane.
Engine purring, I whipped along with top down and radio set to KMOX,
"The Voice of Saint Louis." (My little station shut-down at dusk.) That
summer the Kingston Trio, Perry Como, and "The Yellow Rose of Texas"
were as familiar to me as road wind's singing rush. And flying by above
were the dark shapes of old trees up close to the road, with here and there
salt-and-pepper star-strewn summer sky. Life was beautiful; the past was
past. Fate smiled on me.

✿

In late July of that summer I got a pain in my belly that resulted in a nine-
inch scar for one small inflamed appendix. At my girlfriend's house I

recuperated in a spare bedroom looking out on apple trees weighed down with green August apples. With me hobbling around, barely able to go up and down stairs, her mother regarded me with less suspicion. Plus, soon I would be gone. My orders to Quantico had been forwarded to me from home, and I was to report in a few weeks. My belly burned along the incision; sometimes it bled. My girlfriend was preparing to go back to college.

I returned to Baltimore. Mother told me to postpone training: "Have you taken leave of your senses? Are you crazy?" Dad was sure I would make the right decision. A Baltimore surgeon said I would be "back to normal" in a month's time. When I asked about marine training in two weeks, he laughed, "I don't know about that, son. I just don't know." What worried me about postponing was the prospect of being thought a coward—that and having nothing for six months.

At night in bed, looking out across the valley at Sheppard Pratt's familiar lights, I told myself fourteen weeks of marine boot training was not impossible to tough out. With a half-healed scar on my belly, I could prove how tough I really was. More than exercise of good judgment, the fire of a boot camp trial appealed to me—it full of yip-yipping of rebel yells and the rolling thunder of Manassas, Antietam, and Chancellorsville. And the knife-names of Iwo, Tarawa, Okinawa. Dad's trunk in the basement still contained his army uniforms.

That September I said goodbye to Dad at Ruxton Station. The big diesel I heard coming a long time before it abrupted out of the pearly fog. Pitching my suitcase up the steps of the coach car, I felt the incision; it wasn't bad.

✶

At Washington's Union Station, I changed trains for Quantico. Right here I had gazed at marines, chests full of medals, returning from World War II. Pacing under the station's vault, I was sure this USMC trial was what I should now be doing. Wiggling myself into Saint Louis was fun, half pretending, half real. But this Marine Corps ordeal, there lived my passions. And going to boot camp now would earn even more respect. That summer at Parris Island a drill instructor named McKeown drowned most of his recruit platoon on a forced march through swamps. At almost the same time at Quantico, DIs were putting officer candidates through disciplinary punishment when two suddenly died. These incidents, highly publicized, got my blood up. I wanted this training to be hard, a challenge, an ordeal. And I had burned my bridges. If I failed out of OCS at Quantico, I would be sent down to Parris Island, restart boot camp, and serve my three years in enlisted ranks. That would be okay, too. What did scare the hell out of me was my hair-trigger temper. Usually I was thoughtful, a good-citizen type; then a bump, a sign of disrespect, and a fierce alien presence suddenly inhabited my body. Anger roared, I was strong, ready to fight, with no thought whatsoever of consequences. With incidents such as the one with Auto Mechanics, I had learned to keep more to myself, especially to avoid provocative people and situations. That sunny September morning on the train down to Quantico, catching glimpses of the broad, peaceful Potomac, I understood that in OC boot camp I was seeking out exactly what for years I had struggled hard to avoid.

I managed four sit-ups on the first PT test. My T-shirt was wet with blood. The lieutenant, a round-faced Irishman just out of training himself, slammed me against the bulkhead of the platoon office. "You want to make me look bad? You want to wreck my platoon? Are you hearing me? *Are you hearing me?* You'll pack your sea bag and your butt'll be on a Parris Island train before the end of this week. Got that? *Have you got that?*" His finger jabbed my breastbone.

"Sir, yes, sir!" I yelled back.

Our physical exams had been done by a navy doctor, sleepy-eyed, less military than I. Noticing the incision, he told me it was not healing well. He then said that as far as he was concerned I was fit for duty. If he had given me an excuse for my poor PT test, I would not have used it.

The lieutenant raged on—spit flecks hitting my face, eyes. His talcum powder I still smell. He told me it would be a personal pleasure to escort me to the Quantico depot. He told me he would *enjoy* putting my sorry ass on the Parris Island train.

Daily the lieutenant ripped up my bunk, often with the platoon present. Yelling that I was a class A screwup, he wildly threw blankets, pillow, mattress, and sheets around the squad bay. Then he went and got the stuff, threw it again, all of us standing at attention. (My blankets were squarer, tighter, than my bunk mates'.) At Saturday inspections, when Captain

Burritt had praised my immaculate M1 rifle, the lieutenant returned to the squad bay in a rage, spit flying, shouting that my open footlocker looked like shit. Lifting it above his head, he heaved it down the squad bay through motes of morning sunlight. Retrieving it, grunting, still yelling obscenities at me, he threw it a second time. My uniforms, gear, letters, and civilian clothes, which I had spent hours arranging, scattered down the squad bay.

I learned the tea ritual of perfect shines; my boots darkly gleamed. Brassoed to perfection, my boot eyelets flashed in autumn sunlight. Weapons I could field strip and reassemble quickly. My test scores on tactics, weapons, fighting doctrine, USMC history, were near the top of the company. My cleaning details satisfied the DI sergeants, both Korean War veterans: toilet bowls glistened, to a fingertip were squeaky; the blankets on my bunk were tight enough to bounce a quarter; the GI cans gleamed from two hours of Brassoing. Although I winced on the obstacle course when my belly hit the belly buster log, I otherwise was faster over the course than the big Notre Dame fellow the lieutenant liked, and I was faster, too, than the All-American tackle from Oregon. Landing Party Manual marching I did well, biting off corners, keeping exact cadence. The ballet of squad drill was difficult, but I learned its intricate steps. When we learned a new movement, I counted on being made squad leader that afternoon, when I would have to know the intricate commands for executing that movement. And perform them with the lieutenant two inches from my face, yelling, taunting me. Whether I got it right or not, that evening before chow an UNSAT chit would come down from the lieutenant. He was building a case for my dismissal. My PT test numbers had risen to above the platoon averages.

The grinder, a hundred-yard-square slab of hot asphalt, was terrible. There we marched, too, but the platoon laps, around and around and around, legs going rubbery, then numb, some couldn't take. They staggered off to the side, dropped rifles, peeled off packs, grabbed canteens. Most soon were on trains down to Parris Island. But the real breaker of men was the daily forced march over Quantico's mean, sharp, knee-burning hills. Sometimes as a platoon, sometimes as a company, we ran these flat out with full packs, cartridge belts, canteens, and rifles. Three miles, five miles, seven miles, fifteen miles. The Hill Trail. The Power Line Trail. The

Chopawamsic Trail. Some just quit, stopped to rest. Others collapsed, blood from their noses pouring out through their fingers. Some rolled into the brush, passed out. Some wept; their burning knees had just quit on them. Still others slowed, dropped back in the column, and were swept up by the medics, who had no sympathy: "Sure you're sick. Yeah, we understand," they said, knocking that OC tumbling off the trail. Willpower, as Mother called it, was *not* what kept you going. After the first hour you had no will-power. After the second hour you had no idea how you were still putting one boot in front of the other. I never dropped out; somehow I always kept up, kept going.

The lieutenant began assigning me 2–4 A.M. fire watches, hoping, I guess, to wear me down physically and mentally. But his intentions were reversed: though tired, I was more intensely concentrated on this ordeal. When we fought with bayonets, pugil sticks, hand to hand, he was always there watching. He wanted to write up my lack of fighting spirit. And in the first few minutes, I was hesitant, but once underway, God help me, I loved it too much. Although he daily wrote UNSAT chits on me, none was for a grievous lapse sufficient to toss me out. He needed something terrible, a disaster, to overcome my good physical and classroom performance. As the weather got cold, he ran up the pressure. For platoon inspections he checked my posted duties (latrines, deck, GI cans, butt kits), then after a two-second inspection declared what he saw as the worst he had ever seen and canceled the platoon's liberty. At first my fellow OCs told me how unfair the lieutenant was: "Jeez, the butt kits were perfect. What's he talking about? The lieutenant's got it in for you." But as weeks passed, they got scared of how irrational it was. They were afraid being seen with me would bring the lieutenant's wrath down on them. They stayed away, avoided conversations, even in the squad bay, on breaks, in the mess hall.

That autumn 600 entered OC training at Quantico. By late October 350 had been sent on the night train to Parris Island. At dusk with windows open in the squad bay, I could hear the southbound train stop at Quantico depot. After a couple of minutes its diesels surged, and the train came down through our end of the base, horn blowing mournfully for the crossings. My platoon's squad bay was emptying out. Mattresses had been rolled on empty bunks; wall lockers stood without locks; the formations were noticeably smaller. Surviving into November did not make me exultant or even happy. Instead, it bothered me that, in this crazy ordeal, I was actually finding deep satisfactions.

Tangled up as we were, the lieutenant and I fell into pure struggle far beyond motives and sought-after ends. He doubled my late-night guard duty assignments. Hoping for big mistakes or to finally break me, he escalated the leadership billets he assigned me, ones no one could handle: command of the platoon in difficult squad-drill formations, command of the company in an attack, leading the platoon on the most grueling hikes. But I kept my wits, and my mistakes weren't bad enough. I still had not physically broken down. And his rage rose mightily.

His own situation was worsening. My continued presence in his platoon shamed him in the eyes of the company's NCOs and other officers. If he could not succeed in busting me out of OCS, especially when huge numbers were being sent down to Parris Island, what the hell could he do? He had to break me, my strength, my will, but somewhere in my heritage was the absolute imperative that I would *never, never* break down. I might die but I would not break. This not thought as much as in my bones. And, God help me, I had also discovered an appetite for this struggle, which was not personal, really, as much as metaphysical, that pure and terrible.

And I had discovered something else. The world's physical beauty was suddenly ravishing. Ordinary sensations now ripped through me. At cold dawn, standing in the dark at attention, I was struck by the sight of the base water tower up in lemoning sky, red warning lights winking off-on, off-on. In the mess hall, dark-filled windows murkily reflecting us, the steamy smell of gravy, bacon, sausage, and grits was a knot of overwhelming sensation. Rifle oil's sweet pungency was almost too much. In the hymn our clattering gear made when we ran I lived content; and in the slide of woods-shadow over the pack of the man in front of me; and in the great cool on my sweat-sopped back when I swung-off my field marching pack. Filling me was chuff of boots, needling pains in my shins, and, at night, with red exit lights glowing, bunks squawking with the toss of restless sleep and dream. And I lived in the glittering immensity of after-midnight stars on cold nights along the Potomac. I lived the rip of forbidden pogey bait—Twinkies, Hostess cupcakes—its oily, sweet, jazzed-with-chemicals taste nearly overwhelming. (Like urges from childhood to eat my oil paints—vermilion red, cobalt blue. Like the dank of leaf rot that Dad, at the top of the ladder, threw down when he cleaned the gutters.) I was a switching yard of sensations. If marine training brought out an appetite for struggle, my pride flowering in that dark earth, it also brought out passion for beauty's ravishments.

On a cold night in November, our little platoon of survivors was dug in and shivering in defensive positions on a hillside. Again I was leading the platoon. Again the lieutenant was hoping that a leadership disaster could be blamed on me. He was across the valley with Chinese-style aggressor forces. From the lip of my hole, I saw their bonfires and heard good-time laughter and blaring loudspeakers telling us to come over for nice hot chow and girls. Then I heard an engine throbbing, the chink-chink of treads, and the searchlight, cyclopslike, of an M35 tank started down into the valley between their position and ours. We had no rocket launcher, no mortars, no antitank grenades. I hoped to god I had badgered the platoon into digging foxholes deep enough to withstand that tank's huge weight. Throbbing filled the night, concussed my chest; I felt it in the cold earth. "Get down!" I yelled.

It started up the hill toward our holes, searchlight stabbing the night. Twenty yards down the line, two shadows jumped out of their hole, bugged out for the rear. The searchlight caught them. I yelled but they kept running. Their cowardice enraged me. Better to have the goddamn tank crush breath from your body than to be afraid. Throbbing now filled my brain. Two holes down the tank would strike our line; I wished it would hit my hole. Then, in the gulps of the roaring tank—clanking, chewing of rocks—I heard yelling. Infantry, tanks supported by attacking infantry. Done by the book. Hunker down in your hole and pray the tank does not crush you to death. The earth of my hole, the night, throbbed; it spilled out of me.

Then calm; it was all as clear as icy stars. My poncho off over the top of my head (it was on for warmth), I bounded out of my hole and ran across the brushy hillside straight for the tank that was about to break our line. No rifle, brush switching my legs; exhilarated, as if it already had happened. The lieutenant was exactly where I knew he would be: last man in his file, laughing, firing his weapon in the air, having a great time. He never saw me as I came out of the dark. Using what I had learned, I tossed him to the ground. He was between my knees, helmet knocked askew. The sharp edge of my bayonet touched the soft of his throat. Face shadowy, open-mouthed. I had come to kill him, and he knew it. When the blade of the bayonet raced across his throat, cutting his jugular, his windpipe, my weight would kill him. A pig's throat cut. It was as simple and matter-of-fact as Milky Way stars coming out on breezy autumn nights; as sweet baby-laughing of a creek sliding through rocks. His warm, sticky blood on my hands. But he had quit fighting me. A coward, he had surrendered. *Fight me, you son-of-a-bitch! Fight me!* Then I swung off him. I watched him get up. He ran away down the hill.

In the platoon office, he yelled that I would be court-martialed. Assault on a superior officer, twenty years in Leavenworth. He was afraid of me, and I was not afraid of him or Leavenworth or anything else. The court-martial was not again mentioned, but he put me up for dismissal to Parris Island. He had wanted this, but not in this way. When I had office hours with the company commander, who had a distinguished combat record in Korea, he told me I measured up well physically, that my record in military classes was excellent, that my leadership was okay. He looked straight at me, said quietly: "Your platoon commander has recommended dismissal. You'll have to see the colonel."

"Sir, yes, sir," I said.

Late November, a cutting wind on the Potomac. The colonel had been awarded a Congressional Medal of Honor on Saipan. He had commanded the First Marines at Inchon. Big, with a soft Mississippi accent, he had sent four hundred officer candidates to Parris Island. Every platoon or company dismissal he had approved. Behind his desk were the U.S. and Marine Corps flags. Out the windows, sky low and gray, was the grinder. The regimental sergeant major told me to stand at ease. The colonel asked me to tell him what happened on the night field exercise. I told him. I even told him I did not understand what had gotten into me. He was quiet a moment. He looked right at me, and I liked him. He asked if I could do the twelve-man squad drill we had been taught.

"Sir, yes, sir."

"Will you be a good Marine Corps officer?"

"Yes, sir, I will, sir." My voice was quiet.

Two hours later the dismissal list was posted on the platoon bulletin board. As those remaining in the platoon crowded in to read it, I sat on my bunk. I could stand Parris Island; I could take whatever happened. My strength was that my life was not worth much—not to me or to anybody else. I got off my bunk and went up to the bulletin board. The others quit talking, made a path. Since my assault on the lieutenant, they had kept away more. At the bottom of the list: "Lewis, Clayton W.: retained for commissioning."

"How'd you do it? What'd you tell the colonel?"

I went back through them to my bunk, lay down. Numb, arm over my eyes, I heard the song of our equipment and boots on the trail, in the gravel of roads. The colonel had decided to commission me *because* I assaulted the lieutenant. The violence in me, which I had labored to keep hidden, was out.

The next day with full gear I ran our little platoon sixteen miles in two hours. Grabbed men whose legs were going to rubber. Slammed my hand into their helmets to wake them up. To lighten their loads, took their heavy gear—rifles, packs, BARs. Twice that distance I could have gone. Coming back on to mainside, passing the commanding general's flag, the Marine Corps flag, the U.S. flag—all standing straight out in November wind on the Potomac—one of the DIs resumed command of the platoon. He brought us back to marching cadence and announced permission to sing, for the first time, the Marine Corps hymn. A few voices, short of breath, started, and then all of us began to pick up the tune and sing, and tears were running down my cheeks.

In the base theater I was commissioned. Outside the theater, Potomac wind popping, my gold bars pinned on, one of the platoon DIs saluted me for the first time, and, in keeping with tradition, I handed him a dollar. "You'll be a good officer, sir," said this humane and poster-sharp marine. When I returned the other DI's salute, he winked: "You showed 'em, sir."

When I shook the lieutenant's hand, which was pudgy, soft, he said: "Lewis, you're a screwup." Standing in bright December sunlight, wind beating at my new officer's greens, I looked steadily into his eyes until he looked away.

On a thirty-six-hour pass I went down to Duke to see my Saint Louis girlfriend. On old U.S. 1 that Saturday afternoon I saw familiar gas stations, diners where I had stopped with college friends. Now trees were bare and etched into cloudy December sky. At Duke, the stone of buildings, wet with recent rain, looked trapped in the walls. The bones of my girlfriend's skull I noticed. The student who had been interested in the history of economic thought seemed unrelated to me. That weekend on the car radio, "Hang down your head, Tom Dooley, poor boy you're bound to die" played often.

Trying to act as if I weren't different, we ate barbecue and hush puppies at Clyde's and saw a romantic movie. I asked my girlfriend if she would marry me at Christmas time—not wait until next June or the June after that when she graduated. I'd get a nice place in Fredericksburg. I was *certain* I would be lucky and not receive orders to Okinawa, which would mean fifteen months without wife or family. The dash (and perhaps doom) of my proposal appealed to her. On Sunday afternoon we called her folks back in Saint Louis from a telephone booth in front of Duke Hospital. Her mother was reluctant, but she did not say no. She thought her youngest was getting a sow's ear.

That Sunday night I drove back to Quantico on empty roads. We had planned someday to get married; now it would just be sooner rather than later. That's all. That's all. Married, I would not appear a killer; there would be another way to regard me. Staring into the cast of headlights that brought familiar roads out of the dark, every curve and crossroad known by heart, I did not understand sudden tears stinging my nose, welling into my eyes. Nor did I understand wrenching sobs that didn't stop until I got to Keysville, Virginia.

✡

The wedding was in Saint Louis the week after Christmas. The afternoon before the wedding, I ran sixteen miles on a school track. Sensations of Quantico rolled through my mind—snap of rifles, chuff-chuff of boots on the grinder, wink of red warning lights down at the air-station water tower. When I saw the spread of wedding-present silver and crystal on the big tables in the upstairs bedroom, heard my bride-to-be's happy laughter with her friends, I remembered how cold the earth was on a winter night. How it got in your bones.

In our small room at the Clayton Inn hours before the wedding, Mother shrieked: "A terrible, terrible mistake. You know it as well as I do. *You must not marry her. That family—they don't like you. They think you're not good enough for her."* I had never seen her hysterical. Dad, trying to watch the Redskins-Browns game, said softly, "Aw Betty, leave the boy alone." Ellen's eyes were big; she was frightened. Mother was not deterred: "If they're so snooty, *to hell with them. We'll just go home, that's all. Let's pack!"*

Anger I must avoid.

The wedding and reception, with a big heated tent over the terrace, went without a hitch. In the photographs Mother is composed, as am I.

At a motel near the airport we spent the night. We slept right through a serious fire in another part of our motel—three fire companies, all TV stations. After the flight to Washington, I discovered that my too-smart plan to avoid parking fees had resulted in my car's being impounded. I paid fees I could not afford, and we drove down to Fredericksburg, where I had rented the top floor of an old house. Stopping at the A&P for groceries, I locked my keys in the car. I broke out a wing window to get in.

Our apartment, where the rooms were high-ceilinged and empty, rattled with every step and sound. A box spring and mattress were our furniture. My wife had terrible headaches. At 3 A.M. the second night I went out for Bufferin—got it in a sleazy back-street hotel. When she at last went to sleep, I tried to make the anxious humming of my body stop. Then in cold air I smelled the sweet of rifle oil and the tang of Kiwi boot polish. I slept.

Old Wars

While living in Fredericksburg and commuting to Quantico for advanced training, I was struck by an obsession. For all its grand history, the town was pleasantly southern, shabby, and calling the shots were cops with big guts who hated us buzz-cut marines. (This we considered a high compliment.) In our first months of married life, my wife and I were doing fine but definitely not finding instant marital bliss. In our apartment I was newly and awkwardly intimate with a female; up the road at USMC Schools, I was learning the demanding male business of war. For weekend fun I checked out a USMC-issue .45, which I took out to a sand pit where I blasted one hundred rounds of ammunition, my ears ringing afterward for several hours.

Historical markers about the Battle of Fredericksburg were all over town. The house on Caroline Street, our apartment was the second floor, backed up to the Rappahannock River. Out front was an historical marker about a Mississippi brigade firing from here at Union engineers trying to lay pontoon bridges across the river. At the town library I checked out Bruce Catton's *Glory Road*, and there discovered that Union artillery had blasted the Mississippians here, brought down the houses they were using for cover. Barksdale pulled back, the Yankees finished their bridges, and the Union army marched into town. Exactly here, where I was reading this, this had occurred! On the ruins of those demolished houses, this house was built!

Right here! Immediacy, depth in time: a raging interest was touched off. I read every book I could find at the library on Burnside's blunder, the slaughter of his brave Union soldiers, and Lee's effortless victory. As a child I often had heard from Mother about her grandfathers, who "fought with Lee and Jackson." She still angrily blustered whenever I failed to stand up for the playing of "Dixie." But in those years I did not have the slightest interest in the Civil War. Now, gasoline-doused fire raging, I was obsessed. On our itchy living-room couch, twilight turning to darkness, I refused to turn on the light until the words of yet another tome on the battle were lost in total darkness.

Soon the town's library had no book on the Battle of Fredericksburg I had not read. Books in hand, I tramped and retramped every corner of the battlefield. Where the worst slaughter had occurred—brigade after Union brigade cut down, wounded crying out for help that could not come—were now quiet streets of little houses, dogwoods, and blooming tulips. Although my wife was annoyed, I nevertheless widened operations to include Civil War battlefields at Chancellorsville, Spotsylvania Courthouse, and the Wilderness. Every hour spared by the Marine Corps I spent on the Civil War. My desire to walk these places into my life was a physical hunger I still do not fully comprehend.

✡

Completing training in July, I was ordered to the Third Marine Division in Okinawa. Although my wife was pregnant, these orders still meant a fifteen-month separation. When I returned, our child would be nine months old. We drove soberly across the country to San Francisco, where we sold the car. She flew back to Saint Louis to live with her family, and I flew across the Pacific, stopping at Wake Island, passing in sight of Iwo Jima, to Okinawa. Before I had unpacked my sea bag, my battalion was ordered aboard amphibious ships. A typhoon coming, we went out to sea so that if ordered we could land in Hue, South Vietnam, for fighting in Laos. My ship, LSD *Tortuga,* took thirty-degree rolls. If while sleeping I was not holding on to my bunk, I woke midair an instant before slamming into a bulkhead. Heads sloshed with vomit, mess gear slid off tables, a comedian in the galley served chicken a la king for dinner. Almost everybody, navy as well as marine, got sick. I was okay but queasy. And most of my waking hours I devoted to nostalgically sweet Virginia of a hundred years ago. Not ordered to land, typhoon gone elsewhere, we returned to Okinawa.

My Civil War obsession now was fueled by boredom, anxiety about going to war, and the loneliness of U.S. military pretending to be in America when in the middle of a foreign country. (Of course I was living on another battlefield, Okinawa of 1945, but it did not fire my interest.) In my BOQ bunk, under an olive-green mosquito net, I read the Civil War to shut out the racket coming from the O-Club bar. On its patio with spectacular views of steep coastline, aquamarine lagoon, reefs, the dark of the ocean, I disciplined my mind to stay with Early and Sheridan's 1864 struggle in the Shenandoah Valley. Aboard an LST in the Sea of Japan on Thanksgiving Day, my bunk rocking, I put myself in Maryland with Lee turning to face McClellan at Sharpsburg. At the foot of Fujiyama, then a marine training area, the squad tent where I was sleeping caught fire. We all escaped, but in the soggy, charred remains of my gear I found what was left of my copy of Freeman's *Lee's Lieutenants*, volume 2. It was a mess, completely unreadable. But for weeks I could not throw it away. The fire and the burned book were signs, I thought even then, but with my rushing obsession to dwell in Virginia, Maryland, and Pennsylvania of the 1860s, I could not comprehend what they meant. Back in Okinawa the company first sergeant, a grizzled veteran of the Pacific and Korea, told me the Red Cross had called.

"Lieutenant, your wife had a girl."

"A girl?" For some reason I had always thought the child would be a boy. "A girl?"

"That's what the guy said."

I tried to act appropriately.

✡

Returning from Okinawa, I was stationed at the marine air base at Cherry Point, North Carolina. At nearby New Bern there had been a minor Civil War battle (Burnside beating Confederates a few months before he was beaten at Fredericksburg). There was not much to see. I tried Fort Macon, at the entrance to Bogue Sound, which before the war had been redesigned by Robert E. Lee himself. Unfortunately the fort was adjacent to a public beach, and the sight of all the tanning bodies, beach umbrellas, and children splashing in surf ruined the pleasure I might otherwise have had walking stone walls Lee had walked. Absent local pleasures, I packed up wife and daughter one weekend a month for the seven-hundred-mile round trip to Washington, ostensibly to visit my folks. But in fact to walk, rewalk, and re-rewalk, books in hand, the battlefields of Virginia, Maryland, and Pennsylvania, even those around Fredericksburg. Leaving my wife and daughter with my folks (she not-so-quietly objected), I fed myself not only with imaginings of *then* (the dead, the havoc, the Brady pictures), but also with memories of previous trips to many of these fields in the springtime of my obsession.

In our Cherry Point duplex I continued to read book after Civil War book. My obsession now was fueled from without as well as from within: it was 1961, and the rush of Civil War centennial books had begun. My military duties included sitting on a permanent court-martial board that heard all AWOLs picked up east of the Mississippi. So much sorrow, yearning, so little slack in military discipline. Once a week at least, I was the all-night officer in charge of base MPs. I regularly checked the station brig, then one of the cruelest in the Marine Corps. And pulled brutal MPs off helpless drunks they were flailing with nightsticks. And weekend duty usually meant attending to a marine who had managed to kill himself (and/ or civilians) in a twisted-up, blood-soaked, glass-splattered wreck. Off duty I sought the fan-blasted stuffiness of the base library. Behind our duplex were scraggly pine trees that looked tortured and ancient against the hot white southern sky when I glanced up from reading of the complexities of Grant's Vicksburg campaign.

When I was discharged from active duty, we moved to Saint Louis. With damaged hopes I halfheartedly took up my plan to belong in that closed world. I knew I should not, but still I plunged into reading about the city's role in the Civil War. Among gaudy movie houses along Grand Avenue I tried to imagine Camp Jackson, where southern sympathizers had trained. With Gettysburg and Fredericksburg burning in my mind, Jefferson Barracks, where Lee and Grant had served before the war, ignited no interest. My enthusiasm for visiting Wilson's Creek and Pea Ridge, both nearby battlefields, was too weak. Fussy old General Halleck represented my predicament: Nicknamed "Old Brains," Halleck had an administrative headquarters in Saint Louis that cut him off from the actual fighting, buried him in administrative red tape, isolated him from everything real and significant.

Working for a big advertising agency, I had an office window that looked out into an air shaft. The lobby of the building was walled with black marble murkily reflecting me and other stone ghosts who waited for elevators. A second child, a son, had been born. We lived in a third-floor apartment with casement windows that prevented the installation of an air conditioner. We dreamed of a house we could not afford. Riding in and out of downtown Saint Louis on the bus, I read Eliot's *The Waste Land*; its high-pitched despair mirrored my own.

As my Civil War interests waned, I tried Churchill's *History of the English-Speaking Peoples*, all four volumes, and book after book of Bertrand Russell, but nothing fired my mind. In a crowded, dish-clattering basement cafeteria during lunch hour, I read a chapter of Barzun's *The House of Intellect*. Walking back to the office, I did not recall a single idea I had just read. Headaches pounded. The Civil War, that rushing excitement; now it was just something I remembered. My chest had pains, but the doctor told me it was just emotion.

Two or three times a week I hurried through lunch, or skipped it altogether, to go up to the Saint Louis Public Library on Olive Street. In the periodical reading room radiators sang warmly and old derelicts paged newspapers, sounds like the dry beating of bird wings. In this weary scene there was something that attracted me as strongly as the sense that this big library could tell me almost anything I wanted to know. Browsing periodicals, then card catalogs, I rarely took a book home. In the reference room I randomly pulled books off shelves to read about anything unfamiliar. Listening to the reference librarians on the phones up at the desk, I speculated what questions they had been asked. In the dead of winter I began to poke around the genealogy collections on the back shelves. Casual browsing touched off a second obsession, one drier, less passionate, but also more desperate.

My efforts centered on Dad's side of the family. My names are from his family and I associated Saint Louis with the West and Oklahoma. I knew my grandparents had been born in Mississippi, the same county. (Both were dead.) About 1900 my grandmother and her Wilson family moved out to Indian Territory. My grandfather had followed. Dad remembered being taken back to Mississippi by his father to see his grandfather. This and Dad's few stories of his childhood were all I knew. Living in Saint Louis in these years, 1961–64, I was aware of construction of the Gateway to the West arch. Its two stainless-steel stumps were evident in much of downtown where I worked.

Using the collection of Mississippi genealogical materials, I made long lists of all the Lewis, Wilson, and Clayton surnames I encountered. I then went through the *Dictionary of American Biography*, making notes on surname entries that *seemed* to be related to my family. I trusted to hunches, luck. Nothing really clicked. Nothing connected directly to my grandfather and grandmother. At this time I was writing copy for Purina Dog Chow and reading Turner's *The Frontier in American History* and Webb's *The Great Plains*. My headaches were fierce. I randomly thumbed genealogies. Finding my surnames, I would be torn between feeling that this name—say Putnam Lewis in Rhode Island—*might* be connected to my relations, and the equally strong feeling that there was only a tiny chance that this would prove to be the case. Should I make a note about this name, the birth and death dates, or should I move on to another name? By this time I was staying downtown at the library at least one night a week and returning on Saturday. My heart ached all the time. Again I was in the throes of an obsession, and my daily failures drove me on. If I just kept working, something of my family would turn up. Why I didn't get in touch with Aunt Martha in Dallas, my father's sister who had the family Bible, and ask her about Mississippi relations, I do not know. My desire was not just for simple information.

After three months my ability to believe in what I was doing collapsed. The pretense that this scribbled information might connect to my relations could not be maintained. I was miserable. One bright Saturday morning I watched my son, now an energetic two, run lickety-split across winter-brown grass in front of our apartment building: limb-shadow, which he was completely unaware of, skimmed over him, his pale blue snowsuit. The sight leaped at me, and today remains part of the breakup of this genealogy obsession. I stopped going to the Saint Louis Public Library.

In my lunch hours I now wandered streets where old buildings and houses were being demolished for the riverfront memorial park. When the idiot ball or bulldozer struck, brick walls were reduced to piles of rubble.

Sometimes bedrooms with floral wallpaper were open for the first time in over a century to winter sunlight. Bombed-out London of World War II looked like this.

After months of searching, my wife rented us a little house in Webster Groves that was owned by the highway department and about to be demolished for a new interstate. Also about to be demolished was the old Gaiety Burlesque. One afternoon I sneaked out of the office to see the matinee. In the balcony were kids playing hooky from school. In the rows immediately in front of the stage were old men with gleaming bald heads. Somewhere in the middle was me. Beautiful women, weary with smiling, danced in the warm, dust-swirling light. My heart hurt badly, but the doctor again told me I had simple stress, "just emotion."

On the track where I had run just before our wedding, I began to jog and do marine calisthenics. Though I was getting fast promotions and raises, my job left me feeling empty. No longer did I desire, or believe I could obtain, a secure place among Saint Louisans. I had failed myself and my family. I had no place to hide. When William Faulkner died, I bought *The Sound and the Fury*. Aching loss and gorgeous beauty passed whole into my heart. In the backyard of our rented house, an apple tree bloomed spectacularly that spring. Its scent came into the bedroom, mingled with my dreams. My genealogy obsession was gone and, like its predecessor, left heartache. But in that great absence, I found stories—in those mirrors solemn consolation for despair.

✿

Wanting to be a Saint Louisan turned into its opposite, wanting to be a writer of stories. In a dusty bookstore I found the current *Sewanee Review*; its stories of violence by Fred Chappell, Andre Dubus, and others satisfied ignored hungers. My reading went out from there to Peter Taylor, Hemingway, Dostoevsky, Hardy, and Robert Penn Warren. Persistence of the past and violence—these mirrored depths that frightened and enthralled me. Just here I was offered a job back in North Carolina working in the administration at Duke. (Also out of the blue at this time, the CIA offered me a job. With the Marine Corps as cover, I would be assigned to covert operations at embassies. So like a bad novel, I could not believe them.) So I moved us back to Alma Mater in North Carolina, where I hoped to chase my new passion for literature and writing. That autumn my nerves sang with Sherwood Anderson, Stein, Faulkner, and Dos Passos. Reading when I could in the library's reference room, I took the same tables at which I had read economic history. Six years of blunders, self-deceptions, and the U.S. Marine Corps were swept away; I almost believed I was starting over.

Reading Shakespeare, the British romantics, and the American tantamounts was fun and my confidence grew, but long-banked and upsetting emotions also flared up. These were all associated with childhood. Saying goodnight to my two-year-old son, I noticed the shadow of the closing door cut across his face; his sweet innocence returned to the dark. Unmanly tears welled up in my eyes, stung my nose. Similarly, when I came home from work, my five-year-old daughter ran exuberantly down the long hall from the kitchen, throwing her welcome into my arms, and tears again immediate and stinging. My wife, with two children to care for, was back at the university she had left (to marry me) without a degree. She was frustrated and terribly unhappy. Children in bed, we sat in the living room, dusk coming down, lights off, trying to figure out what to do. Her desperate unhappiness threatened us both.

That summer she took the children to visit in Saint Louis. While they were gone I attended a three-week work-related seminar on campus. During this I became enthralled by a young woman from Chicago. (I had always liked Marilyn Monroe's *Some Like It Hot.*) With dark hair, strong and athletic, she had grown up in a German Lutheran neighborhood and graduated from a Lutheran college in Iowa. She was no talker, but, for being so was no less self-assured. She was suddenly the center of my universe. My mind was empty of all else. I was wild to be near her. So out of control (no doubt obvious to colleagues), I still could not voice my affections to her. Sensations again ripped through me: pine woods behind the chapel at hot noon; fan blast in the wood-paneled cafeteria where I had eaten as a student; her vigorous, unselfconscious walk through old quadrangles where lurked a decade of memories. In afternoon volleyball I foolishly dived and lunged for balls; I welcomed abrasions, scrapes, dark-crusted scabs. In a corner of my mind I knew I was ridiculous, even crazy, but self-consciousness was but a faint light on a dark, storm-tossed sea.

On the last day I drove her and others out to the airport. I watched her airplane disappear into North Carolina summer haze. For several days I was alone, rattling around our empty, mildew-smelling duplex. Elizabethan lute music I turned up full blast. A fifty-page letter I wrote to her, confessing what I had not been able to say in person. (As if a confession were necessary!) My life depended on seeing her again, maybe in the North Carolina mountains where I had had romantic successes. While I was alone, a long letter arrived from a *Hudson Review* editor who had liked one of my stories. This was the first serious response my writing had received. The story was based on something Dad had told me about his folks. He said they had used Wilson, his bigger, older brother, to administer punishments. They had watched from the front porch as Wilson whaled Dad with his fists. Dad was three years younger, built smaller.

When my wife returned with the children, I confessed my enthrallment. She was devastated, and we began together to see a psychiatrist. Misery filled our house, and the children felt it. The following winter was very cold, below-zero weather in North Carolina, and as my affections cooled I was eaten alive by guilt. When I could not stand it, I moved into a rooming house for several weeks. But my children, who, in spite of my failings as a father, loved me and I them, got me to return home. To rebuild my self-respect, I read the Bible through the remaining winter and spring. (In spite of myself, I looked for infidelities such as David's.)

Again blood marked a turning point. While on a work trip to Charlotte, I fell in a motel bathroom. Regaining consciousness, head aching badly, I crawled back into bed. Soon I noticed that my pillow was soaked. Light on, blood. I threw up. And again. And again. The X-rays showed a brain concussion and skull fracture. A colleague drove me back to Durham. Drugs made me content to watch blocks of sunlight move across our bedroom floor. When the X-rays showed healing, my wife and I again tried to talk, this time at the kitchen table. We decided to leave North Carolina for Iowa City, where with the GI Bill I would study writing and literature and she would finish her B.A. While we were packing up to leave Durham, the Marine Corps wrote to ask me to return to active duty. It was 1967; Vietnam casualties were heavy. My war, now at last I would know. Plunging my life's mess into it, at least I would come out with new problems, I thought. Another new start. If I was killed, that would be okay, too. My children and my wife might then remember me in honorable terms I had otherwise lost. But I chose Iowa City and writing instead. (Thirty years later, regrets remain.)

Although I had bouts of depression in Iowa City, I thrived and so did my wife and children. My Marine Corps past I hid from professors who despised the military as much as they hated the Vietnam War. My silence about this gnawed at me. Speaking in classes at all was difficult. But the literature—O'Connor, Tolstoy, Sterne, Blake, Robert Lowell, Barth, Cervantes, McCullers, Flaubert—continued to satisfy strong hungers. And my story about Dad's boyhood (the one *Hudson Review* liked) was published and won a prize; I read it over campus radio. Another about struggles between a mother and her career-driven husband was published. Talk in Iowa City slop chutes (that is, bars) had as its foundation hostility to the Vietnam War and avoiding the draft. I did not like the war, either, but listening to them, my gut tightened with loyalty to both marines and my southern heritage. Worse was understanding what this talk did to marine grunts over there stepping as absolutely carefully as they could, and in an instant, catching a trip wire, a metallic click, then one way to oblivion. In Iowa City I stood clear of both writing neophytes and the illustrious. My defense was silence and distance. At this time, unbidden on a summer evening, that forgotten 1957 Christmas Eve burst into my mind.

I had good luck to get a teaching job at a western New York college. The village was old: houses dating from 1810, flashy Queen Annes, a town common of grass, and a lecture hall where Emerson and Twain had spoken. Whitman himself had eased through the village on the Big Tree Road. After a year we bought a pre-WWI house with an old, rattling furnace, high-ceilinged rooms, and a pleasantly overgrown yard. We made some friends, I was publishing fiction (all rooted in my Bethesda years, 1948–50), and the children were happy. To lighten depressions, I jogged along country roads, past 1830s classical revival farmhouses, up onto a ridge that looked far across the Genesee River valley. A clump of trees on the valley floor was where Iroquois tortured and disemboweled two Revolutionary soldiers. A few miles north, also visible, was a roll of plowed ground where the Iroquois' large village had stood before Sullivan's American army, in retaliation, burned it to the ground. Mass starvation

ensued that winter. Returning home from jogging, winter twilight, I passed
the village cemetery. In dark silhouette was the rather grand tomb of
General James S. Wadsworth, who was in the Army of the Potomac and
was killed at the Wilderness. (This battlefield I had walked, books in hand,
in the springtime of my obsession.) Obsessions with the Civil War and
genealogy I now regarded as unfortunate episodes in my life, now safely
behind me. Out of their ashes had grown my true love of literature and
writing. My life was making sense, on track at last. Except for Saturday
morning basketball with other faculty, where my irrational temper
reappeared weekly.

✡

While at the college I went to a literary conference at the Library of
Congress in Washington. My folks were living back in Washington, so I
stayed with them. At a reception among the ornate mosaics of the Jefferson
Building, shrimp were huge, beautifully arranged on ice, and delicious.
While talking to people I knew, I remembered coming here in 1944 with
Dad's Oklahoma cousin, Homer. In one frantic Sunday, Mother showed
him all of Washington. She included, for some reason, the Library of
Congress, the only time I was taken there. Under my feet were gold zodiac
signs inlaid in marble. In 1944 I had asked Dad what these were and what
they meant. Then and now, marble gave voices a light echoic quality.

The conference speakers, mostly literary superstars, were entertaining
but said little on the topic, teaching literature and writing. Since arriving
at the conference I had been aware of being inside the library of libraries.
During a lunch break I went over to the Library of Congress Annex, the
Adams Building, and located the genealogy section. I spent the remainder
of the day browsing Mississippi genealogy. The local histories and
biographies of Mississippians, though full of my surnames, were finally
as unconnected to my family as all the notebooks I had filled and destroyed
in Saint Louis. After ten years I understood the difference between *is* and
the whirlpool of *might* be.

As I left I told a librarian about my disappointment. He offhandedly
suggested I try the National Archives. One of the few times I had been
there was also on that 1944 Sunday with Homer. Outside it was a bright,
snapping January day. I was tempted to start home for New York, but

decided instead to stop by the Archives. I was wary of being caught in another maze, but at the same time I wondered how this cold, banklike building might connect to the immediacies of my life. The white marble of the Archives blazed in winter sunlight, and I had to squint. As I walked to the foot of the steps, wind whirring in the supple bare limbs of elms along Constitution Avenue, I was almost certain that this visit would be as wasted as I presumed Homer's was on that Sunday in World War II. (He had survived both Patton and the Germans.)

My first surprise was being sent around to the back, to an entrance on Pennsylvania Avenue.

The reading room on the fourth floor contained microfilmed census, military, and ship-arrival records. The carpet was lush green. Quickly one of the librarians, a big, good-natured man, helped me find the 1880 census for Copiah County, Mississippi. The man was black, and this struck me poignantly. In less than half an hour I was looking at my grandfather's name. In July 1880, when the census taker stopped at his family's house in Mississippi, he was one year old, and with him were his twin sister, his older brothers and sisters, and of course his parents, my great-grandparents. This was a direct record of their life. For a long time I looked at the screen of the microfilm reader, at this moment of my family's life in time before I was here. I thought about the Archives, about this record's being here all along.

I remembered a blue dusk coming down around my grandfather and me as we sat on the porch of his house in Oklahoma. Smell of sun-scorched grass was in my nose. My mother and father had gone, leaving me with my grandfather. He held me in his lap, while I held his big watch attached to him by a chain. He had a bittery smell. This was the first of four times I saw him. It was the summer of 1940.

And this memory came also. On a particular winter afternoon I was walking home through the grounds of Sheppard Pratt. It was sunny but chilly. The road wound through pastures, fields, by caretakers' houses and barns, and gently ascended toward the hospital buildings, which at the moment I cannot see. I was free of the jostling, emotion-throbbing high school. I was not yet home, where Mother's off-key humming will fill silences left by Dad's week-long business trips. I was glad I was not at school or at home. When I got up to the main buildings, the original baronial mansion, our ball field, I would have to compose an expression for the insane who will watch me from the secrecy of their dark rooms and wonder why the boy so often walks through here. What did he want? Where were his friends? But not yet where they can see me, free of constraints, I only thought to recite the bones of the skull, which I had learned that day in biology. My books were heavy. This was 1952. In stalemate the Korean War ground on.

In these years I flew with my father out to Oklahoma. My grandfather's strokes had continued and he was taking big slugs of straight garlic juice for his blood pressure. Although his thoughts were scattered, he told me of hunting quail in his early years in Indian Territory. He killed forty, fifty birds a day. Fried them up in bacon fat, good eating. "You still hunt, Granddad?" He laughed, shook his head no, quail too fast for him now. These were his last words to me. Behind rimless glasses his blue eyes, mine exactly the color of his, were hazy, unfocused. He was slipping into absence. Twenty-two years later a census record returned him to me.

✿

Not long after I found my grandfather at a National Archives microfilm reader, I thought to check whether his father, listed on the 1880 census as A. C. Lewis, was a Confederate soldier. Back at the National Archives, I was less than half an hour finding Albert C. Lewis in the Confederate company muster rolls. (Dad's name exactly echoed his.) Enlisting at Corinth, Mississippi on May 2, 1862, he was a private in Company K (the "Dixie Guards" of Copiah County), Thirty-sixth Mississippi Infantry. Here it was, the living connection with the Civil War, what I had desired (without fully realizing it) for fifteen years, ever since Fredericksburg. Here was flesh and blood in the Civil War; it was not simple history any longer.

His oldest brother, Edmund Rayford, had joined the Dixie Guards the previous winter, February, and had been in the Shiloh blood-bath in April. He was now a sergeant. Their regiment was in a close-quarters fight at Rienzi, Mississippi, in September 1862. At dusk the Thirty-sixth Mississippi charged with fixed bayonets. This was great, exactly what I wanted. The story of these brave rebel brothers was right out of a romantic southern novel. But no. In October at Corinth, Mississippi, their regiment again charged the Federal line. With Yankee artillery firing point-blank at them, the Thirty-sixth stalled. They fired several close-in volleys at the guns; their colonel's leg was sliced off by a cannonball. Then Yankee infantry countercharged. And right there, in all the roaring, A.C. heard a wet splat, turned, saw his brother's face (better known to him than his own): a mass of blood, glistening bone. E.R.'s legs collapsed—that quick dead. And A.C. left him there as the Thirty-sixth, with the entire brigade, fled in a rout. This was not noble or glorious, and the battle was not a Robert E. Lee affair like Chancellorsville or Gettysburg. In fact, the Confederate general, Earl Van Dorn, was drunk during the battle and later was killed by the irate husband of one of his lady friends. For A.C. the battle was simple, brutal killing. He was never the same again. Nearly twenty years later, 1880, he still remembered that morning, felt his brother's absence, and named one of his sons Edmund Rayford so that this memory and absence would remain in the living world.

Dad's grandfather was in the battles leading up to Vicksburg. In the siege his brigade occupied an exposed position in the defenses. Day and night he lived the sniping, horrendous artillery barrages, and the hunger of those trenches. Soon they ate whatever moved, rats very much included. In the siege his brigade had 219 killed and 455 wounded before being surrendered on July 4, 1863, one day after the other devastating Confederate defeat, at Gettysburg. Thirteen months of fighting, marching, and sieging had got his brother killed, hundreds of others killed, maimed, crippled for life, and all those high hopes of springtime were shattered, utterly destroyed. For those who fight wars, there can never again be a home to go home to.

Here was the Civil War.

✳

The Battle of Fredericksburg had been a centerless abstraction of movement and countermovement. Discovering Mother's paternal grandfather, who had lived that battle, inverted the movements of Lee and Burnside. Now there was a real person, blood kin, at the center of this mighty event. (Yes, Fredericksburg!) Five feet, seven inches tall, twenty-one years old, he was a volunteer from Rowan County, North Carolina, and serving as a private in the Seventh North Carolina Infantry of Lane's Brigade. He had already fought at Seven Days and the Battle of New Bern. (Living close by at Cherry Point, I had not known!) On the flats south of Fredericksburg, his brigade was split off by a little hill. Flank exposed, they took casualties. He was shot in the shinbone and limped the rest of his life. Since 1959 I had known the history, but not the individual who had lived that history and conveyed its consequences to me. He was Mother's paternal grandfather; this was a Grandpa she kept mentioning. He was in her experience and, through her, in mine as well.

And the Battle of Chancellorsville became a twenty-five-year-old man, a draftee from Davidson County, North Carolina in Company I, Second North Carolina Infantry, Ramseur's Brigade. He was Mother's maternal grandfather. In his first engagement in May 1863 he marched and countermarched with his regiment on the roads west of Fredericksburg. (My own marching at Quantico was twenty-five miles and almost a hundred years from there. That clayey grit I have tasted.) On May 2 he marched in a giant column down the narrow lanes I have walked, waded a bright little stream (then muddied by the army's passage), and in the Virginia dusk deployed in A. P. Hill's second echelon of Jackson's Corps. From beneath my steel helmet I saw the soft mists of such a spring evening.

His brigade, led by the young West Pointer Ramseur, was at the flank of that ferocious attack—felt its blood-surge, the Yankee rout. In the May darkness whippoorwills singing in the pauses, "war moon" full, his brigade prepared for what Jackson planned as the *coup de grace* that would destroy the Yankees, throw them in a second rout back against the Rapidan River. But Old Jack himself was shot that night. At daybreak the attacks went through thick May woods straight into the teeth of the Yankees. In fifteen minutes three-fourths of his brigade was wounded or killed. He was shot in the neck but recovered and rejoined his regiment.

The Chancellorsville that I had held in mind was not the blood, death, and fighting close to butchering that I now saw. I had regarded that battle as a wish-fulfilling fantasy. Like most Civil War buffs, I had identified with Jackson's daring maneuver. In at least ten written accounts, and more than that many tours of the field, I had studied that heady attack, which rolled up over a mile of poor Hooker's flank. Concluding this romantic fantasy was Jackson's mortal wound, which returned me, chastened, to the ordinary business of getting up, putting on shoes, going to my job. Mind candy, these fantasies; how much better what I now have.

Writing of the man who fought the slaughter of Chancellorsville, I have remembered standing across the street from the Iowa Memorial Union in the crazy autumn of 1967. With a mixture of amazement and admiration I watched faculty and student demonstrators block Marine Corps recruiters (who were not in sight) from entering the building. A mob of students jeered at the demonstrators. From this mob some tough wrestler types emerged. They grabbed one of the demonstrators, a girl with thin arms and long hair. Roughly they pulled her away, shoving her and spinning her until she fell to the pavement. The guys bully-laughed and went back for another demonstrator. The courage in the girl's face was something I could not have imagined outside the pages of a book. I was very conscious of being a former marine. This was the first time I realized that I was also a coward.

Another event from my own life I have recollected while considering my maternal great-grandfather's first combat in the Confederate army. One, mentioned earlier as part of my obsession with the Civil War, opens now in wider view. It was the night at Fujiyama, holy site to the Japanese, the U.S. victor's military training area. The instant the oil stove exploded in our tent, the corporal on fire watch *happened* to be entering our tent. He yelled: "Quick, sirs! Fire! *Fire!*" My eyes opened to the stove in flames, the fuel line, the roof of the tent. Everybody was yelling, cots screeching. A sick moment yanking at the zipper of my sleeping bag. In the light of leaping flames others hurried down the aisle between our cots to the opposite tent entrance. Then we were all outside and the whole tent was in flames, the canvas collapsed, and in the dark it all seemed cheerful, almost festive. Under my cold, bare feet was Fuji's black volcanic ash. Somebody gave me a field jacket. The Japanese fire department from Gotemba arrived after the fire had burned itself out. They pointed, exclaimed, laughed, and left. I borrowed some boots and poked around the still smoldering char of the cot where I had been sleeping. I found the remains of loose gear, my duffel bag, the copy of *Lee's Lieutenants* I had been reading before going to sleep. The char smell made me almost sick. I realized what had happened, how close it had been, how cold the night was on my bare legs, how sudden and beautiful and terrible it had been. For three or four days we were all very quiet.

Recovered but limping from his Fredericksburg wound, Mother's other grandfather, her father's father, returned to the Seventh North Carolina. On the first day at Gettysburg, they were in the thick of fierce fighting. Major General Dorsey Pender, who commanded their division, was killed. It may have been a mistake that, having taken these heavy casualties, they then were assigned to the great assault on July 3. Mother's grandfather came out of the trees along Seminary Ridge (I have stood on that very ground), went down into the shallow valley, across fields, and up the rising ground to the fences, road cuts, stone walls, smoke, and gory killing of Cemetery Ridge. How exactly that terrible hour changed him, I do not know. His records say he was "sent home sick," of what is not specified. But I do not doubt that he had seen too much slaughter: the sudden carnage of Seven Days, the panic of being flanked and shot down at Fredericksburg, human gore through dogwood-blooming May woods at Chancellorsville, and the pure spirit-breaking slaughter of Gettysburg. How could these experiences not have changed him? Do we suppose men lived such days and hours only to return home unchanged? Unable to read or write, he tenant farmed after the war and eventually married a girl whose two brothers and father were killed in the war. He brought up a big family, including my ornery, vigorous grandfather. For consolation while tenant farming, he built fine furniture, chairs, chests, and beds. But fifteen years after the war, he had not escaped his wartime experiences or put them to rest, when he named his son, my grandfather born in 1880, after the South's great hope of 1861–65, then dead. My mother adored her father and was brought up in large part by his mother, who had her own terrible wartime losses. I do not doubt that Mother was affected, deeply so, by the legacy of Civil War experiences she inherited. Not just by the idolatry of the Lost Cause, but by the actual experiences of slaughter and loss carried by the lives that most influenced hers. Is my obsession with looking back part of that legacy which has been passed on to me? As a small child I felt the daily presence of the past, its inescapable weight.

Although a cold January wind is now humming in the eaves of my house, I am happy. The voices of the dead of one's family have wondrous, scathing, humbling, and often beautiful things to tell us. Now I am learning to listen, and I am discovering how much the past, as living force, is with us in every minute of our lives.

✡

After a year of researching family, traveling to the places where they had lived across the South, walking ground they had walked on, listening more closely to the stories of the old, I began to see the deep, beautiful inter-generational patterns in the families I belong to. While I believe in chance as well as history, and most definitely in individual freedom, I also know that these complex inter-generational family dynamics—more deter-minative in damaged families, perhaps—were here before our birth and will continue to be here after we have gone to our graves.

My Lewis kin, who had been in Virginia for a century, were suddenly seized with religious fervor in the 1750s and '60s. Turning their backs on fences, gentry, and all else Virginia stood for, they moved as New Light Christians to the swamps of South Carolina along the Little Pee Dee River, to wait for the end of time. Their last son, Joseph, born there in 1763, joined the South Carolina militia as a teenager; he was in Francis Marion's swamp-wading army. After the Revolution he never stopped moving deeper and deeper into wilderness: to Canoochee River swamps, 1790–1811, in what then was raw wildness but would become Bulloch County, Georgia; to raw Choctaw lands in Mississippi Territory, 1812; and late in his life, 1831, to Louisiana swamps with a new wife. Urged on similarly, three of his broth-ers were killed in Indian wars in Kentucky. Joseph was a hardshell Baptist preacher who owned little. That break with Virginia, which occurred before he was born, he carried with him and, not a bit less, the intense, personal, revelatory religion that had caused that break. A time-deep heritage (much of which I cannot now discern) he carried into America's Revolution and out into the new nation's frontier wildernesses. Both astonishing experiences changed Joseph B. Lewis. And who he became in turn became the heritage passed to his fourteen children, and through them, to many others down to some in living generations.

His eighth son and Mississippi firstborn (1813), Hugh, slipped out of the patriarch's sphere—that, or he rebelled flat out against the old man. Hugh Lewis became a tinker who built carriages, ploughs, other farm implements. He scorned what his father and grandfather so fervently embraced, otherworldly visions, and took up the hard practicalities of wood, iron. He was a sheriff, a Whig (as opposed to the rabble of Jacksonian Democrats), but he was also restless, unsettled as his father and grand-father, moved his family and tinker shop hither and yon in the vast extent of Mississippi wilderness. Several of these 1840s villages now are woods, farm fields.

For all his shifting about, Hugh remained tightly knotted with his father, the family patriarch. When the old man's first wife (and the tinker's mother) died, the old man at age sixty-nine, 1831, married Tabitha Morris, age twenty-one. Tabitha was the sister of Elizabeth, Sarah, and Dasda, all of whom were already married to the old man's sons! *My god, what can be said of this?* The father-patriarch pioneered in more than one wilderness! And what indeed when I add that his youngest son, this Hugh, then chose to marry in the Mississippi spring of 1836 yet another of the Morris sisters, in this case Izzie (probably Isabella). A man marries the sister of his brothers' wives and the sister of his stepmother! Allowing for impossible-to-resist charm on the part of these sisters and the appeal of proximity in sparsely settled wilderness, this youngest son, Hugh, still achieves both an act of family obeisance, binding himself more tightly to them, and simultaneously an act of outrageous rebellion against family (akin to what I might call incest by proxy?). Brilliant, and yes, probably unconscious. In that wilderness more comic than tragic. The deep, inter-generational dynamic I trace could not be more clearly illuminated.

In turn, this tinker's middle son, Albert C., rebelled against his father's wandering about and tinkering. As you know, he had passed through the fire of the Civil War, losing his oldest brother and two uncles, finally all but starving in the hell of Vicksburg. But after surrender and parole, he went home, all of twenty miles. Not fleeing into American-spawned dreams Out West (thereby carrying forward that part of his heritage), he married in autumn 1864, of all times in Mississippi to marry, and rode with ir-regular calvary that with rope and pistol attempted to keep the peace in the midst of total social collapse. He took up a farm originally purchased out of Choctaw lands by his father and on which he briefly had lived as a boy. In devastated Mississippi he put down roots, while his wandering, tinkering father gave up tinkering to carpenter only beautiful coffins and become Hazelhurst's first undertaker. (In the simple facts of this man's life, poetry.) His son farmed on shares to the bank, barely survived post-war debts, then paid all of them off, and added land to the original farm. He built onto the house where he had lived as a boy. Here was born in 1878 his eighth child and last son, my grandfather, Edmund Rayford. My grandfather as a young man set out for the territory, Indian Territory, exactly as his great-grandfather had done. But the old man's dreams of boundless wilderness, of space on God's earth in which to unbridle and abide religion-spawned visions, were not Granddaddy Lewis's. His dreams instead reversed his father's slow, patient building-up of a farm. No more for him the steady swing of a mule's rear end. Going out to Indian Territory, he yearned for the status and authority of his new wife's banker family. (I did much the same in Saint Louis.) Married into that family, he would become a man of some substance. In a single stroke the youngest son would surpass his father and older brothers, still farming back in Mississippi, and in the new town would become a man of some moment and stature. He would cut a wide swath for himself.

And his new father-in-law did set him up in Bokchito selling confections and ice cream. He built his son-in-law a nice big house on Main Street and probably engineered his becoming a deacon in Bokchito's first Baptist Church. As my grandfather was named for his father's brother who had been lost in the War, he named his second son (my father) in 1906 for the Mississippi father he had lost, so to speak, in his move out to Indian Territory. At the first opportunity Dad rebelled against his father and family. His dream was not to marry money or receive as a gift a damn thing. He fervently desired radical self-made, *Gatsby*-esque individuality accomplished in *Arrowsmith* realms of medicine (as far as possible from little old Durant, Oklahoma). He did not become a doctor, but with the single-minded fixity of his religious heritage, he became a very successful salesman of X-ray and medical equipment. He aimed for Gatsby and late in life realized he had got Willie Loman. When he named me in 1936, he gave me a piece of his name, from his grandfather, that is, Clayton; and a piece of the name of the father-in-law, the banker, the family hope that was already a husk when the name came to me, Wilson. With it Dad may have hoped to earn favor with the family he had rejected (and which had rejected him); with the name of his banker grandfather, Dad also may have hoped I would get what in fact he had gotten from the old man, that banker's hardheaded business sense. But of course I did not, else I would not have lived the life you see here nor taken so much of it writing this.

When placed within the dynamics of such a four-hundred-year-old story, aren't we seen differently? My Dad with all his nervy success, drinking into oblivion our family Christmases? My grandfather with his broken dreams, come to killing large numbers of something as rushingly alive as quail? Me, obsessed to recover the past my father and mother had fled? But my tale is richer even than this. Mingled with Lewis kin are of course other families with their complex, equally beautiful but of course different dynamics of obverse and reverse, repose and counter-repose moving through generations. Mother's as well as Dad's. Why would anyone suppose that we are not profoundly influenced by these giant inter-generational stories composed of heritage as marked by history? Is it not here in what I have recounted? Is it not present, too, in how I seek to have myself regarded by you?

These matters occurred to me, first, as an obsession in Fredericksburg in 1959. In 1985 I discovered that those Lewis kin who were seized in the 1750s and '60s and moved off as New Light Christians to the Little Pee Dee were from the counties in and around Fredericksburg. (The ground itself calling out to me in 1959?) My story here is not one in the usual sense. Instead, I aim to illuminate a vital, shaping force in human life. Faulkner, Warren, the Bible itself: these tell the tale I could not evade. Like Jonah, I was in the belly of the whale before I went to Ninevah to tell what I knew I must tell.

✿

With regimental histories from the North Carolina Archives, and maps from several sources, I arranged a trip from Washington out to Fisher's Hill, Virginia, in the Shenandoah south of Strausburg. Here my great-grandfather, the one who had been wounded at Chancellorsville, was captured by Sheridan's Union forces on September 22, 1864. He was part of Jubal Early's raid on Washington, and, according to reports, before retreating he had seen the incomplete dome of the Capitol itself. My son, age ten, came along. It was a warm June afternoon, and a soft mist was in the air. We bought Dairy Queen cones in Strausburg.

Using my 1864 maps I found the area south of Strausburg. We turned off U.S. 11, the Valley Road, onto a little blacktop road that had evidently been rerouted a little between 1864 and 1974. Many, many times I had passed this road (on vacations, on my father's business trips, on trips with family) without imagining it might be significant to me. We stopped several times. When I switched off the engine, the complexly rich song of katydids poured into my head. For a while we traced the winding stream that had divided the armies. My son splashed rocks.

Locating the hill where my great-grandfather's regiment had been, my son and I crawled through the barbed-wire fence (ignoring the No Trespassing signs), and began to climb the hillside. The sun was warm. Elbows pumping, he began to run up the hill. Following a gully, my feet scuttered in loose rock. When my great-grandfather was here in 1864, how had this hillside looked? Were the men thin, faces skull-like and brown from summer marching, only eyes alive? I saw the slouched, weary way they sat and stood, their clutter, and the raw red-clay soil of newly dug entrenchments that zigzagged across the hillside. My great-grandfather may have looked on that mountain ridge to the west, or that tree, or this gully. Now all was peacefully ordinary, and I resented the years of hard frosts and rains and springtimes that had intervened between then and now. Failing again to recover the exact past, that experience, even now with my newfound sense of personal relationship to a man who had actually been here at that time.

A voice startled me.

I stopped, and looked up. From the skyline, from the top of the hillside I was climbing, my son waved exuberantly to me. He and his clothing and the waving itself seemed splendid and alive in the field and sky and June sunlight. The sight sang through me. My shoes in the loose rock still slipped and scuttered, but the sensation was delicious. I had an urge to run. I laughed. I waved. I was sweating, the sun hot on the back of my neck. I saw the weeds and thistle and dry grass of the hillside—leaping and throbbing in all that sunlight—and the eroded gully I was following, the undercut, root-exposed clumps of grass and weed on either side, and my shoes making a song in the sun-sheened rocks that lay in that music of sight where the last gully-washing rain had flung them. These and my son, who was now looking over the wider scene. Right then I understood how rich, fragile, and irrecoverable each moment in each place is for me and my son and my great-grandfather. This was leaping awareness. I thought I might split open on that hillside in 1974, with my son, where his great-great-grandfather had lived a few significant moments of his life. All of us, in different ways, in *this present!*

Later I saw that my great-grandfather's experiences on that hillside are finally as irrecoverable as my experiences on that battlefield at Fisher's Hill with my son. Irrecoverable as any experience in time. On the way back to Washington we bought fried chicken, and we stopped by a quietly flowing stream to eat it. Some children were splashing and playing out of sight upstream from us. Back in the car going home in the Virginia dusk, we boisterously sang over the roar of road-wind "Dixie" and "Glory Hallelujah!"

If You Don't Weaken

In the summer of 1981, I was returning with my wife to our new home in Oklahoma. We had vacationed in Maine, an island in Penobscot Bay, and in late afternoon were coming into Saint Louis. On our left was Chokia burial mound—all that remained of the largest pre-Columbian city in North America. On our right in pearly haze out on the flats along the Mississippi was the ugly jumble of East Saint Louis: railroad yards, power lines, warehouses with busted-out windows, and blocks of abandoned row houses. On the other side of the river I saw Saint Louis itself, the skyline. Those mirror-wall buildings were new to me. And what had been two stainless steel stumps when I lived here was now the spectacular Gateway Arch, finished. It seemed to me a huge, sun-gleaming parabola dropped down from another universe. In 1961–64 I was confounded by the demolition of old buildings (some dating to 1810) to build the arch and commemorate the Westward Movement. Then twenty-six, worrying over ironies that bothered nobody else, I knew I was out of step. Now forty-five, remarried, I would *not* let myself worry about the past. It was done and gone. Now I had a big, American, second-chance start underway. And it was in Oklahoma, out of which Dad had fled in 1922 and to which I had returned in 1979, fifty-seven years later. Crossing the Mississippi on a brand new bridge, heading home to Oklahoma, I remembered Dad being a runaway kid here.

Upstream were the gently arched spans of old Eads Bridge. My first wife's family was involved in building that bridge. Her great-grandfather, I was quite certain, fell from a partially completed span to his death in the muddy river. My second wife would not be interested.

Our route through Saint Louis she had figured perfectly. The interstate was new, but I recognized huge cylinders of a grain elevator; exits rang familiarly of Saint Louis—Grand, Kingshighway, Big Bend. There was a sign, WEBSTER GROVES. This, I realized, was exactly the interstate that took the little house my first wife and I rented in the spring of 1964. Marked for bulldozing, it was our first. There I discovered literature, how it could talk to me, and there, too, suffered a terrible impacted wisdom tooth. In August 1964 we left Webster Groves and Saint Louis for good. Now two decades later, Saint Louis again, passing through.

That bridge arching over what then was a double-track rail line into Saint Louis and now was interstate: "This is it," I announced. "We used to live right along here. In 1964." But a half mile farther on were little brick houses identical to ours. These were immediately behind the one where we had lived. "Maybe it was here," I said.

My wife glanced at me skeptically.

We were doing sixty; there was no chance to stop, nothing really to see. The little brick house that meant so much to me actually stood at the second location—somewhere in the air above the shoulder of the eastbound lane.

✡

In 1976–77 my life shattered exactly when I got what I had worked thirteen years to get. Editors and agents were taking an interest in my literary efforts, my job was good, colleagues were friends, and our family was well regarded in the village. I had an upstairs book room that got warm sunlight on winter mornings. My daughter, born in Saint Louis while I was in the Far East, was a good student and a talented cellist, and was playing championship volleyball and soccer. Our son, born while I worked in Saint Louis, was thirteen, also a good student (with a special love of American history), won awards for French horn, and played good Little League football. My wife and I had a reputation for big, high-spirited parties. But behind our closed front door, rivalry and resentment steadily boiled.

On money matters I was the skinflint, she the spendthrift. In our professional lives she was anxious, torn with worry and self-doubt; I was Mr. Bring-Me-Your-Problems, although upstairs behind the closed door of my book room, I rode out bad depressions. The wonder was that, for half a dozen years, it all hung together.

In the spring of 1977, my wife became convinced I was secretly rendez-vousing with a friend's wife. I was not. I was not even thinking about it.

"But how can I trust you?" she asked. "How can I be certain you're telling the truth?"

Foolishly, I tried to convinced her, but as dawn paled the sky, my hours and hours of talk had the reverse effect. The more I argued the contrary, the less she trusted me. I had to admit that my romantic obsession in Durham ten years earlier provided a good reason *not* to trust me.

"But I haven't done anything now. I haven't. I just haven't."

"How can I know for sure?"

Dawn rosing the sky, I walked out in the country. In rippling puddles full of sky, clouds were scudding, green grass, dead leaves. Deer came up out of a dark, wooded ravine into an abandoned orchard; delicately their mouths pulled off apples. In the rising morning, a chained farm dog barked.

It was her sanity and calm, her deep family roots in western Pennsyl-vania. (A direct ancestor had fought in the Army of the Potomac.) It was her Yankee competence and the sensible middle-distance way she talked to you and the old farmhouse out in the country where she lived what I thought was an idyllic life. In a corner of my mind, I knew she was what my wife was not.

On my wife, my children, my friends, I inflicted grievous harm. My wife was despondent, my wonderfully confident children, devastated. In six months I was an outcast, shunned in the supermarket (friends ducked down other aisles). And I understood why. My moral debt to my wife, children, and friends could not be discharged in five life times. Remarried, I wanted badly to leave all the damage I had done in that upstate New York village where I once had a home. Taking a job in Oklahoma, I reached back and out to my oldest and most profound dreams. My second wife and I moved west in 1979.

We were now west of the Saint Louis suburb of Kirkwood on the hills above the Merimac River. Also taken by the interstate was the house where

I had lived that hope-filled summer of 1958. It would have been right here. This was the view from their living-room window. Descending into the Merimac River valley, my heart lifted. Let sleeping dogs lie, I told myself. Ahead was all the hope of our new lives in Oklahoma.

✡

That Christmas of 1981 Mother and Dad visited us in Oklahoma. In over fifty years, Dad had returned fewer than ten times. When he came off the plane, he had a black eye and a bloody, nasty bruise on his right cheek. "Aw, it isn't anything," he said. Then, with him right there, Mother told us his drinking had gone from bad to worse. After golf one day last week, he took stiff snorts of vodka, then, stopping at Roy Rogers, "drunk as a skunk," he fell flat on his face.

"Knocked himself out," she said, eyes popping with indignation and shame. Riding home from the airport, in rolling plains, Dad was silent.

On a bright, cold day just before New Year's, I drove them down to Bokchito and Durant. Since moving to Oklahoma, I had twice gone down there to look around. I assumed Dad would be interested; it was almost forty years, 1945, since the three of us had last been together in Bryan County.

Dad sat by me in the front seat. Warm end-of-year sunlight was coming in on him: a short, white-haired old man with big ears and big nose made bigger by drinking. Dad was silent.

In Bokchito the lot where the house of his birth had stood was now a miserable brick duplex in a trash-strewn yard. Dad shrugged. When I asked, he pointed out again the empty store that had been his father's, the lot of his grandfather's house (where now stood a 1920s house), and the lumberyard from which his grandfather had fired across the street at men robbing his bank. We drove over to Durant and by the bungalow, now shabby, that we had visited in 1945. My belly churned. We stopped and got out, and Mother took a picture of Dad and me in front of the bungalow. My camera, I later discovered, had no film in it.

From the back seat Mother said Dad's sister Mary E. and his aunt Nell, both long dead, had separately told her about the nice house where the Lewis family lived when they first moved to Durant in 1918. Prepared as usual, Mother pulled directions out of her purse. The house was a big, pleasant Victorian. The difference between this prosperous house and the cramped bungalow surprised me.

"That's the house where you all lived when you ran off, isn't it, Al?" Mother asked.

"Yeah, that's it," he said, surprising me with his certainty.

Mother understood from Dad's aunts, Mattie Mae and Nell, that in the early 1920s Granddaddy and Grandmother Lewis had ugly arguments late into the night. "Terrible fights," Mother said.

Just then Dad ran away. Since he had never mentioned any reason, I had assumed he was in pursuit of boyhood adventures. No, that was not it. I expected Dad to contradict Mother, but he did not. He looked out his side window at passing houses he had known as a boy.

Mother went on, talking slowly, matter-of-factly. According to Mattie Mae and Nell, both of whom liked Dad better than his own folks did, he wanted to come home after his summer in Wisconsin.

He wrote to ask to return to finish high school.

His parents wrote back no. He had made his bed, he could sleep in it.

I was shocked. "You know this, Mother? You know this for a fact?"

"I certainly do."

Dad still looked away.

"They wouldn't let you come home, Dad? They wouldn't even let you come back?"

"I could've paid them board." He still looked out his side window.

Then Mother declared we ought to drive out to Colera, a railroad hamlet five miles south.

Dad snapped, "Aw, who wants to go out there?"

Saying I would be interested, Mother insisted. She was right.

Finally, he said, "To hell with it, I don't care what you do."

Driving down to Colera, Mother told me what I had not known. She had got it from family, not Dad. In 1930, after almost ten years in the army, he mustered out of the Medical Corps at Walter Reed in Washington. He took the train home to Oklahoma, where he planned to take premed courses at the teachers' college. He had saved money enough for tuition, books, and board to pay his folks. He needed only a roof over his head.

It had been a long time since he had exchanged letters with them.

Arriving in Durant in August 1930, he found their house, the prosperous one we had just seen, occupied by another family. They said the Lewises had "gone down" and, as far as they knew, were living now out in Colera. Dad hitched a ride and found his folks living in an abandoned store: blankets strung up for room partitions, cots to sleep on, a potbellied wood stove for cooking. They told him *no*, he could *not* live under their roof. Hadn't he run off? Hadn't he always been a black sheep? Hadn't he never lifted a finger to help them out? No, he had no home with them.

Eventually Dad went back to Washington and rejoined the army. His family had rejected him a second time.

Where the store had stood was now a vacant lot between red brick walls. Many years ago it had burned down. On both sides were boarded-up stores. Dad and I looked out at an ugly scar of weeds, trash, brick rubble. He did not move a muscle. The end-of-the-year afternoon was in blue shadow; amber sunlight caught high in the bare limbs of a cottonwood that had sprung up at the back of the vacant lot. I got out, stepped into shin-deep weeds. I wanted significant meaning from this place but found only silence and my hope-choked need for it to be otherwise. *Nothing.* I turned, got back in the VW. He still stared through the windshield at the empty lot. Mother was silent too. *Nothing.*

Here, August 1930, his dream of being a medical doctor died. Here his father's Mississippi dream of life in the lap of luxury also died.

I was a spectator of this American story, but now I see that I was blindly living its imperatives.

✻

The following autumn, 1982, was gorgeous. In moonlight, cottonwoods along the creek beds shimmered in balmy winds. Dancing sunlight, warm days that promised to last forever. My son was off at college, my daughter starting law school in Washington, and my second wife and I were expecting a baby in November to certify our new life in Oklahoma.

Then Mother called to tell me a surgeon had just cut a malignant tumor out of her abdomen ("the size of a cantaloupe," she added). She told me that Dad was drinking worse than ever. She feared that his drunk driving would kill a neighborhood child. "It's more than a body can stand," she said. "I'm at wit's end."

My troubles were also closer to home. When senior colleagues expected me to be obsequious, I did not oblige. In fact, I went out of my way to be insulting. It tickled me to see them scurry in and out of each others' offices plotting how to fire me. To them, my lack of fear was the worst affront. A colleague purveyed the story that I had engineered the baby's birth to gain sympathy for keeping me on the payroll. His face I should have beaten into a bloody pulp. But, up to here, I had not let concern about them or deep worry about Mother break in on the hopes I had invested in the baby we expected shortly.

On a high, bright autumn afternoon, assembling the baby's crib, I began to weep. I had no idea why. The music box mobile I hung over the crib, with its sweet, tinkling music, ripped my nerves. I had trouble sleeping.

My wife and I recently had added to our house a Sante Fe room with glass doors, Mexican tile, bookcases. We hoped it would give us more be-alone space. But when complete, the room felt alien. I doubled my jogging through a crumbling World War II navy base. The auditorium where the Dorseys and Benny Goodman had played during World War II was demolished by an idiot ball. Now it was twisted iron, splintered beams, sunlight in windowless backstage rooms.

Rising anger made me touchier at work. Knowing I should do the opposite, I fought them. What the situation required was flattery, but I insulted them or ignored their presence. My troubles were deepening.

Once more Mother called from Washington. She was again in the hospital. The cancer had spread, and she was having heavy chemotherapy. She said: "It doesn't make me better, just sicker." Then: "If I kicked the bucket right now, it would be okay with me. You gotta die of something." Her crackling laughter almost rang true. She added that Dad, "dead drunk," had bashed up his VW and forehead, cracking into the windshield. He had twenty stitches and a nasty scar. He was drunk pretty much around the clock.

❋

She was tall, darkly and flashily beautiful, and from Dad's Little Dixie section of Oklahoma. She often came to my office after class. Recently returned to school, she told me she felt lost. In her luminous brown eyes were glimmers of sunlight in yellow-leafed trees outside my office windows. After dropping out of a small college in Florida ("it was a joke"), she had been a model in Dallas. She had run with a rich, fast crowd, by which she meant money, sex, pills, major cocaine. She told me, shyly, about oil men who took her everywhere (Aspen, Tahiti, Paris, New York, Greek islands) and bought her cars, clothes, fancy condos, jewelry. After two years of the fast life, she got depressed: "What was the point of it all?" She came home to rural Oklahoma, not twenty-five miles from where Dad was born. Now, finishing her college degree, she wanted to write stories about her experiences.

My mind burned with her presence. What saved me from being a worse fool was the certainty that she came to see a teacher. If I dropped this pretense, I was sure she would flee. I knew all about the dignified old professor in *Blue Angel* who became a pitiful fool at the feet of Marlene Dietrich. Even so, my appetite for details of her life raged on: her growing up in southeastern Oklahoma, her torrid romances in Saint Augustine, the Sodom of her years in Dallas. As afternoon blued, she sat next to my desk, legs crossed, foot pumping. Then the sky was hot embers, her sweet Oklahoma drawl slowed, and any moment I, like gasoline-soaked newspaper, would explode into flames. If she failed to show up at office hours, I was both devastated and relieved; anger gnawed at me. Clutching the leaking and nearly swamped life raft of my self-respect as a teacher, I flattered her writing. Her okay sketches I likened to Sherwood Anderson's country Gothic, O'Connor's droll grotesque, and Carver's restrained humor. I felt light-headed, drunk. While holding in severe contempt teachers who take advantage of student trust, I was doing exactly that.

I lusted, pure and simple. Honorable ideals I held concerning myself ignited, burned to ash. Again sensation ravaged me: enormous autumn skies full of sun, high cirrus, vibrant baroque space; a maple tree where I parked igniting yellow, its leaves unearned blessings tumbling onto my beat-up car; plains wind dancing three backyard Lombardy poplars, golden with autumn. Desire was anguish; morality, up in smoke.

On a bright Saturday afternoon, 1982, the Oklahoma-Texas football game going on down in Dallas, I walked from my office, where I had been trying to work, through the deserted campus to her nearby apartment. The town was emptied for the big game, so I stood out like a sore thumb. Nerves on fire. Her address was a battered house converted to student apartments. When she had mentioned that she would be home this afternoon (not once but three times), I half-believed she intended an invitation. Not a simple innocent, she might feel as I did. I was of course also sure that this thought was complete self-delusion.

It was astounding to find myself standing in that dim, sour-smelling hall. Her door was scarred with lock changes; crowbars had pried it open. I knocked.

Silence; she was not home or was not answering the door. My knocking again—rattle-banging dropped into roaring. Nobody home; my god, what an old fool! Rage and self-disgust ripped like wind-driven fire through me. My dignity, such as it was, now nothing but char. My brain was inhabited by somebody I did not recognize. I was afraid for my sanity more than in high school, more than at Quantico, more than in Durham. How could I stop myself?

I was outside, hurrying for my office. By a bookstore, up the walks of the campus where oaks shimmered with bright wind. The campus buildings, so pleasantly familiar, now hulks of brick.

That evening in the new Sante Fe room, I sat in one of two new chairs. The TV glared. I heard words, recognized them as English, but meaning was lost. All afternoon, coming in waves, I had been weeping; it was beyond cause, bottomless. Now I was empty. Belief in words, that uttering one and not another—even to myself—would affect life at all, was lost. A line from *Lear* rattled like an advertising jingle: "The worst is not / so long as we can say, 'This is the worst.'"

Then I was aware of sitting in the wide chair, slumped, turned a little sideways, elbow on the chair arm, head resting on my hand. This was familiar. Something stirred. He sat exactly like this, drunk, a hundred nights in front of the TV.

This overwhelming sense of loss he tried to keep out of sight. All the vodka in the world could not dissolve it. (Nor my flights to women, nor moves to new jobs, new places.) Coming out to Oklahoma had brought me back full circle to the losses he had suffered here and fled from all of his adult life. As a child I knew there was something; later at Christmases I was certain.

✡

Two days later I came home from work to an empty house. My wife, now in the final days, had gone to a baby shower. As twilight charcoaled the new room, I sat in the same chair; preferring twilight, I left the lamp off. On the stereo was *Chariots of Fire*, popular then (my son had given me the recording). Volume up full, huge waves of music swept through me. Something old was breaking open. I looked out the French doors, up to a huge harvest moon riding the lemon sky. About 1944, from a vacant lot in our Hillwood neighborhood, I had looked up on a chilly October evening and seen exactly this moon. How wonderful my life would be, I had thought then, how good the future would be, how proud my mother would be of me. (That had been the night of her birthday, Halloween Eve.) The loss of my hopes, collapsing into absence, crashed through me. Unwept grief I could not control; I wished to die.

In the following week, my daughter was born, and with her what is most painful of all, new hope. When I called to tell Mother, she hardly heard me. Dad's drinking was horrible. Weeks on end he wallowed in bed, drunk as a skunk, looking at a nasty old *Playboy*. Mother told me she was beaten down. She had stopped her chemotherapy: "I'm ready to kick the bucket." Later that week of my daughter's birth and my mother's announcement that she preferred death, my colleagues at work tried to engineer a vote to fire me from my job.

✡

When I woke up to the baby's cry, it was as if awakening to my own. Unable with walking and singing to soothe her, anguish burned. Without her to care for, I knew I would be adrift in a boundless ocean. Guilty, fearing shame, I managed to maintain some professional composure when the beautiful student visited my office. I fought the vote of my colleagues to fire me. Although the decision at each level was reversed, I was no less afraid of losing my job and of having *nothing*. From dreams I awoke to the copper-penny taste of fear. My wife, alarmed at me and our situation, strove to maintain her composure.

Mother refused to die in the hospital: "I want to be in my own house, not in this old place." I could not go back to help. Dad did okay for a few days, as best we could tell, but then my grown daughter, who was starting her own life in Washington, found him passed out on the hall floor, the house dark, Mother awake in the dark upstairs with no one to get her the tiny bit of food she ate. My sister flew in from Calgary to set up a hospice arrangement. In Mother's last week I went to Washington to be with her. When I arrived, Dad was drunk, blundering into walls, hiding his vodka bottles in the garage (as if after twenty years we didn't know his habits).

At twilight on a rainy Sunday in February, with my sister and me at her bedside, Mother died. We watched a burly funeral-home attendant carry her frail body, wrapped in a white sheet, bare foot dangling out, down the stairs, out the front door into the rainy dark. Grief churning in my mind, that night I walked grocery aisles amazed that canned goods, paper towels, and cellophane packages of cookies were here, and not Mother, her skin and bones soon gone to crematory flames.

✡

That winter, back in Oklahoma, I regularly telephoned Dad in Washington. He slurred fat-tongued assurances that he was playing golf, seeing friends, cooking himself good meals of fried chicken and mashed potatoes, doing fine. But we knew he had closed himself into the little town house. With him were the remains of mother's life: jars of grape jelly she had put up, her incomplete afghan project, North Carolina barbecue in the freezer, the country furniture she had restored and polished to a gleam. Also there were his own half century of vodka-fogged memories of her. And gnawing guilt. To sustain him, Dad had his old-fashioned belief in himself, which had served him well, and vodka, which was rapidly destroying him. His fifty-some years of family life were now a shell, a cheaply built town house, vitality gone, and he was back in lost hopes, Oklahoma despair.

When hungry and unable to fix for himself (or with bare cupboards), he drove to a nearby Roy Rogers for roast beef and a Coke. They knew the staggering, bad-smelling old man. When he needed vodka, he stocked up at Pudgies Liquor, where they knew to help him find the VW Rabbit he had lost in the parking lot. At the bank, tellers laughed with embarrassment at his staggering, the mingled smell of vodka, urine, and sweat, as they filled-out his deposit slips for dividend checks. They knew to give him two hundred dollars in cash.

Although I was out in Oklahoma, I saw him vividly in mind's eye staggering through the town house's small rooms. Rocking the baby in the dark, singing to her squirming unease, I was gnawed by futility. Old songs I sang badly: "Red River Valley," "O Shenandoah," "Suwanee River," "Streets of Laredo," "Erie Canal," "Dixie," even "The Marine Corps Hymn." My voice was tight with crosscurrent emotions, the baby unsoothed. The innocence of her pellucid gaze, her baby hands opening, crashed into thoughts of Dad, now an old drunk, deep in despair, hope lost, drinking himself senseless. Once he was a baby like her; I had seen sepia pictures. It was almost too much.

Although prospects for saving my job brightened, I still woke up sweating. Fear of having no job was an inextinguishable fire. I thought of my Oklahoma grandparents living miserably in that abandoned Colera store. And of my father in 1930, "fresh out of dreams," as he put it: no school, no job, no home. One day during these months, the sun just up full, hot as blazes, I noticed a hitchhiking couple out on Interstate 35. Teenagers, both scruffy, weary, grass on clothes and hair. They were inside a cloverleaf on which I was turning 270 degrees, and they were wading through tall grass back up to the southbound lane. I saw the beaten-down patch of grass where they had slept. As I got closer to them, I saw that the girl's thin arms were carrying something. Then, prickles leaping up my back, I saw that it was a baby, about a year old. They were just coming up onto the southbound shoulder, sun full in their faces, when I passed also going south. The baby was a boy, towheaded, round-faced, badly sunburned; he looked like baby pictures of me. In all that violent blast of noise, road wind, summer glare, he held to his mother as babies do, and surveyed with a baby's innocent wonder that wide, ugly world. According to newspapers, thousands from the Rust Belt were heading south in the hope of oil field jobs that were not there. Anguish from out-of-sight sources welled up for days— made more burning for my failure to stop, offer help. Walking night-filled rooms trying to comfort my little daughter, I thought, too, of Dad as unconsoled by his vodka as the baby was by my walking and broken singing.

On the abandoned World War II navy base, I jogged even longer distances. The pool, where 1943–45 aviators took swimming tests, had sprouted big cottonwoods, thigh-high weeds. Barracks, years ago tumbled down, hauled off, now were concrete slabs in tall weeds; even tornado shelters were caved in, open to the weather. The base movie theater, where war-hero movies played, now was moldering, a wall-sagging hulk about to collapse. Interlocked slabs in the weeds were once a shower house; undressing rooms were now in bright sunshine. Big shower rooms recalled Quantico showers. Sweat soaked my T-shirt; wind riffled cottonwoods next to the slabs. When one of the old buildings, quickly constructed in 1942, fell down, or for safety was bulldozed, I stared at the splintering of the beams, at the tumble of two-by-fours, shingles, and window frames. Sometimes one had an unbroken pane of glass.

✿

On the exact anniversary of Mother's death, late February, neighbors found Dad on the hall floor, blood everywhere. He had drunk enough vodka to kill him, fallen down the stairs, cracked his head open, dislocated his shoulder, and had lain there for at least twelve hours. He was too beaten up and toxified for a detox house on the Chesapeake at Havre de Grace, Maryland. So he was taken to the local hospital, where he thrashed about, angry as hell, and had to be restrained. He called for Dr. Sawyer. (The same Dr. Sawyer had presided at his birth in Bokchito, and a few years later, 1912, saw Dad through bad malaria. The source of Dad's dream of being an M.D., he died in 1938, his tombstone in the overgrown, ill-cared-for Bokchito cemetery.) I flew to Washington and drove up to Havre de Grace. Drying out, scalp stitched, ribs taped up, Dad talked wildly: "Get me out of this damn place!" He saw people in the room who were not there. On an X-ray the curls of his cerebral cortex had loosened, flattened out. The doctor said his condition was alcohol dementia. When Dad was released from the hospital, I drove him directly to a Washington hospital with a detox floor.

He would be in a month-long program. When released, he would not go home to that dense weave of death, guilt, mourning, awful drinking, and a lifetime with Mother. Instead I arranged for him to move directly to an elegant retirement apartment. My sister agreed to fly in from Calgary, with her baby, to move his things, get him settled. In new surroundings he would have a fresh start. On the detox floor at the hospital, he was a model patient, well liked, cooperative, although not talkative. Within hours of his release from the hospital, he was tossing straight shots of vodka.

"I knew it wouldn't work," my sister said on the phone to me in Oklahoma.

"I did too. The old story, we got caught hoping he'd quit."

A pause, then we both laughed hard.

At the retirement community, with its lush carpets, big Monets, Mozart Muzak, Dad was usually drunk and smelled of urine. And if this was not shocking enough to the lady residents, he often appeared for meals with his fly wide open. The director, so full of smiles when we could pay cash for Dad's apartment ("Oh yes, yes of course"), demanded at a distance of one thousand miles that I immediately reform Mr. Lewis's behavior. I was Oklahoman enough to laugh.

When I begged Dad not to drive drunk, he replied with the great indignation he could summon only when drunk: "I would *never* hit a child with my car!" The Maryland police refused to watch his car, arrest him, lift his license. This would violate his rights. My stomach burned.

Celebrating my birthday at a restaurant with my wife, I heard an old guy at the next table bully a young man who never quit bootlicking the old guy. Scarcely controllable rage churned in me. With my fists I wanted to hurt both; I wanted to toss them through the restaurant's quaintly bowed window. In chest and stomach, hot skewers. At home I lay down on the living-room floor. After an hour the excruciating pain subsided. Later that night, looking at my baby daughter asleep in her crib, I realized that anguish was a life raft in the nighttime ocean of abject despair.

My wife, struggling against the tide pulling me out to sea, constructed a machine that determined when exactly each of us would care for the baby. The machine's authority was absolute. I stood my watches; I walked my rounds.

April, and wild redbud bloomed along the creeks and cottonwoods leafed gold-green; spring returning with its burden of hope broke my heart. On a bright, beautiful Sunday morning, I received the telephone call I had been expecting. In Washington Dad, of course drunk, had fallen asleep in his chair with a lighted cigarette. The chair caught fire, smoke filled the apartment and hallway, terrifying the resident ladies, setting off clanging alarms, and bringing the fire department. In his call to me the unctuous director had changed his tune: "Your father must leave at once. He is not suited to independent living."

I again flew out to Washington, lined up the only nursing home that would take an active alcoholic, and arrived unannounced at my father's apartment. He appeared sober. He said there had been a little accident but nothing was harmed, except his old arm chair, and he was not aware of any major problem with the director of the retirement community. Hope sparked, but I put it out. I told him they had said he must leave. He looked surprised. In the dark of the picture window I noticed four murky reflections. My heart swelled with love of him as I explained the phone call from the director, the arrangements I had made at a place where he could get the care he needed. "There's no other place to go, Dad. You can't stay here. Ellen can't take you. With a new baby, we can't take you." At some point I wedged in "nursing home." He didn't flinch.

"Well, if it is necessary, all right."

Rain in Washington this Easter week, and in a rented car I shuttled his clothes, some personal items, his golf clubs, and a chest of drawers down to his sterile room at the nursing home. Windshield wipers slip-slapping, I listened to Handel's *Messiah*. The soprano of "I Know That My Redeemer Liveth" clogged my heart with hope and despair. In the wet glimmer of the windshield were watercolor blots of cranberry azaleas, intense jonquils, lush greens. I wept for the man who once took me, a kid, night swimming at the Takoma Park pool, let me ride his big shoulders through dark water, then in the dank men's dressing room, dropped his black wool trunks plop, naked without much embarrassment, and dried himself vigorously with the white towel. He matter-of-factly traded remarks with other men, then helped me tug down my swimming trunks—my hairless little boy parts embarrassed me. He vigorously dried me off, helped me into my underwear and shorts. At home in bed, looking up into hazy summer stars, I thought he was the best father of all.

Leaving him, I looked back from the hall. Slump-shouldered, he sat on the edge of the bed. After I bucked open double doors out into the rainy, sweet springtime, sobs broke through. Back home in Oklahoma, hugging my baby daughter, I was certain I was too weak to bear up under responsibilities to her and Dad. How often had Dad bravely and humorously repeated: "It's a good life if you don't weaken." Telling myself there was no alternative to the nursing home, I knew this was not true. If you are willing to pay the price, an alternative is always there. This thought twisted in my stomach. We hired a private social worker specializing in the elderly to visit Dad twice a week. At least four times a year I would be back to visit him.

✡

A week later, my wife and I drove down to Fort Sill for dinner with acquaintances. This was our first outing without the baby, and I talked with so much excitement about the redbud, its gorgeous magenta color, and greening cottonwoods, and the expansive spaces of the plains, I got myself lightheaded. The man, a lawyer and army first lieutenant, had grown up in Washington, D.C., and the woman was from Chicago's South Side and a newspaper reporter. Both were Catholic. He wanted to discuss conservative politics and theology; she loved the wide world of artillery rounds falling short in backyards of country taverns, a 1920s circus wing-walker now living alone in a trailer out on the plains, and a crusty old sergeant major with tales from three wars. She wrote for the Oklahoma City newspaper and talked with Chicago's brisk clarity. Her accent, dark hair, vigorous manner, and directness recollected the woman from Chicago I went crazy over twenty years ago in North Carolina. On this cool spring evening, we were shown around Fort Sill. Passing old barracks, I recalled that Dad did recruit training in the Oklahoma National Guard here. Only sixteen years old, he lived in these barracks. He saw those small mountains, the Wichitas, where the Kiowa once wintered. We left the post and drove east, out onto the slow, oceanlike rolling of the plains. As a kid in Washington, I was fascinated by the plains—rolling, open to the sun, free, all associated with western movies and Dad. Spring sky darkening from lemon to rose, we drove along a creek bed where Geronimo and other Apaches were buried; like most boys in the 1940s, I had loved what I romanticized as the outdoor vitality of Indians. Hope was re-entering my life and I hated it and welcomed it for showing me that I, who prided myself on withstanding adversity, was so weak that I could not live without it.

Back home that night, pitching and tossing, I moved to the spare bedroom so I would not bother my wife's sleep. The bed in that room was an antique from her Pennsylvania family. April moonlight poured over me. I caught the scent of sun-warmed pine needles and cologne and, immediately, I was on a bench, a girlfriend too, at lakeside at the North Carolina resort where I had worked. Then, summer 1958, Saint Louis, and I was walking from wearying heat into the sweet cold of air-conditioning. Then, dammit, Barbara Stephenson sauntered through my mind. Old bed scrawing, moonlight on my face, I refused to close the blinds to its disturbance. Not all this again. No, but the moonlight, its hope and burgeoning promise.

Next day in church "Morning Has Broken" overwhelmed me, its childlike simplicity burning with contradiction. My daughter asleep in my arms, I could not stop weeping. Again swept with tides of emotion I could not explain. The old despair I had tried to leave behind in upstate New York, in Saint Louis—all now here. Hope roared with anguish. And my wife's trust, the baby's, the bonds I had patched up with my grown children, even my pride in withstanding adversity—all set afire in the warm Oklahoma springtime.

I drove down to Bokchito, saw the sites my father first knew as a boy. Then over to Durant, the house he ran away from, the house we visited in 1945. And finally out to miserable Colera, where Dad's young man's dream died. When I looked at the vacant store-space in Colera, at weeds, trash, broken and glimmering glass, I could not with my thoughts connect it to what burned, roaring, in my chest.

I heard the throb of a KATY diesel coming up from the south. It recalled nighttime locomotives and the clanging and banging of railroad cars in the Southern yards, East Spencer, North Carolina. South of town along those same tracks was Chestnut Hill Cemetery, where Mother's ashes had been poured into North Carolina dirt beside her folks' graves. Dad's name and birth date were cut into the other half of her tombstone. Abruptly appeared, then, down the empty Colera street, a KATY diesel, grimy yellow, huge, passing, then freight cars. Its sudden, ugly force changed everything. I heard it horn for the next crossing, mournful, dying out over the brushy plains. Then, just as abruptly, the hamlet of Colera was again a silent bell. Seven miles north that KATY freight would pass, horning again, within sight of Highland Cemetery, Durant, where my Mississippi-born family were all buried. I got back in my car. In the comfortable, dusty smell, I waited for the banging-closed of the car door to be silence. I started up.

✿

A few weeks later, summer beginning, I bargained for time out of the baby-care schedule for a Sunday morning drive by myself down to Chickasha, Oklahoma. It was Father's Day. My camera I took to make photographs of some of the sights that struck my eyes these days. In blue morning light, sun not full up, I photographed cutting sweeps of a thresher in a field of winter wheat-mow left to dry in warm, sunny days. And just down the road, a cotton gin, rusty, tin-roofed, in the loading bay weeds growing up through cement-slab joints; and along the roof beam, eight or ten pigeons strutting—little clicks, tin wanging—then five rose into the huge sky, flew in shifting arrangements a big circle, returned and settled, and another flight soon lifted, arced away, circled out, and returned. I captured the beautiful instant the pigeons lifted from the roof. And at the edge of Chickasha I photographed gauzy light on a big, four-cylinder grain elevator—POGUE in two-story-high letters. (Later, in the exact center of the frame, I discovered a STOP RR CROSSING I was not consciously aware of.) Then, early summer light exalted in the sky, in fast-running clouds, Oklahoma living in brisk, warm winds, I walked abandoned fields, weeds to my knees, racing and swishing in wind, glanced with sunlight.

✿

My wife had month-long professional commitments in Colorado Springs, and I had agreed to go along to care for the baby. We left about six in the evening and drove west into the summer sun's huge presence—blaze and glare I could not visor out. Leaving the route of old U.S. 66, the *Grapes of Wrath* road, we worked northwest along the Cimarron River. The baby fussed—sky flamed apricot, then slid down into blues—but she finally slept. And with the thumpa-thump of old cement-slab highways, we approached and passed by places—the grave marker of Sam Chisholm (of the Chisholm trail); the town of Cushing, where Edna Ferber lived while writing *Cimarron*; and old Fort Supply, which was Custer's base for making war on Plains Indians. And grain elevators (some tall enough to catch the setting sun's direct apricot light), water towers, lights of softball fields brave in the night's huge bell, and blocks of brick stores (half empty, boarded up) and the smug quiet of big old Main Street houses dark but for a single lighted and curtained bedroom. Out of night appeared, slid passed, returned, presence half-remembered.

My wife and I talked about crashing out of difficult marriages directly into each other, and unwisely moving to Oklahoma, and losing the knack of talking to each other, and owing to my male pride in enduring suffering and her class pride in maintaining superior equilibrium, our disastrous underestimation of how birth, death, job, and assuming responsibility for my father would, a mighty storm, split us apart.

As I drove the Panhandle, my wife slept. For stretches I turned off the car lights. In that enormous dark, I saw the vault of a quadrillion bright stars come down to touch the black horizon. At Guymon, dust devils blowing around the deserted square, I turned north into eastern Colorado and worked northwest again across those giant plains. Over the north horizon flashed the concert of a thunderstorm. The storm was moving through Denver toward Boulder, the radio said. It was beyond the earth's curvature, over 150 miles north. An hour later I saw, with the silent kettle-drum concert, etches of lightning strike the earth. Thrillingly beautiful, sights only the universe's Maker should see.

I turned east on a two-lane road that cut one hundred miles west, straight as a die to Colorado Springs. Struggling with the urge to sleep, I searched the dark ahead for first pink light striking Pike's Peak. My mind was playing tricks on me. Dangerously sleepy, I pulled off into the weedy entrance to cattle grazing land. My wife and the baby still slept. I took a blanket, lay down in the dewy grass by the car, and looked up into stars filling the depth of night. But that thrill, mixed with fear of the implacable universe, kept me awake. Rolling over, I slept in the blanket's dark, and, seconds later it seemed, I pushed aside the blanket. I saw mist-rising dawn, and, nearby, antelope frozen in concern of what I was. Another thrill leaped hot through my chest. I watched until they went back to grazing. When I awoke again, stood up, they were nowhere in sight—perhaps emissaries from a gentle world beyond ugly striving. Starting up, getting back on the road west, and in thick morning mists, I never caught sight of Pike's Peak.

Mornings in Colorado Springs parks with my little girl, sprinklers whirled—cast wet iridescences. She loved to play, exuberantly, in the circling casts of the sprinklers, but otherwise was downcast, moped, and when I failed to keep track of her favorite doll, finally declaring it lost, she was inconsolable.

I understood. My wife and I did not share a bed. We fought unceasingly. Although the baby, now nearing two, could not say so, she understood the terrible storm that had ripped through her world, destroying everything. When she dabbled at lunch with her chocolate ice cream, her absolute favorite, and I gazed at the crown of her head—hair raggedly parted by me—suddenly guilt was overwhelming, my terrible selfishness, bringing hurt to her innocent life. My heart ached for her. In late afternoon there were sudden, dark, mountain-booming thunderstorms, followed immediately by strong sunshine that evaporated all moisture. During the first week she began to cry in great fear of these storms. She remains afraid of storms.

✩

My second wife and I divorced that autumn. My one-bedroom apartment was a few blocks from the house. I moved in a too-big round dining-room table (bought in Virginia and refinished by Mother), a desk (which my first wife and I bought in Saint Louis the months after I discovered *The Sound and the Fury*), a small dresser (refinished by my first wife while I was in the Marine Corps), two cheap ladder-back chairs (from my grad-student days at Iowa), a bookcase (bought when we moved to upstate New York), and a bed. I liked thinking I was unburdened. In four liquor boxes were all the family photos, Bibles, and genealogy. It thrilled me to be so unencumbered, but at night all this washed-up debris of former lives made death seem near.

For solace there was Oklahoma landscape. I did not yearn for scenes suitable for watercolors. I hungered for ordinary rural houses on fragile islands of green lawn, neat flower beds of zinnias, bird baths, and surrounding it scrub oak and dun-colored plains out to the horizon. And in eroded red-clay yards old trailers with rotten steps, a woodpile, a busted-door shed to one side, a rusty pickup, all half lost in the immensity of scrubby rolling plains and sky. Buying *Ghost Towns of Oklahoma*, I visited at least twenty. I saw tumbled-down brick walls out of which inkberry bushes grew; and roofs collapsed, brick walls standing, and in tangles of rotted timber and floor planks weeds springing up. There were abandoned rail lines, the cross ties and tracks ripped up, sold, trestles wobbling. At a country church with a poor, unfenced graveyard was buried an army PFC killed in Vietnam, 1966, age nineteen.

I got to know a Vietnam vet, also divorced. In 1966 he was a medic in the First Air Cavalry. In a year of heavy fighting, all eight medics in his unit were killed or wounded except him. He had gone through bankruptcy, owed the IRS big, and was hounded by creditors. He moved every six months to a different apartment and to support himself worked grave-yard shifts in emergency rooms as a physician's assistant. He also kept three women convinced each was his one and only. Born in Oklahoma like my father, he also had failed in his ambition to be an M.D. But undaunted, manic, funny, he lifted my melancholy spirits. He and I agreed that my depressions were exactly what he fled with all his manicness. He wrote of his Vietnam experiences with high-speed language and unsteady irony. Slowing down for even a second, he feared descent into memories of rice paddies, claymores, zinging bullets, rolling over a guy with no face, a friend with his arm bloody pulp screaming for morphine that might kill him. When he talked about the war, he said, "No big deal, no big deal." He told me I had managed to get screwed up without even going to Nam. I laughed; he was right.

My other ally was a psychiatrist, a big-shouldered old fellow. He came from tough Germans in south Texas. When he was a kid, men as a joke enticed him to pee on the magneto of a threshing machine. Shocked him bad, never forgot. He went into the hard life of Texas A&M and then to infantry combat in Europe. The killing changed him. After medical school he worked at the Menninger Clinic. Like Dad, he had roots in the South. But the old doc had traveled the path my father had abandoned at Colera in 1930. He went into the inner world that Dad had sealed off airtight. He treated vets, convicts, emotionally disturbed children, and me.

My job now was okay, safe. The dislike of some of my colleagues I considered a compliment.

Every weekday evening at five I saw my little girl for two hours. As we played blocks and drew pictures, or, the autumn weather holding, visited parks, I noticed her lack of joy. Her life had been split in two: toys and books at Daddy's, at Mommy's, and never the twain did meet. Her favorite dinner, macaroni and cheese, I fixed, and we roughhoused and read books together, but all rattled hollowly. Hearts loaded with loss and yearning, we clung to rituals: every time we got in my car, she chimed, "Seat belt, Dad"; for Saturday lunch, always a certain deli's gooey egg-salad sandwich; and on winter evenings, when it was too dark and cold for parks, always art projects—wild, color-splashing, exuberant—on the dining-room table. Aching, we worked to make our time happy.

I also liked being alone. As at Quantico, my days were sustained with brown leaves riffling and chattering in sunlight; sun warming a windowpane; wind's cold bite where hills dropped into bleak plains (this where the Cimarron Trail crossed the Washita River); the rolling tumble of tumbleweed; the music of echoing voices in a room. These and drives without destination in Oklahoma countryside.

Often I took my little daughter to a downtown park. As blue dusk gathered, a chill in the air, I pushed her in the swing—"High up in the sky!"—and we sped together down the big slide, and I held her hand as she walked benches in the outdoor amphitheater. When the mournful horn of a diesel carried down to us from one of the north crossings, we looked at each other, laughed. Picking her up, both of us still laughing with simple joy, I ran for the Santa Fe track bordering the park. There I swung her up on my shoulders, throbbing diesel now close, looming, and we waved wildly, often got waves and smiles back. After the solemn passing of the freight cars, that nice clickity-clack, we waved again at the trainman in the caboose's cupola. He usually waved back. Then red lanterns slid silently away into blue dusk and we were happy.

✶

In August when my ex-wife moved to a better job in Iowa, she took our daughter. The child would have better opportunities there than in Oklahoma, I thought. But when she actually left, the town was riddled with her absence, and my anguish was unbearable. I doubted I could survive; I could not lift my head. My Nam vet friend said, "Buddy, if you can't live without the kid, then I want to say it's been good knowing you. It's yours to decide." We were in a Greek gyros place smelling of burnt lamb.

That August was scorching; tar in patched cracks of streets melted;

heat was loud noise. One evening, sun descending, I walked deserted city streets in Oklahoma City. Electric wires hummed; hot air smelled burnt. When I found the ice cream parlor, it was closed without explanation. Peering in through dirty windows, I saw in the dark inside chairs inverted on tables.

Later that week, 3:30 A.M, I could not sleep. I got in my car as I used to do to put the baby to sleep. Memory put her absence in all I noticed. At city park, where cicadas and crickets screeched insanely, I stopped, parked. Mottled shadow from streetlights; slides dark, and in big poplars, cottonwoods, no wind stirring. Into the outdoor amphitheater I went, sat down. Twenty rows up, the raised grass stage was empty, dark, and overhead the Oklahoma night was stars splattered in endless confusions.

That day at noon in the old doc's office I had wept hard. No windows, each of us in Lazy Boy loungers, mine with the Kleenex box. With shame I pulled out those soft white flags. No words to speak entered my mind.

"What . . . ?" I managed.

"Losing your daughter reminds you of something—old losses before remembering."

Wallowing; not enough belief to . . .

In long silences, thoughts of Mother. Her voice saying, "Clay, you storm through life." And, "You are just an old bull in a china shop." And, "You have a strong back and weak mind." And, "Clay, you're all boy." In her voice a biting edge, some humor, and love I'll never stop craving.

Then memories. As a kid, diving into a flooded excavation to save a friend who had slipped in, could not swim, floundering; both of us nearly drowned before I got him up the slick clay sides. Nearly forty years old, throwing a borrowed ladder up against a house, climbing up, fire singing its fearful song, house smoke-choked. At the second-floor window, trying to force myself in that thick, roiling smoke. I could not. And the old man the firemen found dead was just under the windowsill. For the hell of it, and because it was a blustering March day, I signed up for the Marine Corps. Incision on my belly bleeding, I plunged ahead to officer-candidate boot camp. Assaulted a superior officer. Lunged into marriages and plunged into divorces. Uprooted family for ill-considered career switches.

"You took your licks," I heard Mother's voice say.

I thought I was brave. That I had guts. But no. I was just helpless and afraid. In fact, at the heart of my lunging and plunging, I was what I now saw, *nothing*. This in the silence at noon with the Old Doc. There was no *I* to say.

In the dark amphitheater, to my mind came Winslow Homer's painting called *Defiance: Inviting a Shot Before Petersburg*. In it a Confederate soldier near defeat in the trenches at Petersburg, Virginia, leaps up on the parapet to draw Yankee fire; below, down in the trench, a black with banjo, grinning, plays a sad jangling thrum; far away Yankee puffs of smoke—bullets coming toward the dancing Rebel. Fool's joy, drawing fire. I should tell the old doc about that.

Once I got jailed in Petersburg, Virginia. Arrested for an invalid registration that was valid, cash required, I spent twenty-four hours behind bars. *No*, this more bluster, bravado. No *I* to say. Pain of *nothing* worse than anything I had endured, worst's worst.

Silence.

Taking risks, jumping up to draw fire, but my secret was that my busted life was not worth a damn to me.

Thought myself oh so independent, but in fact did not risk a goddamn thing.

In this hot, still night, this clearer than in the old doc's office at noontime.

Then, consumed by pain's fire, I wept, reasons ignited, bursting into flame, hot coals swept up into surrounding dark. Only now, a park amphitheater at 4 A.M. where I had come for what I had lost, was it clearer.

Then silence, maybe half an hour.

I looked at his dark eyes on me, a hulking man, not so strong anymore, with Freud's mustache, Freud's nose, and socks flopping down to expose pale ankles.

No words. Whatever I say will bluster emptily, plea for attention, beg somebody to put me out of my misery. Any word I say perpetuates my will-broken life. Silent; chilly sweat. His eyes, which recognize me, I do not want to stop looking at. Saying anything, I'll just start it again. That's all I know how to do. That's pitiful. I'm nothing.

After a long while, I got up.

"If you have difficulties," he said, "telephone me."

I walked stooped over.

I went to Po' Folks, a cheap food chain, and ordered a southern lunch Mother would have liked: green beans and blackeyed peas, both cooked with pork fatback, mashed potatoes sopped with gravy, and a big glass of iced tea. When a waitress in gingham, forcing cheerfulness, slid the food in front of me, my stomach knotted.

When my ex-wife was preparing to leave town, I kept biting my tongue. Eating a hamburger, a donut, sharp pain racing into my scalp, then salty-blood taste. I came down here, to the park, this dark amphitheater, to make my daughter's absence burn.

North up the Santa Fe track, a freight train's horn sounded down over flat prairie to me. When my wife and I were together, I would be tossing in bed, late at night, worrying, and then hear in the dark this mournful horning. Lying there, I would listen to the freight coming down through the town's crossings, by the university, by the cement slabs (that had been sheds) of the stop at the old navy base. Too many night trains; too many in mind's dark. In my scrawing bunk at Quantico, heard across the dark base the Seaboard pull in, stop, pick up that day's dismissals, then pull out, horn down through the clanging crossing signal just outside our barracks. Here in this park, twilight, freights called me to run with my daughter to the track and wave. Now that joy burn of absence. Where Mother herself was born, that house, in the old bed with her, while out in the dark of the big Southern yards trains chugged, then silence, silence, then bang, bang-bang, bang-bang-bang; without rhyme or reason. Then a huge steam-snorting locomotive rushed down on me . . .

Horning again, big diesel, north up the line, closer.

Standing up, I walked down the amphitheater aisle, up the steps to the empty grass stage, then through the backstage cedars. Passed the swings, the long slide—her happy shouts recalled—and the jungle gym, the sandbox, the benches where I had sat. I went up the embankment to the track. Its polished edges gleamed in the dim carry of street lights. Horning even closer now, diesel's headlight switching back and forth; engines big, chest-concussing; knife edges of track.

Yelling my courage, I'd hit the exact bite of wheel to rail, into that thundering, mind-overwhelming, delicious presence. No more absence.

When the engine struck me, it would begin horning for the next crossing fifty yards down the track. Mind calm, peace rising like dawn mists, thought annihilated, all self-consciousness pulled into that Santa Fe engine's rushing presence.

Then I was listening to the sing of boxcar wheels on iron rails, and screech of brakes, and my heart was going hard. I had not jumped; at first, a coward, afraid to take hold of my life. But the dark presences of the boxcars, in that nice clickity-clack, were rolling by, and the song of it was happy, reminding me of my little girl, and when the caboose slid by, slowly its red lights disappearing down the track, I was left there at the track in beautiful silence, the ringing of a giant church bell hummed down. I was sleepy.

✡

I became seriously interested in Wiley Post, the one-eyed pilot from Oklahoma who flew a record-breaking solo around the world in 1931. (That was the year Mother's mother died; it was also when she and Dad met and got married.) As an oil-field roughneck Post for ten years had dreamed of flying. In 1923 he lost his eye to a steel splinter, but he did the opposite of giving up his dream. He took his workmen's compensation money from the accident and bought his own plane, then learned to fly it. Handicap became strength. Within eight years, Post flew alone in the *Winnie Mae* around the world, setting a record, and stood on the White House lawn shaking hands with President Calvin Coolidge.

Every source of information in Oklahoma I chased down, including people living who had known him. With the woman from Chicago, in windy summer days and lightning-crashing thunderstorms, I located the exact Oklahoma places of his life. Another obsession drove me. My emptiness slowly began to fill, but Post's character I could not fathom.

There was a schoolteacher in Marlow, Oklahoma, writing a book about Post. When I called for some information, she wanted to meet me at the Git 'n' Go. Her now-dead father had been Post's friend. She told me Post (and his family, including present-day surviving members) took pains to hide the fact that in 1919 Post, poor but dreaming of flight, had attempted highway robbery. He was unarmed, the men in the car he had stopped overpowered him, and he was tried, convicted, and sentenced to ten years in prison at Granite. (The clerk of the court of Grady County remembered Post's trial file. Somebody, probably family, had stolen it.)

Granite's grim rock walls are out on an expanse of high plains—horizon twenty miles away, huge sky. His ten-by-six cell turned inside out Post's dream of flight in Great Plains sky. Doing time there, he got near to death of "severe melancholy," the doctor's report said. The doctor recommended parole, and the governor granted it. Not a year later, Post lost his eye, got his money, and was on his way at last. Eventually he even played himself in a Hollywood movie. (But look at this film or any photograph of Post, into his eyes, and there you'll see the broken spirit of an ex-con.)

If he had not done time at Granite, I doubt he could have managed to fly countless hours alone. If he had not done time at Granite, in abject mortification, and with honorable yearning set forth to show himself and the world the exact contrary, I doubt Post would have become disillusioned in 1935 with flying, with his own achievements, so exhausted he lost the razor edge of his judgment. He bought floats too heavy for the plane he would take to Alaska, and, near Point Barrow, forgot about carburetors in Arctic air, and killed himself and Will Rogers. Tragedy, I thought. American—in Great Plains light, flat, solemnly beautiful.

✳

I drove out to the road south of Ninnekah where Post set out to commit robbery and ended up in prison. It was a sunny winter day, high cirrus and mare's tails, scrubby trees bleached yellow, sumac bloody along the road shoulders. I pulled off, got out, walked. No passing cars broke the winter day.

I did not expect a historical marker. Forlorn and empty as most of Oklahoma. But no. Right here Wiley Post's life was irrevocably changed. From here he circled the globe, visited the White House, starred as himself in Hollywood movies, and crashed in Alaska.

Down in Colera there is that weedy lot where in 1931 there was an abandoned store. Now vacant, *nothing*, but what happened there burns in every breath of Dad's at Friends House and in every breath that I draw walking on this road shoulder under a heartachingly high winter sky. There when I raged at Dad. And that night, also cold, at Quantico when I almost killed the lieutenant; and in all of my violent lunging through careers, divorces, marriages. Burns also, God help me, in the lives of my children.

I stopped. Warm sun, coming through gauzy cirrus, fell across my shoulders. All of us wounded, hearts dipped in gall, but that hurt's persistence testament to love's indomitable yearning.

I knelt down on the road shoulder, with acute awkwardness and embarrassment. Words failed me. In my mind was a garish Sunday school picture of Paul struck on the road to Damascus. That violent man struggling for dear life. And Genr'l Nathan Bedford Forrest, as fierce a warrior as ever lived (great-grandfather's brother survived two life-consuming years with him), after the war turned remorsefully to Jesus and for his wife carefully set the dinner table. Still kneeling, nearly laughed at these knotted incongruities. Above, the sky, implacable, empty, but my heart a burning knot that would not leave me until life did; this for good and ill my human inheritance. On most days I can still touch that moment on the road south of Ninnekah.

✡

The outside of my life held steady. I worked, visited the woman from Chicago, who now lived in Oklahoma City, made trips to Iowa to see my daughter and to Washington to see Dad in the nursing home and visit my grown children. But I also tracked inward paths. As one learns a beautiful but haggard face, I learned Oklahoma's landscape—not pastoral or mirror of being alone but earth itself in somber autumn light.

One day I drove dirt roads that ran straight as the survey lines that determined them. Through rolling and barren hills I descended to a creek bed. Dark trickle; on steep, erosion-cut banks, were brush, stunted and scrawny trees with spiny limbs holding scatter of torn black plastic, ghost-white milk containers, and washed-out fenceposts tangled in barbed wire, all carry of gully-washing storms. Above the creek, and these gullies, an old farmhouse abandoned and resembling the Joads' of *The Grapes of Wrath*. It was cheap, banged together poorly, falling down now and life gone from within its walls. Down the road, I noticed some abandoned trailers half hidden by high weeds and sumac. A shack, probably inhabited, had its porch propped by a two-by-four and ripped plastic sheets nailed over the windows. At a crossroad I pulled off, stopped; weeds along the road shoulders were dusted red. I got out, walked the sandy ruts. A scrubby pasture by a dry creek, a few cows lifting their heads. The sun low, air thick with dusty rose light, and the shadows of fence posts, eroded hillsides, creek woods were rich burnt sienna.

To the east, on a bare hilltop above the plain of the South Canadian River, I saw an air traffic installation for the approach into Oklahoma City, a stubby beacon surrounded by wire fence. High enough, it caught the last of the direct rosy light. Now I was in umber, not burnt sienna. I stopped, feeling the cooler night approaching, and I loved this stretch of earth in the solemn tolling of days, seasons, which one day would gather me in. The earth that filled my heart.

Later that week I drove down to the Highland Cemetery by the railroad tracks south of Durant, where my grandmother and grandfather were buried. The scale of their lives was so grand, simple, and their end so abject. Nearby I found Aunt Nell's grave next to Uncle Bob's. So unearned, those brass spurs she gave me. No gift ever meant more. The family stewed in outrage that she would spend so much on Al's boy. Aunt Nell (for N.L., Nancy Lockwood) was family too.

I listened to Woody Guthrie on a tape the woman from Chicago gave me. In my car I sang Steve Goodman's "The City of New Orleans." Tears broke into my eyes, voice, at the words "Don't you know me, I'm your native son." I talked weekly to my little girl in Iowa. When she wanted only to make funny noises, I understood. When I visited her we made new rituals at Ground Round's silly restaurant, the Amanas, Herbert Hoover's birthplace, and at Al and Irene's Rib-Haven in Cedar Rapids. When I left, I hugged her hard and she hugged back; this seemed all that was best of life. I rode I-35 watching with joyful tears Handel's *Messiah* in a summer evening of pink and rose-edged cumulus clouds.

✿

I passed a last trial in Oklahoma. When I turned fifty, a medical exam found a lump in the back of my right thigh. The doctor cut it out, just old scar tissue. He also found three little lumps the size of peewee marbles in a testicle. He sent me to a urologist, Dr. Blue (yes, his real name!). When he examined me, I saw alarm in his eyes. He told me I should have an operation immediately. He told me if the lumps were malignant, he would need permission to remove the testicle. My Vietnam friend, unusually sober, told me testicular cancer was a killer; he told me to let Dr. Blue cut. I agreed to the surgery, but I was not afraid of death, freighted with abstraction, but of the loss of the universe's presence, of cottonwoods riffling and chattering in the wind, of blocks of sunlight on the cheap shag carpet in my apartment, of the actual physical sight of my children and the woman from Chicago. At first I did not believe that, without me, these gorgeous sites would continue to be present in the universe of earth and sky, light and darkness. Then I understood, yes, and I was mightily afraid of death's darkness. In a new way I understood being alone.

I resolved not to mention the operation to my children. If there was a good way to live, there was a good way to die, and that was what I wanted. The woman from Chicago held my hand as I waited to be wheeled on the gurney into the operating room. She, the Nam vet, and the old doc were my allies. They and the knowledge that other men had crossed here.

I felt strong; I gripped my fear. I was calm.

There was Shakespearean aptness in dying of a disease in my sexual parts, the urges from which had led to my chief sins: passions, lust, wives left, children hurt in divorces. Such a death would have dramatic symmetry: my adult life beginning in 1958 with a large scar on my belly and ending, nearly thirty years later, 1987, with another large scar exactly opposite that scar which had pulled in healing. I thought of the still larger Greek appropriateness of coming to Oklahoma, the home of my father, and there suffering a final wound from which I would not recover. And, opposed to this tragic, the comic and romantic appropriateness of marking the final transformation out of my troubled and repetitive past with a scar that marked the end of what had begun with the appendectomy in 1958. In a detached sense, I was eager to see what would happen.

The lumps were old scar tissue. They were excised, biopsied, and found to contain no cancer cells. I had suffered scar-causing trauma I had forgotten, Dr. Blue said. Life remained open, its force in me strong. And Oklahoma I did not yearn for anymore; its mixture of loss suffered and desperate desire, always part of my flesh and bone, now I also comprehended.

Anna's Tombstone

A boy of five in 1911, Dad traveled with his father back to his father's birthplace in Mississippi. Just the two of them went, because E. R. wanted *his* father to see the towheaded boy, this grandson, who had been named as a compliment to the old man. E. R. was hoping to gain favor in the eyes of the patriarch. That summer old A. C., born in rough-and-tumble Mississippi in 1840 (newspapers railing against too-frequent murders), was seventy-one years old.

When I was about age five, 1941, Dad told me he had two memories from that trip back to Mississippi. He remembered drooping, gray Spanish moss; this appeared otherworldly to eyes accustomed to bleached-out Oklahoma. And he remembered swinging off the train at Crystal Springs, walking with his father up the platform, then being told that the tall old man walking erectly toward them—the man with the long gray beard—was his grandfather and namesake. Terrified of that fatherly presence, Dad ran away; there was no more to tell. The old man must have looked like Father Time.

In 1986, seventy-five years later, one of us next journeyed back to Copiah County, Mississippi. All my poking around in records had got me to thinking I had been to Mississippi. But I had not, not at all.

✡

I left Oklahoma in a January blizzard—open plains blowing with snow, snow devils on the roads, life hunkered down. Just to go out my apartment door required pride in facing adversity; wind bit with needle-fierce teeth.

As I drove empty roads, sun broke through, spectacularly haloed in swirling ice crystals, blowing snow. Clouds then quickly closed out the sun, but later my flight broke back into pure bright winter light. I descended into sunny, mild January weather in Mississippi. My eyes, accustomed to Oklahoma, feasted on Mississippi's lush green. The huge crowns of hardwoods were so full. Lack of rain had not stunted them. They were not frostbitten as in upstate New York. I had come here to discover more of my father's inheritance buried in time.

For several days in Hazelhurst I crawled through courthouse marriage records, deeds, and land records, tracking that huge Lewis family which for nearly a century had been right here where I was. This the slope of land on which they had walked, here the county-seat of Gallatin (now a cow pasture) where they lived in the 1830 and '40s.

☆

A fellow in the Hazelhurst post office told me Robert Harper's wife, Ruby, had been a Lewis. She turned out to be Dad's first cousin. Older than he, she claimed to remember his 1911 visit with them in Mississippi. One of her daddy's brothers and his little boy, her cousin, had come back from Out West. That evening I was invited to supper. The house was a Mississippi cottage, Queen Anne style, bay windows, gracious wide porches, and it was chocked too full of beautiful antiques, all polished to high gloss. A black maid, an embroidered handkerchief pinned to the pocket of her peach uniform, served with good humor delicious fried chicken, mashed potatoes and gravy, lima beans, slaw, and apple pie with ice cream. Ruby Rosebud, for that was her given name, had hands badly twisted with arthritis, and she took pain pills that were irritating to her stomach. But Ruby was of good cheer and talked sweet-to-the-ear Mississippian, and her direct gaze was both welcoming and to me disconcerting. Her father was Ezekiel Obadiah Lewis, the oldest son of A. C. and of course my grandfather's oldest brother. She pointed out a picture of herself at age twenty, blonde curls, sweetly beautiful in a white brocaded dress. When she told me she no longer looked like that, her laughter was genuine. She told me she and Robert had no children. She said, then, that there was something out in the barn she wanted to show me. It took a good while to get ourselves out there. At her direction I shoved around trunks, pushed aside old settees, and finally pulled out, banged opened, a very old looking trunk.

Then I met Lovey, who had been dead for sixty years. This trunk was hers, packed neatly by her as death approached and conveyed to Ruby as the only one of her relations still living in the county. She was a maiden lady. All the property she had in this world was in the trunk, according to Ruby. Lovey's father was Joseph B. Lewis, named after his Revolutionary War grandfather, and he was the brother of old A.C. In the Confederate army too, Joseph B. miraculously survived over two years of hard fighting with Genr'l Nathan Bedford Forrest. Strong-looking in her photographs, eyes fierce, Lovey devoted her life to caring for the old veteran. After he had passed on to his reward, she was poor but managed to get by tending children. As she was about to die, she wrote on a child's tablet notes about the Lewis family, their Virginia and South Carolina roots, the Morris sisters, details of old A.C.'s quiet death at the home of his daughter, details of her father's god-granted survival of Forrest's cavalry, three horses shot out from under him, hat and coat cut by bullets. And Lovey wrote about her Grandpaw Hugh, maker of caskets and Hazelhurst's first undertaker. Holding these age-browned pages in my hands in that dim barn, understanding that these had been left for me (even though I had not then been born), I wanted to yell thanks or weep or pray or jump up and down. It was a living connection of words to the world I was laboring to recover.

"You be sure and take your revolver now," Ruby said.

"My what?"

"Your pistol."

"Why?"

"Cause you'll need it out there for the rattlesnakes."

"Out where?"

"Out at Grandpa Ab's farm."

"Well, I had thought I'd drive out there, look at the land."

"The house."

"What?"

"The house is still standing. Nobody lives in it, but it is still there. Least it was the last time Robert and I were out in that part of the county."

My ears rang, burned. My god, this and Lovey's notes in the space of ten minutes! Granddaddy born there, and Dad visited, and the land was bought by Hugh, the son of the Revolutionary War veteran, in the 1830s from Choctaw lands. There all along. All those years of my looking.

I never did find out whether Ruby assumed that all males would as a matter of course carry revolvers. Although I wrote, sent cards, she died before I got back to see her. After returning to Oklahoma, I realized that her eyes struck me because they were the exact color of mine (and of my older daughter's).

✡

Courthouse records had shown me the land of my great-grandfather's farm, but discovering that the house still stood there was astounding—*actually here* out of that time. It was out in the northwest corner of Copiah County, near the hamlet of Carpenter, close to the Natchez Trace. In a rented car I drove west from Hazelhurst on a meandering country road. At a fork I stopped to ask directions. On the porch of a little white house set back in some tall, wide-crown pecan trees was an older woman and a young man, probably her son. Stopping halfway down the drive, I got out, walked toward them, then stopped again. (My North Carolina grandfather had instructed me in country manners.) I do not talk southern (only *greezy* and *Warhshington*, that I know of, remain of southern speech), but the woman on the porch cheerfully answered me, told me the way, and was interested that I was looking for the house where my grandfather had been born.

"Well I hope you find it," she said. "Good luck to you."

I think she meant it.

I went through some low hills, and then along a flat valley that was mostly pastureland. My map showed White Oak Creek to the north. The grass was lush, and there were grazing beef cattle. Utica Junior College I had seen on the map, but, spirits high about finding the old house, I was surprised suddenly to be in the middle of a knot of grim Victorian buildings. Students on the walks were black. Something akin to grief filled me; hope was making them so vulnerable.

A half mile farther on, I slowed. There was the broken-down barn and beside it the mailbox scrawled with ANNIE O. JONES. I eased the car through a deep mud puddle, then into a rutted lane that curved, twisted, disappeared several times into deep puddles of muddy water.

The road skirted a small field—bare, wet earth surrounded by thick woods. I stopped by a tin-roofed shack. Told to ask here for directions, I was certain this shack was not anybody's home. The planks of the walls had gaps my hand could pass through and the porch roof had come down on one end. Absolutely nobody lived here. Then two black children, little girls, came around the corner—solemn faces, faded dresses, fear mixed with curiosity. People did live here, and my heart dropped.

"Hello," I called.

The children, about six and eight, stayed around to the side of the porch.

"Hello," I called, and I walked toward the open door of the shack. Inside I saw scraps of linoleum on the floor, newspapers stuck to the walls, and a cluster of pictures of Jesus. A Washington slum, a New York one, has a violence in its ruin, a sense of something destroyed, but this shack in rural Mississippi looked to be assembled into its present condition—made of picked-up scraps, things hauled in from the woods, from trash bins. Out of the dark inside a woman appeared, Annie O. Jones. Her hands were wet. She eyed me with anger, suspicion.

Clumsily I explained that my grandfather had been born here, that my name was Lewis.

She nodded at the name, but didn't speak. Then she said, "This old A. C. Lewis's place."

A terrible clot of hot feeling was in my chest. Out of all that time had come from this black woman my father's and great-grandfather's name. I had hoped she was not intelligent, for this would account for why she had so little and I so much.

"Could you tell me where the house is?"

Her manner was gentler. She stepped out. Sunlight touched her brown face. She grinned, a little embarrassed; several of her teeth were missing. The children came up beside her in the mud in front of the house. She pointed across the field.

"Go through the gap, and you'll see it." She pointed a limp hand toward a gap in the tree line.

Then she and the children turned, disappeared into the shack. With me and Annie O. Jones there was deep history, and we came close to failing altogether in even such a simple communication. My family did not own slaves, never did, but they were deep in a community that did. They were there when racism was at its worst.

I drove on the lane, across the soft, muddy field, and stopped at the gap. In the tree line there was a beautiful, clear, fast-running stream—cutting the bank, going quickly over rocks. For a moment I listened to its song, remembering the creek where I had played as a kid. Then I crossed on a log, and from the other side, out of the trees, I saw a pair of fields cut at right angles to each other. In the autumn they had been harvested, plowed under, and the rains had softened the furrows. The field to my right sloped gently up to some trees, which, with long-needled pines higher up, covered a small hillside; in among the trees, just back from the field, was a large tin roof. It was right where Annie O. Jones said it would be. I knew this was the house where my grandfather was born, where my father had visited.

But for reasons I am at a loss to explain, I quickly headed off up the other field.

No, I told myself, that roof I so plainly see cannot be what I'm seeking.

So I went up the other field, looked for the house in the trees back of that, my heart beating hard, nearly frantic for not being able to stop what my clearer mind knew was absolutely wrong. I crashed through another line of trees to a higher field, and I blundered through another, thicker, dense with undergrowth, into still another field, a bigger one, and I was nearly lost, still very excited, wanting and not wanting what I had first seen from the gap. My shoes had gooshed in the field mud, and I was sweating. These fields theirs; they cleared them, plowed them for a nearly a century. A wild, lifelong hunger answered in muddy strides.

The house I feared, the intimate knowledge it contained. I was sure my thrashed-down life had been theirs back to the 1830s.

Through muddy fields and thick-grown tree lines, I worked down to where I had started. Across the stream, my rented car. My nerves steadied. I started toward the sun-gleaming roof at the edge of the trees on the hillside above the field. Nearer, I could make out what had been a yard between the house and the field's edge. It was now overgrown with dark cedars, huge thorny hawthorns, flower beds of crushed-down stalks, and redbud trees taller than the house eaves. Set up on shoulder-high cypress logs, the house had a wide porch across the front, the roof coming down Mississippi style from the side-to-side roof beam all the way out over the porch. It had chimneys at both ends, still straight. Through the front door, which was missing, I saw down a long, wide hall and out the back door, which was also missing.

The front steps were rotted, so I worked around through the overgrown yard, thick with vines too, to the back of the house. I had expected a hard, severe house, everything reduced to an absolute get-along minimum, but instead found a house with a little country grace. Off the back there was a kitchen wing made of logs, but its roof had collapsed. I wondered if this was where my grandfather's father had lived as a boy—the log house built here first by his father, who had purchased this virgin land after the Treaty of Dancing Bear Creek in 1832. Scrambling over some fallen logs, rotting, vine-tangled, I got through the back door and inside the house, into the unique quiet all houses have. I walked through the rooms of the old house, floors perfectly level, footsteps solidly kathunking, and heard the soughing of pines further up the hill, the song of the creek behind the house, and a luffing sound.

It was wallpaper, linen, a floral design—color now ghosted to rust. Where paste had dried to nothing, the linen had peeled up, luffed when breeze came through the old house. In the parlor, a corner fireplace of fancy brickwork was tumbled in. The flue had been ripped out of the old brick. Some window frames had also been crudely ripped out. Looking out one, I saw tangles of vine-grown trees and grotesquely overgrown yard bushes; beyond these, dark-earth fields open to the sky, still worked. My grandfather as a small child looked out this window *exactly here.* And stepped with the same light thunk. And his father. And his grandfather who had built the attached log house. Their voices, all of them, had spoken here. My father, too, as a five-year-old; and he too looking out this window, stepping these floors. Consolations welled up. Through words (census, land records, family stories, memory) to *this living presence.* I was standing in that presence, not in what I imagined, but the presence itself—what the words had come out of, what they had brought me home to. Through this place on the earth I belonged, at last, in time. From here life came forward toward my birth, our lives in Washington, my life in Saint Louis, North

Carolina, New York, Oklahoma. And stretched back to Georgia, South Carolina, and Virginia.

In what had been a side yard, now gloomy with overgrown bushes, I found a lane going off down through the hillside of woods, curving, seeming to meander. The worn trace was clear, a buggy lane, although now fifty-foot hardwoods grew in it. Old A. C. had not made the lane straight; excitement was rising. He had not taken the lane straight out to the field, then, easily, down its edge to the gap. He wanted what was more pleasant than that; my heart was beating hard as I followed the trace. The awful, busted-down defeat I saw in A. C.'s son, my grandfather E. R., was not family as I always had thought. It was his sweet, dependent character marked by hard-times history. His young man's frontier hopes and dreams in middle age had gone bust. But old A. C., he desired to go back and forth on a pleasantly winding lane to the road. He had seen his brother killed by Yankee bullets at Corinth; suffered Vicksburg, surrender, defeat; and in 1866 watched their first child, age one, die. He had also been equal to the rough, swift violence of irregular cavalry. All this, and he still wanted this pleasantly winding lane.

In the lane I walked, in the well-built country house I had just left, in the yard plantings, all grotesque now and going to ruin, I saw the cipher of a fuller sense of life. Not just standing up to adversity. But inclusive, too, of pleasure in things, in care and respect for the immediate world. Not holding where we are in disdain but embracing it. The care invested here I had not invested in my own life. I stopped in the lane. Rocking back on my heels, I looked up into the huge hardwood crowns, limbs tossing gently in afternoon breeze, and my heart spilled over. This moment, don't just remember it.

I said goodbye to Annie O. Jones, who grinned, the children still behind her skirt.

Across the county road I stopped at the White Oak Baptist Church, to which the Lewises belonged. It was a plain country church, white clapboard but in good repair, stubby steeple, and towering above it several enormous live oaks, dripping with wind-swishing Spanish moss. Behind the church was White Oak Creek, which flows into Bayou Pierre. To one side was a little cemetery, unfenced, soil too sandy for much grass, and there was one Lewis grave, that of Granddaddy Lewis's twin sister. The tombstone, handsomely cut, announced her to be the daughter of Albert C. and Virginia Lewis. When had flowers last been placed on her grave?

Family and Ruby said she was a stunningly beautiful young woman. She was also willful. In her teens she announced that she did not like *at all* her birth name, Edna (sound-twin of Edmund?). Then she declared herself henceforth to be Anna. That was to be her name. And with force of character she made it stick. Anna was ardently courted by young men from three Mississippi counties, even several from Vicksburg and Jackson. She was not easily swept off her feet. In 1902, age twenty-four and still the center of a whirlwind of courting, Anna contracted influenza and died. Ruby as a small child saw her Aunt Anna in her casket out at Grandpa Ab's: "In her lace and white satin dress, the most beautiful creature I ever hope to see." Her folks honored her self-declared name. On her tombstone was ANNA LEWIS for me to see.

Until that moment I had thought Granddaddy Lewis's twin sister had died *after* he had gone out to Indian Territory and married. But the Wilsons had pulled up their Mississippi stakes in summer 1901. Although betrothed to Oneta, E. R. did not go with them. In fact, he was still in Mississippi a year later when Anna died, June 7, 1902, and he did not finally decamp until eighteen months after that, December 1903.

Standing at Anna's tombstone, where E. R. had stood in June 1902, I wondered why a young man would have remained two and one-half years in Mississippi while his betrothed was out in I.T.

In his early twenties, plowing, planting, picking, still living with his folks, he was given on a silver platter a well-to-do bride and booming, rosy-hued opportunities in Indian Territory. He did not like farming, for he always chose town jobs, storekeeping. He was not terribly close to his family, since in the rest of his life he returned to Mississippi only two or three times. Why did he delay that first year?

And after the sudden death of Anna, why did he remain eighteen more months?

And a related question: Why did Anna, a great beauty, hotly pursued by suitors from all over central Mississippi, remain at home and unmarried at age twenty-four?

Standing at Anna's grave, above her last remains, this mystery rose in my mind. Something crucial to my understanding of my grandfather, my father, the family, and myself was present, I knew.

Mother had told me of the correspondence that went on between Oneta and Edmund before he came to I.T. Oneta's sisters, my great-aunts, saw her letters. They reported that Oneta pleaded with E.R. to come on out, to see the wonderful opportunities, and of course to marry her. I do not doubt that Oneta, a woman of storming emotions, was mighty aggravated that her fiancé did *not* join her. His absence, implying at least lack of romantic ardor, publicly shamed her. Not one to suffer in silence, Oneta soon turned up the heat in her letters to E.R. He did not budge: one year, then his twin sister's death, then another year. What held a get-along young fellow so tightly to the Mississippi farm of his birth?

His twin sister, Anna, I believe. Living on a remote farm, E.R. and Anna were the youngest of eight, five years separating them from the next youngest, Carry. The family indulged them, and in the unique dynamic of twins, Anna took up headstrong willfulness while E.R. was left quietly expecting the good things of life to be brought to him. Bonds, complex, deep in the human mystery, existed between the twins. In countless ways both obvious and forever hidden (even to them), their separate characters reversed each other. They were life-companions, soulmates, and existence was the dialogue between them. This held E.R. to the Mississippi farm.

From the Wilsons' departure in summer 1901 to Anna's sudden death the next summer, E.R. was held by Anna. Considering her well-known headstrong nature, I do not doubt she demanded that he remain. (And by his continued presence he silently insisted that she not marry.) When Anna died, E.R. was lost, adrift, and as strongly bound to the absence her death created as to her living presence. In every room, field, the church, the turning seasons; in the towns (Utica, Crystal Springs, and the county seat, Hazelhurst); in the passages of moon, sun, and stars; in the soughing of wind—there was Anna's absence. The house I had stood in and the fields I had walked knew his grief. To leave house, farm, and Anna's grave would be to leave all that remained of her on earth.

He did leave, finally, but his profound loss of Anna went with him, an incompletely mourned grief, and as years passed this became what the man was. In every photograph I have seen of him, he is downcast, dispirited:

with Oneta in fancy clothes at their long-postponed wedding; with his young family, including three-year-old Albert, on the front porch of the new Bokchito house; in bathing costumes with Oneta and wonderful Aunt Nell; and at Lewis Grocery, Durant, in what I think were good years. His grief for Anna, that profound loss.

Standing at Anna's tombstone on that warm, breezy January day, I, his grandson, had turned full circle. Right here Granddaddy Lewis's sad adult life began. The loss of his twin sister, Anna, was not requited by the West, marriage, family, work, or the passage of time. Her shadow never left him. And since Anna's death so profoundly marked Granddaddy Lewis's life, it has become part of the heritage my father and I carry.

Although Dad offered to pay whatever was needed, Oneta, her daughters, and her favorite son, Wilson, put Granddaddy in the cheapest nursing home that could be found in the state of Oklahoma. In Noble, it was of course miserable and 150 miles from any living soul he knew. He died within a few weeks, August 1954. Of course the family, led by Wilson, brought his body home for a most respectable funeral and burial. (They asked Dad to pick up the tab for that, too. And he did.) What we sow, I am afraid, we really do more often than not reap.

Considering my grandfather's legacy, I have noticed for the first time that my grandmother's given name was not simply Oneta. It was *Anna* Oneta.

I drove north to Utica, the nearest town, where my grandfather's grandfather Hugh lived in the 1850s. Then I went up the Natchez Trace highway, through Raymond, which Grant had shelled. I noticed the white junior college, the other side of Utica Junior College. In the sweet, earth-smelling dark, I drove up to Jackson.

✻

From that house I took two hand-wrought nails and several small pieces of linen wallpaper. The house I have described visiting is now gone, torn down; board, timber, and brick have been hauled off, sold I am sure. When I revisited, I had trouble locating where the house had once stood. Annie O. Jones's house was gone, too. Standing on the property now, protected by NO TRESPASSING signs, is a cheaply slapped-together hunting cabin. Fields family cleared of original forests in the 1830s and farmed until 1916 are now rented out. I have what I remember, what I've written. But the real treasure I brought back after finding the house, the farm, I did not understand until a number of years later.

Locating that exact place on earth where blood kin lived, worked, and brought up children for nearly a century, at last understanding *there* with my senses, I finally was able to bring into full daylight the story I had dug at for more than two decades. Its strong presence I felt, first, in 1945 on our trip to Oklahoma—especially during our brief homeward-bound stopover in Saint Louis. It rose mightily when I met, in 1957, my Saint Louis wife-to-be. And again, in 1962–63, when, living in Saint Louis, I first became consumed, as by a raging fire, to find out about Dad's Oklahoma family and their Mississippi roots. How blindly I moved inside its imperatives when, in 1979, I hastily took a job in the state of Dad's birth.

Walking that Mississippi land, stepping inside the house, and quietly standing by Anna's grave, I began at last to understand this American story.

✡

The old Confederate veteran, A.C. or Ab, was thirty-eight in 1878 and middling prosperous when he named his twelfth child and last son for his brother, killed at Corinth. He gave the twin sister a go-together name, Edna. Edmund and Edna, who was as high-spirited as she could be, were together constantly. Since they were the last of the children, and since to witness them together was good for the heart, A.C. and Virginia let them be. The twins played in the creek, they teased, they fought, they went to town, they talked more than all the rest of the family put together. The boy had no knack for farm work, and Anna was certainly not cut out for housewifely chores. Both of them relished cutting a figure in church and town, and if it were not for their being the youngest and his having other hands for the work, A.C. would have borne down harder on them. He knew it was wrong. He caught himself hoping they would marry rich. But they were not marrying at all. Their courting kept going on and on. If Anna (they called her that now) married, then probably Edmund would leave. But she would not. If E. R. married, Anna would without question accept the next marriage proposal she received. But he would not. This state of affairs hung there, suspended. Indian summer might just really last forever. Then Edmund got tied up with the Wilson girl just as the Wilsons, a well-to-do family, were heading out to Indian Territory. But the boy still dragged his feet; it looked as if he would never get himself off dead center and go on out and marry the girl. Then Anna, his beautiful child, died, a sudden and mighty blow to them all but hardest on the boy. He came unhinged, and the Lord could find no way to comfort him. He went out into the upper fields, the far woods, and bawled and bawled. He spent whole days at her graveside. A year and a half later, he surprised the family when he actually did decide to go on out to Indian Territory and marry the Wilson girl.

E. R.'s father-in-law-to-be, old man Wilson, put him into a nice little confectionery store in Bokchito. He sold candy, other sweets, and fresh oysters iced on express trains all the way up from Galveston. (The ads for his store I've seen in the *Bokchito Commercial Appeal*.) But after a few years E.R., needled by Oneta, who was savagely jealous of her sisters' husbands' successes, determined that the profits from his little store did not measure up to his expectations. He switched to the grocery business and took a larger Bokchito store. When his father-in-law moved in 1918 to the county seat, Durant, E. R. followed, established Lewis's Grocery, and, again with the help of his father-in-law, bought the pleasant, up-to-date (that is, with interior plumbing) house we had driven by in 1981. There were a few good years right here.

Then the bug bit again. Oneta got in a big stew over the still-rising status of her sisters' husbands. Mattie Mae's Gat Grubbs was just over thirty years old and already a millionaire in the oil business. Nell's Bob Stinson, with his fancy Washington and Lee College law degree, had risen to become Durant's most respected attorney, a southern gentleman of the old school. To add insult to injury, Oneta regarded E.R. as hurting his prospects by not acting warm toward folks. He was friendly enough, but with everybody, even her and the children, he also kept his distance. It did not take long for Oneta to reach her boiling point. She told E.R. that she deserved more than to be the wife of a grocer catering to the Saturday farm trade. As she assailed him, E. R. withdrew himself further. He said less than ever at family meals. So Oneta turned to her oldest son, Wilson, on whom she bestowed her urgent and unrequited hopes. He could do no wrong. His considerable streak of cruelty he therefore was free to exercise on the littler, younger Al. And in consequence Al got rebellious: a bad crowd, drinking, fast girls, automobiles, all heaping more shame on Oneta's shame-burdened shoulders. She was about as aggravated as she could get. And her sisters, fresh from the beauty shop, unencumbered by children, wearing their high-priced Dallas clothes, were regularly reported on the society page of the *Durant Bugle*. Although Mattie Mae and Nell were happy to finagle invitations for their sister, Oneta was still resentful and knew the other ladies looked down on her. Then she refused to attend. So Oneta was left to explain to her Sunday school class why her younger son was once again brought home drunk by the police. And all this did not escape the attention of her father, the tough old banker now riding the earnings of his investments, living a life of ease.

It is not surprising that right here Dad hopped a freight. Aunt Nell and Aunt Mattie Mae both told Mother, separately, that Dad at about seventeen wanted to return home at the end of that summer to finish high school. Oneta erupted: "Didn't he shame us in the eyes of the whole town? No sir, good riddance, I say." They wrote to tell the boy not to come home.

Shortly thereafter E.R. decided to become rich speculating in oil leases. The incoming tide of 1920's oil money would lift his boat; less deserving men were becoming rich overnight. His brother-in-law Gat Grubbs, the oil-field millionaire, understood that E.R. did not know a damn thing about oil leases. So did his other brother-in-law, Bob Stinson, who was doing legal work for oil men. And so did his old father-in-law, a hardheaded businessman if there ever was one. For E. R., getting rich on oil leases was the most recent of his Mississippi-spawned dreams of leaping in a single bound into luxury's lap. (Or, more truly, to find in bone-dry Oklahoma what he ached for and had left back in Mississippi—young, beautiful, sweet Anna.) It was a hell of a lot more than a closely figured business decision. E.R. wanted the big house of Bob Stinson out on West Main, and Gat Grubbs's Dallas suits and Pullman trips to Galveston and Colorado Springs. And just once he wanted, for himself, to stroll through courthouse square like his father-in-law, with that air of authority, of ease and wealth, which attracted overeager greetings from everybody. E. R. did not believe the Lord wished him to spend his life in a storekeeper's apron.

And certainly Oneta would not under any circumstances permit him to remain any longer a negligible presence in the social life of Durant, Oklahoma.

He sold the grocery, bought oil leases, faltered immediately. He was not cut out for the swagger, bluff, and icy nerve of the oil-lease business. Oneta, seeing her dream of par with her sisters turning to ash, spared nothing as she assailed E. R. for his failures. Then E. R. did the one thing in his life that totally surprised everybody—maybe even himself.

He simply quit. He stopped trading in oil leases, although he had a safety deposit box full of them (and margin notes to pay), and decided he would just wait for the death of his father-in-law and what he estimated to be a sizeable inheritance that would rightly come to him and Oneta. Unfortunately, old man Wilson was healthy as a horse. (When he died in 1935, he left his money to his widow, of course; when she died five years later, there was little left.)

Late in the 1920s, his oil leases bought on 10 percent margin almost worthless, E. R. fell way behind on his debt. Nothing was coming in, his notes to the bank were in arrears, and if the lease sites had been worth drilling, the bank would certainly have foreclosed. When the depression hit in 1930, E. R. was fifty and in the middle of a lifetime of drift and bad decisions. He always had believed that, when push came to shove, old man Wilson, Gat Grubbs, and Bob Stinson would bail him out. He could not understand that his oil leases were a rat hole nobody would pour cash down. E. R. lost everything: house, leases, car, furniture. When it was over, he had nothing.

As bitter compensation, old man Wilson let E. R., Oneta, and little Martha Ann live in an abandoned store he happened to own in Colera. E. R. got work as a drummer calling on grocery stores; he traveled six days a week by rail from Colera and struggled hard to keep the wolf from their door. Oneta's decades of striking out in resentment and anger were now stunned silence. She and her family were forced to live like country trash, and her sisters were ensconced in big houses in town, her own father too. Kerosene again, baths in a galvanized washtub, a common outhouse, eating blackeyed peas for supper, and ladies from her in-town Sunday school class coming by, saying, "Oh Oneta, dear, we are *so sorrrry!*" when all they wanted was to know how bad off she was so that, back in town, they could gloat and gossip. E.R.'s own father back in Mississippi might have helped, but he had died too soon rather than too late. E.R.'s small share of proceeds from selling the homeplace barely paid two months of interest on the oil leases. Granddaddy Lewis's young man's dreams of Easy Street had brought him to this blanket-strung storefront in a miserable water stop along the KATY. No family or friend to help, nothing.

And with Sophoclean bad timing, right here in August of 1930 Al, their son gone bad seven years, turned up one afternoon. He wanted a place to live while he took premedical courses at the college in Durant. The nerve of him. As Oneta said, if he was too good for them in 1922, he was too good for them in 1930. They had shame heaped upon shame inflicted on them and she would not have yet another. This "bad" son would not drag their name once again through the streets of Durant. No, not even if he just wanted a cot to sleep on. She would not have him under her roof.

Al did not plead.

He immediately hated himself for believing they would give him anything, even if they had it. He kicked himself for lousy judgment. He never should've left the Esau life he believed in.

That evening he bought a bottle and took it in a paper sack down to the loading chutes and cattle pens along the KATY tracks. He smelled the whine of sun-bleached wood, of baked manure. On the slapped-together chutes, he noticed the tufts of hide ripped off by nail heads as cows ran through hard and scared. The cloudless sky taunted him, azure going to rose in the late afternoon. Up into it was thrust a loading chute going to nothing. You goddamn fool. His shoulders slid down a post; felt nails, but none bit. Yeah, come on back and live at home, son. We've got a place for you. We'll share what we've got. He grinned, screwing off the cap of the fancy bourbon he had bought instead of a jar of country moonshine. It burned good; he didn't have a goddamn thing except the money in his pocket. He heard his dry, raw-throat laugh. By god, never again. Trust nobody but yourself.

With the long, good pulls of bourbon, sweating through his shirt, he felt all right.

The next day he took the KATY down to Dallas, then trains on to Houston and Galveston. His compass gone, he was drifting in huge landscapes like tens of thousands of others in Oklahoma and Texas who also were, then, as he would say, "fresh out of dreams." Money getting low, Al took the train back across half the United States to Washington and re-enlisted in the U.S. Army. His sergeant's rank was gone, his money, his life's dream. Right there Dad closed the door on his inner life.

Here was what I had lost, and what I had been so obsessed to recover.

Killing Absences

Mother's death was a shadow I could not escape. On a muggy spring night, I tossed on too-warm sheets trying to sleep. In my apartment not enough air moved; onions from supper I still smelled. Dad was settled at the D.C. nursing home, where he was sometimes agitated but okay. He was a heck of a sight better off there, I had convinced myself, than in a closed-up town house full of Mother, drinking himself to death to kill emptiness—that is, to kill his grief and guilt. Tonight there were tornado warnings. The huge siren a block away was capable of lifting me a foot off the bed. But when I started to drift off to sleep, I immediately awoke with a start. I was afraid I would wake not to the siren's wail but to the tremendous roaring of a tornado itself—discover the roof ripping off, boards flying, clattering, glass exploding and shattering. Nothing in a cheap apartment building on a concrete slab is safe. By the bed the sliding doors were open: in wind gusts the screens sang. On the wall distant lightning flashed.

Then a nightmare; light rosy, as if from an embering bonfire; air dusty. Just-born pups, toy bulldogs, were not squirming as strong hands (*mine*) wrapped thick cord round and round their sweet, plump bodies; pulled it tight, cord cutting deep. After hard knots were tied, the pups were gently laid down in a shallow hole. Their quiet was heartbreaking. This was occurring at the bottom of a big, freshly dug excavation, raw clay walls, teeth marks of steam shovels. Nightmare abruptly jumped several years. Still tightly bound up, the pups have grown into grotesques, scarcely recognizable as dogs. The same strong hands (*again mine*) peeled cord up carefully out of deep-cut grooves. All removed, but the bulldog grotesques lay in red-clay dust exactly as if still bound. Clumps of head, belly, bent-up legs that were hard to look at. Dogs that were not dogs. Free, they cannot move; they cannot even crawl. Then it came to me. Their luminous brown eyes were Mother's exactly. My yell was silent; can't breathe, can't breathe. They *weren't numb;* pain of what was done to them burned every minute of every day. Scalded; raw panic; I must get away, *must get away.* Up out of nightmare I rushed, but there was no escape. Panting for breath; soaked with sweat. Lightning flashed on the wall. Understanding that what happened to toy bulldog pups happened to me—happened to us all. And from us our children have no recourse.

Days later I realized that the toy bulldogs of the nightmare were exactly the toy bulldog I remembered from a picture of my maternal grandmother. That picture, a Brownie snapshot probably taken by my grandfather, was the only picture I ever saw of Mother's mother, who died before I was born. Behind her was a vacant lot, winter-dead weeds with long late-afternoon shadows. Wearing a black skirt down to her ankles, a fitted jacket, she stoops down to bring her toy bulldog into the frame. She pulls the little dog close in to her black skirts. Her shadow is long, inky; her eyes depthless black pinpricks. Her smile, a grimace. At her left temple, a vein's worm Mother inherited. Her skull's vault was Mother's too, high and broad like that. Not desiring to compose her expression for the camera and my grandfather, my grandmother makes the toy bulldog, her "lap dog" they called it, the false pretext for the photograph. Although she is a pretty woman, her gesture and expression reveal submission to, and thwarting of, the well-meant occasion.

Somebody has penciled "Daisy, 1928" on the back.

Daisy Clodfelter Kenerly died three years later, February 1931, at age forty-six. Two months later Elizabeth and Al met, and on the last day of that year they married. Six years and the worst of the Great Depression later, 1936, I was born.

In the 1940s I could not get enough of this old photograph. Dead before I was born; now this was all I'd ever see of Mother's mother. Her grave and tombstone I had seen down in Salisbury; as a child I had speculated on what remained down in that coffin. Then I grew up, lived my life, and forty years later, I had all but forgotten that old photograph. Mother died. As instructed by her, we had taken her ashes down to North Carolina and buried them in the cemetery plot where her mother had been buried in 1931. Now, a spring night several years later, the alien genius of my nightmare had brought back that winter afternoon in 1928. Years later, I realized that that same genius had also understood that I on that night of my nightmare was almost Daisy's age at the time of her death. In the workings of nightmare are life's deepest mysteries.

✡

When I next visited Dad at the nursing home, I went out to the town house, where everything remained as it was. I searched top to bottom for the old photograph of my grandmother. I flipped through photo albums and thousands of loose snapshots. But instead of the photograph, I discovered that Mother as she died scratched her own face out of every snapshot we had. She used a ballpoint. As her life ended, she also destroyed the photograph of her mother. That mortal image, freighted with time, exists now only in memory.

And the tale is darker. In 1983 Elizabeth died of ovarian cancer, exactly what killed her mother in 1931. This I understand. But not why Elizabeth died on February 27, 1983, the exact date of her mother's death in 1931, fifty-two years earlier. Maybe chance, but I doubt it. More likely, especially given Elizabeth's angry denial of her mother's importance, is that in the wellsprings of Elizabeth's earliest life (1916–22) a dark reverse of love's dependence formed between daughter and mother.

Living her last summer, my sister and I home with our families, Mother collected herself for death. She sorted and labeled boxes of letters we had written her, gave directions concerning who got what, and ordered that her ashes should be put by her mother in North Carolina. (Not in Washington, where she had lived a half century.)

She added: "And if you don't, I'll come back and haunt you. Just see if I won't."

Looking into her eyes, I expected a gleam of humor. But no. That very day, all of us thumping around in her little house, grandchildren crying, I am sure she took that old photograph of her mother, salt in her wounds for a lifetime, and scissored it up into little strips. Did she look down at the strips lying in the kitchen trash basket with damp and wadded paper towels, junk mail, coffee grounds? Did she, after we left, as her cancer spread, think of cut-up strips out at the Montgomery County landfill, in with rank garbage, an eye on one strip, half of that grimacing face, and the same on another strip a few feet away? When she destroyed the photograph, a lifetime of anger did not suddenly vanish. In that anger was a child's burning and unrequited desire to lie close to the body that had given her life. Only love and its thwarting, those deepest of passions, account for such great extent through time.

And how naive to believe my own existence was not bound up in this knotted, passion-choked parable.

In old silences, lives stir.

On a summer evening in 1945, while Mother fixed dinner, I climbed through a ceiling crawl-hole up into the attic. Heat roared in that dim flash-lighted space among two-by-fours and driven-through nails. In a beaten-up box I found a few old photographs, including my grandmother's. It was odd that Mother kept her mother's only photograph in the attic rather than downstairs in the black-covered photo album that was in a drawer of the buffet. In the same box, which originally was for Rinso, I found letters Dad had written to mother in the months (1931) when he was stationed at Carlisle Barracks in Pennsylvania and Mother was in Washington. They were tied with faded pink ribbon. His handwriting looped, slashed, swirled, and had other elegant flourishes. In end-of-day heat in the attic, sweat dripped off me, but who cared. Dad's letters were not "lovey-dovey," but the strong things he said about himself and Mother did not at all sound like him. The letters did not square with his tough practicality; he always disdained anything he considered "just pretty."

As Mother stirred around in the kitchen, Dad not yet home, I showed her the photograph of her mother. She glanced at it, said matter-of-factly, "That's Mother." I asked why it was in the attic. She said she did not know; it just was. I asked what she was like. "Well, she was a southern lady. She was strict, I'll tell you that. I just didn't have much to do with her. Afternoons she took her little bulldog with her for walks in the woods. She liked to be alone, not with us." Here her cutting laughter began: "She'd go out in the woods and write poems." There was scorn. "She loved that bulldog more than she loved any of us."

"I found the letters too."

From the stove she looked around at me. "Letters?"

"They were in the same box with the picture."

Then she understood what I meant. She was angry. "You found those old letters and read them?"

"Yes, ma'am."

"You should have sense enough not to go poking in letters that are private." Her eyes burned until I looked away. "You brought the letters down from the attic?"

"Yes."

"Get them."

I got them out of my room and came back down to the kitchen. She took the box, put it on the icebox, and said, "Don't you ever read private letters again. You hear me?"

I told her the letters were great, the words and all. I told her I didn't know Dad was like that. I told her it wouldn't do any harm for me to look at them. At the stove, her back was turned. She did not answer.

That box and those letters I never saw again. I crawled, secretly, back up into the attic. I searched in closets, the corners of the basement. When I asked about them, she laughed: "I burned them."

My grandmother's picture she kept loose in a drawer of the buffet. I never saw her look at it. Studying it myself, I came up with nothing. Asking Mother to tell more about her mother, I just got the story of a southern lady's afternoon walks in the woods with her toy bulldog. Her poems, which I have inquired after and searched for, do not exist. As cancer killed her, she may have burned her poems in the kitchen stove. If I could read what is now ash (or rot or simple earth), I would find mawkish Tennyson and the Poe-like gothic of southern ladies burning with Lost Cause fervor. That is, absence, aching loss. But, in fact, the words she struck to paper there in the woods, seized by unrequited yearning, or lost hope, or desperate ecstasy, have fallen back into the maw of the world. Nothing remains. (As the photograph I remember and Dad's letters are now nothing.)

✿

When Elizabeth mentioned anything beyond her mother's escapes to the woods with her little dog, it was to recount her admonitions. "Mama insisted that a *lady's* back must never touch the back of a chair," Elizabeth said, following with her hard-edged, mocking laughter. "Mama would not permit us to roll down our stockings." "Mama told us a *lady* should never participate in any sport. She would not allow it! She would not even let us swim!" (And Mother, although quick and energetic, never learned to swim or catch a ball.) She told me almost nothing else of her mother.

But she adored her father, Robert E. Lee Kenerly, and took delight in telling wild tales of him. Doing exactly what he knew to be dangerous, walking the railroad tracks to his job at the Spencer Shops, he was struck from behind by a locomotive, dragged a half mile, nearly eviscerated, and then saved by a young doctor who decided to do a bit more than just sew him up for the undertaker. Coal soot from that day had remained in his scars. Hunting on Thanksgiving, he mistakenly shotgunned a skunk, then in the backyard had to strip off and burn every stitch of his skunk-stinking clothing. He drove his first automobile, the entire family on board, through the back wall of the barn. Failing to get the SOB stopped, rafters and roof coming down around him, he roared with laughter. Her stories of him mentioned his hot temper: "Sometimes he'd get started beating the boys and could not stop. Mama had to pull him off." When he retired from the Southern Shops to a little farm he had bought, Bob Kenerly's wild streak was still running strong. For the fun of it, he got his plow horse pulling him in the old wagon up to a gallop through a rocky pasture— stood up on the wagon seat, bouncing, tossing side to side, having a hell of a ride. Then got bounced off, crashed down on rocks, lay an hour in a dusty field yelling and swearing. His hip was broken. At the hospital he cussed a blue streak, threw fists at doctors putting him into a hip cast. Within a week he died of pneumonia in his own bed. So much about him that was robust, rebellious, rule-scorning. And nothing of Mother's mother but strictures, retreats, poetry, and indulgent love of her little toy bulldog.

As cancer closed in, as Al's drinking worsened, Elizabeth turned defiantly from her mother to her father. She cared less about social niceties; she worried little about her appearance. She gloried, instead, in refinishing furniture she had acquired in backwoods Virginia and North Carolina: oak kitchen tables, pie safes, busted-up kitchen chairs. All recalled her father and his family, not her mother's, the Clodfelters, who were country gentry. Her father, she told me, had refinished furniture; her paternal grandfather, the veteran of Gettysburg, had made furniture himself, including a bedroom chest that Mother acquired, lovingly refinished, and then sold rather than have it remain in the family. (So she would not be faced with a Solomonic decision to give it to either my sister or me?) She also acquired in these years two mean-looking kitchen knives that had been made by her father. The blades, one that of a butcher knife, the other a boning knife, he had machine-cut out of a sprung carpenter-saw blade; he then attached oak handles with brass brads. Mother honed razor-sharp edges on the blades, restored the wood handles, and, warning us of their danger, used them exclusively in the last years of her life. She had almost ceased to care about being ladylike.

✡

The opposite of her sister Vada, Elizabeth rebelled against her mother. She liked boys and fast cars and rolling down her stockings after she left for school and sneaking off to fly with barnstormers out of rough pastures in open-cockpit planes. Appalled by Elizabeth's unladylike conduct, Daisy took more excursions to the woods. Then, flush with independence, Elizabeth decided to "kick off the dust" of that tight little southern town and head up to Washington, D.C., where bright opportunity beckoned. Daisy became alarmed: "A lady does not degrade herself, nor shame her family, by running off to a strange city. A lady would never lower herself to accept a common job. I absolutely forbid it. I will not have it." Repeating this maternal admonition, Mother's voice was a scathing parody of her mother's.

At age sixteen, with a high school diploma (she had skipped half of four grades), Elizabeth left old East Spencer and Salisbury behind. Although times were hard, she did not doubt she had grit enough to make her way in Washington. Her first job was at Woolworth's candy counter.

Saving dimes from her pay, she took night-school stenography lessons. She learned fast and never forgot; in the last year of her life she still used shorthand. In three months she landed a job as stenographer and was quickly promoted to secretary. She got herself a Woodward and Lothrop charge-a-plate. She got new city clothes and expensive Christmas gifts to take home with her to North Carolina. This soon she returned to the family and town she had fled.

Early on a December morning, the night coach down from Washington dropped her off in the Spencer yards. Lugging a shopping bag of gifts and a suitcase, wearing her city clothes, young spirits high, she walked through the back garden (sweet-corn stalks brown, busted over; tomato plants frost-dead on stakes; only kale green), by the barn and outhouse, through the gap in the tall hedge and up onto the back porch where, in the kerosene lamplight of the kitchen, her father looked up, grinned broadly. Throwing open the door, he laughed, hugged his rebellious prodigal.

Her mother was in bed ill. Too weak to do for herself, she relied on a black woman for cooking, keeping house. She managed only a morning hour in the parlor, door closed, to read her Bible. The toy bulldog never left her. He growled from her lap, showed his little teeth. But away from Daisy, the master's step scared the dickens out of him, sent him scurrying away. If set outside the kitchen door, he whimpered pitifully at the brawling of the master's penful of hunting dogs out by the barn. Elizabeth, returning home with high spirits and happy independence, was an affront to her mother. Better than anyone Daisy understood why Elizabeth had come home, and, if the Good Lord gave her sufficient strength, she would hold to the high moral principles of a Christian and southern lady.

On Christmas morning in the parlor redolent with pine scent, Daisy sat in her platform rocker. Her little dog scowled from her lap. Rob, Elizabeth's younger brother, was dazzled by the fancy white shirt. Vada, her married older sister, cooed over the beautiful tea towels. Even her father, who couldn't afford such fancy gifts (and neither, really, could Elizabeth), jumped with delight when he saw the silk necktie. But Daisy, who had at first refused to open Elizabeth's gift, took one look at the cameo, shut the box, slid it onto the table by her chair, and said into the hush, "I cannot accept this." I imagine she turned her attention to the little dog, stroked his ears, as he gazed with smug fierceness at Elizabeth. She would not beg; she had her pride. Nor would Elizabeth touch the box that remained where Daisy had put it by the Bible on the parlor table. In her mother's last Christmas alive, Elizabeth fled the stalemate of the white Woodward and Lothrop box on the parlor table for the prodigal's welcome over at her aunt's, where her paternal grandmother also lived.

In a February ice storm Elizabeth again returned to North Carolina. Daisy's cancer, the same terrible wasting that Elizabeth would die of fifty-two years later, was worsening. Her end was near. She was in the downstairs bedroom and, when receiving a rare visitor, always beautifully dressed and groomed by her black maid. Inside her lacy bed jacket, she was skin and bones. The little dog, scowling, sat up on her bed beside her. Undaunted by her Christmas visit, Elizabeth wanted her mother to forgive her for running off to Washington—that transgression of the corsetlike code of a southern lady. But Daisy, stroking her little dog, understood exactly why her daughter was here. She remained icy, aloof, as if Elizabeth were a distant cousin. When Elizabeth began to talk about "bad feelings," Daisy shifted her eyes to a dark corner of the room and refused to respond. This knot of parental scorn Elizabeth, a half century later, carried to her own grave. Love for her father, for his tenant-farmer manners, for his devil-may-care vitality, eased not one iota the scorn of her dying mother, the southern lady.

It was love that was wounded in both; nothing else persists so long.

✳

A few months after Daisy was buried, Elizabeth met Al. In a spring evening he was pitching for the army ball team at Walter Reed. (Elizabeth did *not* know the army's ball field was on the ground her grandfather, Daisy's father, occupied with Jubal Early's Confederates.) Al was sweaty. With mutual friends they went to an ice cream parlor on Georgia Avenue. Her girlfriend whispered: "He blows in the wind. He'll never settle down and get married." This challenge struck a match to Elizabeth's passions. He was six years older, experienced, bootstrapping ambitious, and dashing. He loved sports, the physical; and his manners and talk were western as well as southern. Attractively dangerous, Al was far indeed from the beautifully mannered and considerate southern gentlemen Daisy had preached to her girls. In Washington's lush summer Al and Elizabeth courted: fast drives in Al's Chevy roadster, picnics in Rock Creek Park, twilight window shopping on Sixteenth Street, movies on Saturday nights, dinners Sundays at Aunt Dessie's and Uncle Walter's, where Elizabeth stayed. Swept up, stepping fast, they hardly noticed bread lines and the *Star* full of bad news for the United States. But now and then, I don't doubt, Elizabeth remembered her mother's pallid face—icy anger in her eyes—and the roaring silence that followed Elizabeth's half-asked pleas to be accepted back if not forgiven.

When the weather turned cool, Al left for army OCS at Carlisle, Pennsylvania. Proud to have bootstrapped himself to the verge of becoming an officer and a gentleman in the United States Army, Al was disturbed by Elizabeth's reaction. She regarded the army, in 1931, even officers, as hardly better than criminals and thugs. This was too far from her mother's idea of refined southern gentlemen. But arguments, even hot ones, stoked the fires of their romance. Al wrote the letters I found in the attic; Elizabeth wrote letters that, if Al saved them, she surely later destroyed. When he got a weekend pass, Al drove his Chevy wildly back to Washington to see Elizabeth. As economic news worsened, as the Great Depression darkened, Al asked Elizabeth to marry him. She said yes, but only if he agreed to resign from the army. For Al the army had been a better home for nine years than he ever had in Oklahoma. And Officer Candidate School was his best break yet, a door at last open. But rebel's confidence, as much as passion for what Elizabeth promised, rose up in him. He agreed to get out. He asked Aunt Dessie for permission to marry her niece. A live-and-let-live person (as her sister Daisy was not), Aunt Dessie wished them well, gave her blessing, but said she could not have done so had Al remained in the army. When Elizabeth wrote to ask her father's permission, he forthwith came up on the train to Washington. He was afraid his daughter, his spirited favorite, was marrying too soon after her mother's death—a decision tied up in loss and mourning. He also was afraid she was marrying a Yankee. Al told him, with the southern humor they shared, that where his folks came from in Mississippi, North Carolinians were considered Yankees. It was a bold response, but Robert E. Lee Kenerly loved few things more than a good hard laugh. I heard nothing of Elizabeth's response to the question about her mother's death, if there was one.

On New Year's Eve 1931, a bitterly cold night, Elizabeth Jane Kenerly, age nineteen, married Albert C. Lewis, age twenty-five, in the Washington living room of Aunt Dessie and Uncle Walter. Elizabeth's mother had been buried ten months.

On the exact date of her mother's death, fifty-two years later, Elizabeth died. On that same February date exactly one year later, 1984, Al tried to kill himself with vodka. In the spring that followed I had the nightmare of the little dogs.

Dad's life is tangled in Elizabeth's struggles with Daisy; so is mine.

✿

In her last summer alive, Mother brought to light a big piece of her life's story (and mine), one deliberately kept hidden for forty-five years. Having stopped her chemotherapy, she was planning her death. The town house in suburban D.C. was full of my family and my sister's, all her children and grandchildren home together. I was surprised when she wanted just the two of us to drive down to Stratford Hall, Robert E. Lee's birthplace on the Potomac in Virginia. She idolized Lee, her father's namesake and commander-in-chief of both her grandfathers. In her living room over the mantle hung a large, elaborately framed etching of Lee. He was the pinnacle of southern values, a saint. But this July afternoon as we drove down through Virginia she did not talk of her idol, nor of how the South had suffered. She wanted to talk about the first years of my life, 1936–38.

In her heart something old was stuck. On the way down we stopped at the Fredericksburg battlefield to search out the exact location where Grandpa Kenerly, in the Seventh North Carolina, Lane's Brigade, had received his wound. When we had made similar visits to Spotsylvania Courthouse and Gettysburg, Mother was intensely interested. Now she hardly took note of where she was, saying instead, "When I would pick you up out of your crib, my heart would beat so hard you'd feel it. You'd cry harder. Your heart would start to race, too. I'd be at my wit's end."

I said something about little babies being hard to care for.

Thinking I was not taking her seriously, her anger flared. Then for a while she rode in silence.

In the northwest sky dark clouds were piling up. But her thoughts had not left the first years of my life: "They wanted me to return to work.

Harry Hopkins himself called once to say he needed me. They had a special project they wanted me to work on. But you were too little."

We were about ten miles from Lee's birthplace when the thunderstorm began to thrash the roadside pines. In the muggy afternoon, suddenly chill winds. Mother loved thunderstorms, was thrilled by them, but now she did not appear to notice. "Your father did not want me to work. He thought a lady"—the word was bitter to her—"should raise the children, take care of her husband, mind the home. He thought it humiliating to a man to have his wife work."

How damn southern they both were.

When the thunderstorm struck, it was furious, blinding; I could see nothing. I thought Mother would tell me to pull off on the shoulder, wait out the storm, but she did not say a word. I pulled off. After a few minutes the storm lifted and I saw that we had pulled off opposite an abandoned country schoolhouse. It was a two-story hulk, a bell cupola on top, all its windows broken out, the classrooms where children had toiled opened now to the weather. The wood siding, bleached by Virginia sun, was now darkly soaked by the rain. Busted-down downspouts splashed and sang. I took a photograph of it—a sight more delicious than sad. Mother, who had always been fascinated by ruins, paid no attention. When I asked, she told me that she did not want to get out and look around.

As we pulled back on the road, she said, "When you were about two I had to take you back home to North Carolina."

I thought I had not heard her. "Sorry?" She repeated it. I had heard her correctly. This bit of my past I had never heard mentioned. "You and Dad . . ." I began, but she cut me off.

"No, just you and me."

I was startled. This item of family history they had kept from me.

"Your father," she continued, "stayed in Glendale and I took you down to North Carolina to live with your Grandpa Kenerly. I did not plan to go back."

"You mean you left Dad? You mean you split up?" Emotions roared.

Her purse was on her lap and she looked straight ahead down the road; she remained composed, replying quietly, "The well ran dry."

"What?"

"The house out in the country in Glendale—the well ran dry."

"But you said you weren't sure you would go back. That you were leaving Dad."

"The well ran dry," she repeated, her voice quiet.

The phrase was a personal cipher and she was not about to explain it. (When I was a child we once drove by that Glendale house, a one-story frame bungalow by itself out on a country road. Tall pines came up close to the back door. My barrage of questions did not break their pained silence.) Now as I asked more questions, Mother again did not respond. Her story, with its weight of pain and time, she was untying in her own slow rhythm: "When you were born, your father did not want to be bothered. You were sickly, and when you weren't sick, you were into mischief or trying to run off." He wanted his meals on time, he wanted to read the *Star* in the evening, wanted the room tidy, wanted to play golf at Rock Creek, wanted to dance and be a little wild (and not a little drunk) on Saturday nights, wanted not to be bothered with this baby." Here there was silence.

"In Glendale your father took the car to work. I was a mile's walk from the nearest neighbor. I was by myself all day with you. It got to where I was afraid if a man walked by on the road. I didn't blame your father for not wanting to come home until late, after dark. I was a mess. Left to my own devices, I jumped at my own shadow. I tried everything in the world I knew to do, but I could not make you content; you were the fussiest, orneriest child in the world. I didn't know what to do with myself. I thought I might not be able to take care of you." Never in her life had Mother admitted to being unable to do anything. Never had she even expressed doubts about herself.

Through the car poured sweet cool left by the thunderstorm; it smelled of Potomac bays. Old sensations flooded in: screeching metal bunks, tang of sweat and starch, crunching gravel under boots, commands sung to ranks of us in the dark as dawn spread through the sky overhead. Sweet grief. Thunderstorm smell here near the Potomac had brought back marine training, 1958, up the river at Quantico.

"The well ran dry," she repeated, still in that peculiarly quiet voice, "and I took you down home to North Carolina. Your grandfather had found and married Mama Mae," who was a country woman Mother always liked.

I did not remember that 1938 stay in the East Spencer house where

Mother had been born in 1912. But a later visit when I was nine, 1945, spooked me. Up in the bedroom I shared with Mother, her room when she was a girl, I could not sleep for the trains. Did that junking, banging, out in the dark bring back 1938, when in that same house Mother's life collapsed, me then feeling it without understanding?

And now from the 1946 visit, I remember the wobbling swirl of moths (up around the porch light) on the ice cream freezer, all over Granddaddy Kenerly, who cranked it, and I was afraid to eat the ice cream. And my grandfather taunting my courage: "Don't you want to be a Johnny Reb?" And he and his brother-in-law Pink, who had a farm, roaring with laughter when a surly mule they had gotten me to bring up from a pasture sidled me into a farm-lane electric fence—like getting hit hard with a shovel. They also taunted me for being a city kid who had to learn country ways, to be tougher, stronger. And finally how Mother, except for meals at the kitchen table, was mostly absent, off somewhere else. In this remembering of 1946 resides what I had not forgotten of 1938.

But Mother had not finished in 1982 showing me her great loss of 1938. "While I was down home I learned that your father was having an affair with a nurse at Glendale TB Sanitarium, where he worked. When you and I were in that lonely house, I knew all the nurses chased your father, that he liked flirting. When I left for North Carolina, I told him I was not coming back. He said, 'Well, if that's how you feel, good riddance.' He could quit us that fast. But I don't blame him for finding love with someone else."

The car had slowed, my foot off the accelerator. I was stunned that Dad had had an affair, the first word of such I had heard.

She continued, her voice quiet: "Aunt Myrtle, bless her sweet heart, lived where she had always lived. She told me to go back to Al, to Washington."

Her rebellious and prideful character drove her to do the opposite, which was to stay away, to start another life with her considerable abilities. The terrific energies driving her life were becoming visible. Purse on her lap, gazing straight ahead, she looked composed. She was managing at last to say what she had devoted a lifetime to not saying. As those old losses, locked up forty-five years in her heart, came out that afternoon on our way to the birthplace of the southern ideal, my inmost sense of Mother changed. She had seemed combative, fiercely independent, her self locked safely away, but as the exchanges of 1938 came to light, I understood these qualities were consequences of her losses.

Living her last summer, and knowing it to be so, in her heart she had love this time stronger than loss, absence, and death. Love for her rises in my heart. I wish I had understood before her death. I wish I had understood before I watched her last breath in a Sunday twilight.

✡

At Stratford Hall, I was aware of rain dripping, splotting—a near-song— off immense trees, some appearing older than the great house. Coming into the huge trees was mist-swirled sunlight. Out on the wide lawn the sunlight in the unburdened air sparkled on everything it touched. We were quiet. Trying not to think such thoughts, I wondered how life would be without Mother. From grass underfoot, boxwoods, the old brick of the house, came a rich, sad smell.

As we formed up into a tour group and entered the house, I noticed how thick the walls were and how dark the halls, the rooms we glimpsed. Immediately Mother began asking, in a harsh southern singsong, questions of our overly polite gentleman-of-the-South tour guide. His veneer was thin; he became flustered. The others on the tour looked askance at Mother. In her straw-visored hat, white blouse, and gaudy flower-splotched skirt she looked like a southern crank. The guide tried to patronize her but she did not relent: "What are the dates of that piece?" "Who would have stayed in such a small room?" "How many slaves did a house this big have?" Embarrassed by the absence of the southern etiquette she had so painstakingly taught me, I stayed a few steps away from her. She asked involved and complicated questions about the Lee family. The guide, having dropped his patronizing for pure haughtiness, played the tour group against her, but she took no heed of it.

Standing in the doorway of the room where Lee was born, she and I looked at the cradle in which he was rocked. Mother's furious curiosity was undaunted by the solemn importance of the room where the Confederacy's greatest hope and her father's namesake was born. I was annoyed as well as embarrassed. Later, I admired her for being so fully herself. In the birthplace of Robert E. Lee, Mother, Elizabeth, was the most alive.

✳

That winter Mother died. When I arrived and went upstairs to see her, she was skull, skin, and bones. But she had managed to sit up, smile, and hold out her beautiful hands to welcome me. Three days later my sister and I sat at her bedside as her breath labored, stopped, silence, then the living force in her struggled, another wheezing breath, another. Then what had begun in the house in East Spencer, 1912, ceased. Silence; and out into the rainy twilight her spirit flew. My sister called goodbye. I remembered how much she loved playing bridge on the shade-dappled porches of Orkney Springs Hotel.

Sitting beside her body, touching her hands, I remembered from the 1940s meeting her bus from downtown at the bus stop where after school I caught the shuttle home. Before the big downtown bus stopped, I saw her smiling through the open bus window, happy to see me. She bounced off into the sunshine, soft with May springtime, and handed me a store bag. "Here, Clay, this is for you." She was beaming.

Although I had never owned a book, I drew one out of the store bag. It was Edgar A. Guest, *A Heap o' Livin'*, poems; we read library books and never poems. Excitedly she told me she had found it browsing in a downtown bookstore. Then, my school friends looking askance at us, she read aloud a poem about naughty boys. "When I read that," she proclaimed, "I had to buy the book because the poem reminded me so much of you!" She never looked happier. With all the shuttle-bus windows open, spring air breezing us, we rode together out New Hampshire Avenue. Clutching my treasure, I hoped I understood it enough not to disappoint her. Even though I was not a great reader, I read all the poems carefully. I even memorized some because she got such a kick out of hearing me recite them. And all this leaped with the sweetness of good times through me in the moments after she died.

Her face, now like her father's, and her beautiful, lightly cupped hands, these soon lost to me forever. As twilight turned to darkness, I kissed her cool forehead. As she had wished, she was cremated.

✳

Bound in opposition to Daisy, Aunt Myrtle and Grandmaw Kenerly gave Elizabeth the mothering she did not get at home. Since the death of the limping Civil War veteran, Grandmaw had lived with Aunt Myrtle and Uncle Hayden. As a child Elizabeth considered Aunt Myrtle's bungalow stylish, up to date in comparison with her own house, a plain two-story farmhouse occupying a town lot. Uncle Hayden worked at the Southern Shops with his brother, Elizabeth's father. He was a solemn man, moon-faced, and with innocent blue eyes. A Baptist deacon, he was known for great probity except when behind the wheel of his Oldsmobile. Even around town he drove the Olds floored, at top speed, wild to pass every automobile in sight. A slew of tickets for speeding and three bad wrecks had not slowed him down a bit.

As a little girl Elizabeth walked the mile from her own house, crossing the Southern RR tracks and yards on a humpbacked, plank-clattering bridge, to the refuge of Aunt Myrtle's. She was Grandmaw's namesake and their clear favorite. They indulged little 'Lizabeth, spoiled her rotten, the family said. And she loved it. There in the bungalow she received the reverse of Daisy's cold strictures. And her just being there at Aunt Myrtle's got her mother's goat. (No wonder Mother angrily forbade me to spend time with Mrs. Parker!)

When we visited in North Carolina after Granddaddy Kenerly's death, Elizabeth had us stay at Aunt Myrtle's. The bungalow was dark, furniture-filled, and out every window were overgrown wisteria, lilac, and snowball bushes. (Grandmaw had long ago passed away.) Aunt Myrtle, four-ten and weighing nearly two hundred pounds, gave birth to no children. But in every other respect her daughter was Elizabeth. From the country, no southern lady, her singsong talk was a foreign language to me on the first day of our visits. Her love and hugs smothered: "Oh lordy, lordy, come here and let your Aunt Myrtle a-hug you! 'Lizabeth, I could just eat him up!" Dad told us he was too busy at work for visits to North Carolina. And Uncle Hayden worked the night shift at the Southern Shops, was not home much, or was sleeping in the back bedroom.

At Aunt Myrtle's I sensed danger. Her legendary cooking I hardly could get down: watermelon pickles ("ghost-fingers" to me), corn relish, dark country ham looking road-killed, warm cream-thick milk. It was so strange, as if from a foreign country, I feared swallowing it. As at Granddaddy Kenerly's, at Aunt Myrtle's Mother acted differently—girlish, livelier, unusually happy. Was this her or a bad dream? When I did not respond nicely to Aunt Myrtle's country hugs and talk, Mother got peeved. (It was,

I think, Daisy's strict propriety and admonishments inverted into Aunt Myrtle's indulgences and hugs that so threatened me in the little bungalow.) I tried not to bring down Mother's wrath. I tried to act my normal self.

And every minute I ached for my father. Stuck in Aunt Myrtle's bookshelves was a penmanship book. It was not Palmer method, the bane of my existence. This was elegant loops and flourishes and slashes; it was the handwriting of Dad's letters to Mother before they were married. (The ones I discovered in the attic and she promptly destroyed.) While her voice and Aunt Myrtle's happily singsonged from the kitchen, I tried on an end table in the living room to teach myself that elegant handwriting. While applying all the diligence I had, my efforts scratchy, blotty, I told myself that Dad knew how to do this, that he once wrote just like this. Concentrating hard, I almost blocked out their voices and the accompanying agony of Aunt Myrtle's house.

Elizabeth's love of Aunt Myrtle influenced her move with Al, when he retired, back to North Carolina. By then Aunt Myrtle had a bad heart, cataracts, and rheumatism, and when Uncle Hayden died, she had herself moved into a nursing home. Three times a week Elizabeth visited her there and filled up with that good-natured presence. Meanwhile Al, recently retired and absent anything to shape his life, found buddies at the Lexington Country Club with whom to drink away winter afternoons. He had bad falls, got two DWIs, publicly embarrassed Mother (into week-long silences), and, late at night, wildly drunk, cursed her obscenely. This situation was tighter, tenser, for Elizabeth's now living in the little North Carolina town with her older sister. Vada had heeded exactly what Elizabeth had rebelled against.

One summer afternoon Elizabeth was listening to Aunt Myrtle's country lilt, song older than Elizabeth's memory, when in the middle of a sentence, Aunt Myrtle stopped, smiled broadly, and died. Mother envied Aunt Myrtle's pleasant death. She attended to burying her beside Uncle Hayden in the cemetery where, a stone's throw away, Daisy was buried beside Robert. (In five years Elizabeth's own ashes would be poured into that red clay.) After Aunt Myrtle's funeral, Elizabeth moved herself and Al back to Washington.

Aunt Myrtle was the mother Daisy wasn't.

✿

And so was Grandmaw. When Grandpaw Kenerly died, Aunt Myrtle happily invited her mother-in-law to live with her and Uncle Hayden. It was Grandmaw Kenerly's furniture, from deeper back in time, that filled and darkened Aunt Myrtle's house. (All built by the veteran with his own hands.) In the family Elizabeth was envied for the attention she received from Grandmaw. Vada, up in her seventies, had not forgotten: "Going around town like that with Grandmaw, 'Lizabeth always thought she was so big and important." For weeks at a time the spirited little girl stayed in the bungalow with Aunt Myrtle and Grandmaw Kenerly. Mother told me, her smile unusually big: "Mama was reproached when Aunt Myrtle and Grandmaw would have me stay for a week. She told me in no uncertain terms that a daughter was obligated to live under the same roof with her mother." But how, really, could Daisy forbid Elizabeth's long stays with her aunt and widowed grandmother? Even as a little girl, Elizabeth knew how to drive a wedge.

Grandmaw Kenerly's bedroom at Aunt Myrtle's was the front one. This room Elizabeth had shared with Grandmaw. Both in their nightgowns, she loved watching the old lady, during the Civil War a girl like her, let down and brush her long gray hair. Sometimes Grandmaw let Elizabeth brush it out. Then in the bed where Grandmaw had conceived at least some of her many children, under the quilts with her warmth and close-up smell, they slept together.

Grandmaw died in that bed.

✿

Grandmaw, Elizabeth Jane, was twelve years old in 1865 when her father, James Earnhardt, a countryman fifty-two years old, was hastily mustered in with other old fellows and some boys to defend Salisbury against Stoneman's Yankee cavalry. Already her brother John Wiley had been killed at Sharpsburg; already another brother, Jacob Calvin, had been killed at Spotsylvania Courthouse; of the boys, only Lawson, an eleven-year-old, remained. And now, in May 1865, her father rode off with a ragtag artillery battery. Even a country girl from the German Lutheran hamlet of Lower Stone Church understood the utter hopelessness of matching old men and grinning boys against all-conquering Yankees. The little girl never saw her father again; sudden absence, greatest of wounds.

Compelled by necessity, Elizabeth Jane sold little cakes to Yankees on Salisbury's Main Street, the same Yankees who had taken her brothers and her daddy. That they swaggered along Main Street attested to the futility of his final act. The story, often told, was intended to be about surviving adversity. But that gritty virtue was always overwhelmed by choking, anger-filled loss and humiliation. Little Elizabeth Jane could not forget, even as an old woman, and the child she told could not forget, even as an old woman, and I have not forgotten, either.

Five years after the war (1870) Elizabeth Jane found a living Confederate veteran. She was sixteen, fatherless, nearly brotherless, and Charles W. Kenerly was thirty years old and limping from a wound got in the war that had ravaged her home and family. Charles had been born the same year as her brother Jacob Calvin, who was killed in the war. He must have seemed to her (secretly) that brother returned.

After Gettysburg, Charles Kenerly was "sent home sick." Even though the Confederacy was desperate to refill the Army of Northern Virginia, Charles was allowed to remain at home. His spirit was broken, I think; he had seen too much slaughter. Although most of the eligible men were buried in Virginia, he remained unmarried for five years. He believed that farming, the work of his hands, would cure him of the war. He helped to ease the hot pang of memory with the plowing of cotton fields season after season—that hissing sing of scouring plow blade; and drawing buckets of well water, the sky wobbling down there in the dark; with the warm spill of blood when in autumn smoke they butchered hogs; and even with venting his own all-consuming rage when Dodd (his mule, the only thing he owned) kicked at him and he struck him back repeatedly with his fist as hard as he could against mule skull until his own pain called him back to himself; and with winter nights by the hot stove eating corn bread and collards, thankful for the time being his belly wasn't gnawed with hunger; and, with twisting off the lantern night after night, total dark immediately there. But no. The butchering they had got at Fair Oaks running right into the volleys and scything grapeshot, and his fall (after what seemed a mule kick to his shin) onto the frozen ground at Fredericksburg, and the carnage left scattered through the shredded May woods after their attack on Fairview at Chancellorsville, and Slaughter's slaughter, charging with Pettigrew and Pickett at Gettysburg, the butchered on those fields as he, Charles, with the mob in abject defeat fell back to Seminary Ridge: these were not to be extinguished. And telling himself, "I got used to it up in Virginia and Pennsylvania. I'll get used to this now," he met the young girl with gray eyes and solemn manner.

Elizabeth Jane was the hope he thought he had lost forever in Virginia and Pennsylvania. Her respect for him, one of Lee's illustrious veterans, he did not object to, but he knew, as did others who got home to North Carolina from the war's slaughterhouse, that they did not deserve such high regard. To the girl Elizabeth, Charles's every limping step reminded her of her war-killed brothers, her lost daddy. He was a veteran of the Seventh North Carolina Infantry, of Lee's and Jackson's glorious Lost Cause. He had fought battles with names she would never forget. And at Gettysburg he came within inches of whipping the Yankees, sweeping into Washington, and hanging Sherman and Grant and old Abe Lincoln himself. He had dealt death to the Yankees. He had killed the likes of Stoneman and his swaggering, braggart, cowardly blue-bellies. He had done exactly what she with burning humiliation and anger still desired most to do. He had made Yankee women mourn for dead brothers, for fathers. Elizabeth, choked with grief and rage, married the hot-eyed, short, limping man.

And forty years later, in the 1910s and '20s, she taught her namesake to venerate that grandfather (although he was dead eight years before she was born), and all Confederates of Lee's noble Army of Northern Virginia. Mother repeated to me stories Grandmaw told her of Grandpaw, of his courage and fortitude in the War Between the States ("marching with bloody bare feet in the Virginia snows"), of his wound in the shinbone at Fredericksburg ("they never got the minié ball out"), of God sparing his life in Pickett's great charge at Gettysburg. And she told me how he lost to Yankee carpetbaggers money he slowly had saved to buy land and thus get off sharecropping. These were Grandmaw's stories, not Grandpaw's. His stories he did not tell, as far as I know; they died when he died. But not their effects, which live today in some of us. He could not read or write; he signed his name with an X.

His death in July 1906 I remember because Grandmaw told it so vividly to her namesake, the fiery little girl, and Mother told it to me. Charles hoed cotton on a warm summer morning. He left the hoe cut into the red clay and crossed furrows, knee-high cotton plants, to the shade of an oak. (I was shown the field, the oak.) There he took his water jar out of a wet tow sack, which kept it cold. He sat down, back to the tree, took a sip, removed his hat, put the jar between his knees, and died. He was found sitting peacefully like that. His death was the mirror reverse of the slaughterhouse battles of the Civil War that, miraculously, he survived; in beautiful stillness of a North Carolina morning, body wet with sweat, he passed through to the peace of the dead. For forty years he had carried memories of carnage and gore and the rippling terror when they charged, yelling, into the Yankee guns. Memories not throat-cut by the solemn young girl, by her love mixed with veneration, nor by six children, nor by a lifetime of sharecropping, by the coming and going of seasons along the Yadkin River, nor by the clay-stained rage of spring floods. Only death stopped memory. Understanding this in the last moments of his life, he was flooded with contentment, I hope. Dead, Grandpaw Kenerly remained a father presence that could not fill an unfillable absence in Grandmaw. And since Grandmaw was so significant to little Elizabeth, in fact a mother-presence to her, Grandpaw was therefore important to little Elizabeth too. He was her father's father. And turning toward that dead and venerated Confederate veteran implied a slight to her mother. Grandpaw's absence, like Grandmaw's, like Daisy's, was everywhere at Aunt Myrtle's.

✺

This must be coincidence: Grandpaw died within a month of Al's birth in 1906. Is the weave of loss and hope deeper, more intricate, than I suspected? With her grandmother and Aunt Myrtle, did Elizabeth learn more than simple venerating love of men older than herself?

For years Aunt Myrtle's bungalow was devoted to the Lee-veteran dead, more venerated in death than life, I think. At its center was the religiously regarded Lost Cause engraving on the wall of Grandmaw's room and, several miles away, the final object of that devotion, the grave of Charles at Ellis Crossroads Baptist Church. Elizabeth, who owed her name and well-being to her darkly dressed grandmother, went weekly with Grandmaw to visit the grave. She stared at "July 25, 1906" chiseled in stone. Irreverent as usual, she thought of that Fredericksburg minié ball down there, still in his shinbone. And that if it were not for what happened the day Grandpa passed away, she would not now dwell in shadow and absence but in the vital, sun-warmed presence of life itself. ("No more of these durn cemetery trips with Grandmaw," the child silently declared to herself.) This surged then in 1931 when she met Al, six not twelve years older, but born less than a month after the charged presence of Grandpaw became absent from the lives that had most shaped hers. So that Al, devil-may-care anyway, lively as he could be, was that grandpa absence returning with youthful vigor and thus welcomed with her considerable adult passions. Al, to Elizabeth, both return and lively reverse of her grandfather who came to her through venerating stories. (And fanning the flames, Al's birthday, August 20, just two days shy of her father's, August 22). In more ways than one, Elizabeth married to escape Daisy; that clot of loss (profound with its roots back to her first years of life), rage, and guilt verging on self-annihilation. When she destroyed her mother's only photograph and ballpointed out her own face, which we wanted to remain with us, she testified to the unabated, still-roaring existence of all she had attempted to flee a half century earlier. In Al, so like her father, she threw her arms around her father's family. At Aunt Myrtle's, Elizabeth's losses left no air to breathe.

✿

Twelve years old, I did not desire *at all* to sleep in the same bed with Mother. That featherbed troughed, too, reminding me of a coffin. And they told me this was the exact same bed where little Elizabeth slept with Grandmaw. And that that august lady died in this bed. And that they both often saw Grandmaw Kenerly's ghost at windows, in doorways, and that the sight was a comfort to them.

Even in the dark, I saw in mind's eye Grandmaw's Lost Cause engraving of women burying a young soldier in a dark grave. I smelled Mother, her breathing steady, slow. Night breezed the curtains, streetlights in them with shadows in the folds. Curtains shifted. Next to the chest of drawers was impenetrable dark. My nerves leaped: in that dark might hide anything. Ears roared, an ocean storm, and I became sure Grandmaw Kenerly's ghost was there by the chest of drawers. If I go to sleep, it will swallow me.

What was at Aunt Myrtle's was already shadow within myself. And it was Daisy, my grandfather Robert, and Grandmaw, and her Lee veteran, and Daisy's veteran father, her mother, Aunt Myrtle herself, all of them. Grievous losses, those wounds to the heart, and generations of lunging for cures that could not really cure. All spiraling in counterpoint, in dynamic symmetry. And forty years later, this is what became the nightmare of the newborn bulldog pups being tied up tightly, growing into grotesquely deformed dogs. In this, truth's dark seeds.

✿

Born in August 1880, Robert E. Lee Kenerly was the hell-raising middle son of the Kenerly family. His bursting vitality and orneriness were fist-shaking against his father, almost forty-years old at his birth, a certified hero of the Lost Cause. (And of course at his father's venerated commander-in-chief, already gone to Gloryland's Gloryland.)

In spring of 1903 Robert went to a dance at Philip Sowers's place. His sharecropping family had worked Sowers's land since before he was born. At the dance the tenant farmer's son met the landowner's niece once removed, Daisy Clodfelter. Raised in the tightly laced corset of southern womanhood, Daisy was pure essence of what Robert lacked in manure-smelling barns, sun-blazing cotton fields, and a six-to-six job amid the banging and din of the Southern RR Shops. She was from a refined world, a universe apart from the sudden passions of white-lightning-drinking Southern Baptist sharecroppers with their quick fists, boisterous laughter, and tent revivals down by the Yadkin, where they were saved from terrible guilt and sin.

Daisy was the granddaughter of Philip Sowers's brother Jacob. The brothers owned rich land on both banks of the Yadkin River. When Jacob went off to the Confederate army in 1862, Philip promised to take care of his land and family until his brother returned. Sick in hospitals most of the war, Jacob disappeared when Richmond fell. His wife, Harriet, and girls—Elesia, Tryphenia—waited through the war, through his debilitating illnesses, only to have him die exactly when he might have returned home.

Fate is, in fact, cruel. But Philip remained more than true to his word. He saw Elesia married into a landowning family, the Clodfelters across the river in Davidson County, and he kept up ties with Elesia's children, his dead brother's grandchildren, including Daisy and Dessie. (Always present in these families, this heart-injuring absence from the Civil War.)

Daisy and Robert were married on December 23, 1903, at Uncle Philip's big house, where they had met. Both old veterans were there, Charles Kenerly, Seventh North Carolina Infantry, age sixty-two, and Daniel Clodfelter, Second North Carolina Infantry, age sixty-five. (I doubt they talked enough to know they had been side by side that Sunday morning in May at Chancellorsville forty years earlier.) Both much younger wives had lost their fathers in the war: Elizabeth Jane (Grandmaw) and Elesia (Daisy's mother). Both were forty-nine that day and both had been girls in the war their older husbands fought. The wedding, which reminded them of their own, brought tears, I believe. For profound loss, there is no balm, nor forgetting.

For a wedding present Uncle Philip gave Daisy and Robert a lot in the new railroad town, East Spencer, being cut out of his family land. Robert, who wanted nothing else to do with chopping cotton, was a mechanic at the Southern RR shops. Flush from selling land to the railroad, Uncle Philip built on their town lot a house for Robert and Daisy (one that, ramshackle, stands today). Although forty years had passed since the war, Uncle Philip continued to do right by his brother's children and grand-children. Daisy was his long-dead brother's granddaughter.

Uncle Philip's gift of a town lot and house to Daisy and Robert came with a cost. His brother had an unmarried daughter, Tryphenia (Elesia's sister), who was forty-seven in 1903. Uncle Philip received from Robert and Daisy their promise that Tryphenia could always live next door to them in the house and on the lot he had also provided. And that they would always see to her, be her family. A bitter, cantankerous, hypercritical, child-hating woman, she was feared and disliked by everybody, even Robert with his hot temper, who feared almost nothing else. She was always next door or, when she insisted on renting out her own house, living with her life-hating under their Kenerly roof. She was unpayable mortgage on their lives and family. She was the war's inescapable shadow. When her father went off to the Confederate army in 1862, little Tryphenia was two years old. Unable to remember her lost father, she grew up only with his absence. She was not wounded by Yankees in 1861–65, but she was no less a Civil War casualty. Her heart received a grievous wound. (Mother and her brothers and sisters did not believe ugly old Aunt Pheny even had a heart.) She lived to the ripe old age of eighty-two, dying in September 1941 on the eve of another war. I met her as a child, but I have no memory of that event.

How soon Daisy paid for passions stirred by Robert! Railroad yards out back unceasingly disturbed and often startled her. And coal soot invaded every nook and cranny of her home. It hazed embroidered doilies in the front parlor, which she kept locked up, and was in the bottom of white porcelain wash basins, and even got under her own fingernails. And giving birth to children was a terrible indignity—in the fire of birth pain romance burning to gray ash. And the children's grimy, sticky hands pulling at her. And although the black women, Matties and Sallies, nursed her babies (their heavy breasts revulsed her!), they had not the slightest idea how to go about teaching the runny-nosed little creatures to mind and be Christians. Daily these ill-behaving children with sooty hands assaulted her bearing as a lady and a Christian. When she asked Robert to discipline them, he razor-stropped them out on the back porch, temper roaring hot, not hearing screams of mercy loud enough for neighbors to hear. (Not to mention Aunt Pheny.) Thus it was her Christian duty to instruct the children herself. The Lord required this of her. And when withholding food or sitting stock still did not discipline them, she was forced to resort to a half dozen brisk cuts of a willow switch on the backs of their bare thighs. They *must* be punished. Shirking this duty turned her back on the Lord himself. With the strength he had given her she would struggle to maintain herself and them above the crude, ill-bred manners of other railroad families. And whatever she did, whether good or ill, her Aunt Pheny Sowers scowled and lectured, pointing her finger at everything in this world that was wrong: "I thank God in heaven that your mother did not live to see you raise her grandchildren to be such loathsome hoodlums and heathen brats! Rather she had died than look once on what I must see every day of my life."

To calm her own heart, Daisy left Robert in the kitchen after supper with his newspaper and went into her front parlor, softly closing the door. In her platform rocker, she let *Psalms* console her; she read *Ecclesiastes, Ruth,*

Luke's gospel, preferring it to the starkness of *Mark*, *Matthew*'s closeness to Jews, and the extravagances of *John*. If there was time, she read some Tennyson from the *Complete Works* her mother (who had died in 1910) had given her, allowing tears to well, slide down her cheeks. From *The Humbler Poets*, purchased with her saved egg money, she read poems that fell on her heart like slow, spring rain in woods. On winter mornings after the kitchen stove heated up and Robert had gone off to the shops, Daisy sometimes wrote into the mist on her kitchen windows verses she had committed to memory. Only little Vada exclaimed, "Mama, how beautiful!" But sharp-tongued Elizabeth laughed under her breath, muttering, "Oh woe is me, woe is me!" And of course the boys took no notice whatsoever of the words Daisy had lovingly written with her fingertip.

In the parlor at night, Daisy stiffened when out in the kitchen Robert pushed back his chair. The thump and floor-creak of his footsteps raced prickling needles through her nerves. Sitting erect, she told herself that Robert was before God and the State of North Carolina her lawful husband. He had every right to expect of her wifely duties. Still, hearing the knob of the parlor door turn, she jumped.

His crude invitation caused her to blush. She despised her reaction as much as, or more than, his ignorant lack of understanding.

She held her eyes on the passage she was reading until the words signified again. She urged herself to remember that passage or phrase. When she turned off the lamp, sudden dark shot an icy jet through her stomach.

In their downstairs bedroom, although it was pitch dark, she felt him there on the bed, eyes open, stark naked, leering at her. Before taking off her clothes, she dropped her nightgown over her head. She was repeating the passage or phrase, attempting to hold at bay all else but the rote of getting undressed, letting down her hair, combing it out in the dark. As she turned back the coverlet, slid herself into the bed, she knew he was already excited. This was the lifelong retribution she must expect for her young girl urgings toward Robert; this was the terrible debt she had incurred and never could pay back in full. Her own passions rising, very much against her will, Daisy fought not to surrender again to her own disgusting carnal appetites. But on some nights, oh Lord in heaven save me, humiliation was added to just punishment and her own body betrayed her with joy.

To submit to him in the dark befitted her own sinful nature; coal soot sifted down (after a snowfall, soot dusted the pure snow itself); freight cars banged together out in the dark of the Yard, their musical accompaniment. Her mother had fairly warned her. Their wallowing in carnal sin (sweating, coupling like common dogs, horses, bulls and cows) had proved to be God's own just punishment.

✣

Daisy was a gentle Lutheran, Robert, a hard-shell Southern Baptist. When the second girl baby arrived, Daisy recoiled. The baby's temperament was fierce, unyielding like Robert's; little Vada, such a sweet child, Daisy's heart had already embraced. Favoring her father, baby Elizabeth became a living and breathing reminder of what held Daisy's soul to this ugly, uncouth, coal-soot life of East Spencer with its snorting railroad carved out of her Sowers family's beautiful fields. (She remembered as a girl seeing the Yadkin's morning mists in cornfields on the very land where her house, with other soot-grimy houses, now stood backed up to the yards.) This new, squalling baby had abrupted into her life just as sweet Vada at last had learned to use the slop jar and attained human decency. Bound to her cross as surely as the Lord was nailed, hand and foot, to his.

Soon Daisy surrendered the management of little Elizabeth to the black woman. At about age four, 1916, Elizabeth found Aunt Myrtle and Grandmaw and they found her. Escaping Daisy's cold admonishments, Elizabeth had from her father's family these sweet indulgences. And Elizabeth forgot, at least for the moment, the blue absence filling the house when Daisy left for walks with her bulldog. Lost in the bargain was Elizabeth's father, never mind his explosive temper, whom she loved as fiercely as he loved her. On the other side of the yards, Aunt Myrtle and Grandmaw leaped to the little girl's every demand and whim.

Elizabeth's strong appetites they welcomed as high spirits. Headstrong and lively, she promised to cure the losses they felt most deeply: Aunt Myrtle's inability to have children and Grandmaw's losses in the war. And for little Elizabeth herself, how she liked scorning her natural mother. Loss and loss's hoped-for cure turning together. At Aunt Myrtle's I felt this tornadic vortex, its intense darkness.

✻

So Daisy, Mother's mother, centers these killing absences. But she, too, once was a child without recourse among adults who had suffered grievous losses. In the first years of her life, 1885–87, a world indelibly marked her, just as Elizabeth was marked by 1912–14 and I by 1936–38. The rural Davidson County house into which she was born (and into which her father was born) has been torn down. As far as I know, every scrap of her life—possessions, letters, poems—is lost (like Mother's photograph of her). Only her tombstone and her bones remain distinctly marked as hers. But with heart, and little else, I venture into this absence, pitch dark, in the hope of discovering a most important piece of the heritage I already carry.

✻

When Daisy Clodfelter was born in 1885, her father, Daniel, was forty-five years old. Long ago and of necessity he had made friends with death. Twelve years old in 1850, he witnessed his mother's death. His new stepmother daily reminded him of his mother, absent, lost forever, while also reawakening his abject hope that she would return from the dead. Twenty-four in 1862, he was drafted into the Second North Carolina Infantry to replace the regiment's dead, killed in the Bloody Lane at Sharpsburg. In Stonewall Jackson's corps at Chancellorsville, he was on the flank of that crushing attack. In the May morning that followed, young General Ramseur pleaded for orders to attack through a brigade forward of their position. These men had earlier charged and been shattered, and now the survivors hunkered behind hasty log-works. Ramseur got his order and attacked, Clodfelter with them. As the brigade swept forward, some of the skulkers in the beaten-back brigade shouted, "You may double-quick, but you'll come back faster than you go!" Out through thick woods being shredded, limbs falling, a maelstrom of Yankee artillery firing canister and grapeshot. A man in Clodfelter's regiment wrote, according to Ernest B. Furgurson, "I was very nearly covered in the earth many times by bombshells. The bark from trees often made my face sting, and splinters knocked from the neighboring trees or saplings were stuck in my clothes." They drove back the line of Yankee infantry, a battlefield triumph, but then took terrible enfilade fire. They fell back to the log-works where they had started and had scorned as cowards the men who had been broken as they now were. In those fifteen minutes Clodfelter's regiment of 340 men lost two-thirds, 214 killed and wounded.

Seeing some regrouped, Ramseur, so full of fire for the charge, asked: "Is that all that's left?"

"This is all, sir."

Ramseur burst into tears. "Men," he cried, "I love you."

*

Daniel Clodfelter was wounded in the neck. Desire for glory, the terror of the killing machine, brief triumph, decimation, and retreat; the living that quick gore scattered through shattered May woods. How could a young man from a North Carolina farm not have his heart as scarred as the back of his neck? (Often do I tramp those woods, tracing and retracing that charge, trying to comprehend my great-grandfather's experience there and its legacy to me.)

He was sent to Liberty, Virginia to recuperate. There the man who would become Daisy's father emerges. Having seen the gore of battle and glimpsed glory's absurdity, Daniel Clodfelter deserted. According to family legend, he went home to plant crops on the farm he had inherited from his father. But, according to Confederate muster rolls, he deserted on August 9, 1863, a very strange time, indeed, to plant crops in North Carolina. The news-papers were printing the names of Gettysburg casualties. Vicksburg had fallen to Grant. Daniel also had a new wife, Maryanne Elizabeth, whom he had married just before leaving for Virginia. He deserted so that the killing machine would not kill him. Through that Carolina autumn he hid out in the rafters of the porch whenever provost marshal's patrols came down his road. As the frosts came, he found resolve or guilt or sense of modern absurdity strong enough to return to the killing. On December 17, 1863 he returned to the Army of Northern Virginia, where he im-mediately went into the stockade to await execution by firing squad. The governor of North Carolina spared him for the slaughter of Spotsylvania Courthouse.

In that Bloody Angle he was thrown beyond simple battle, beyond the killing machine, into something "fiercer" and more "horrendous than what had gone before, ever." Sixteen hours of a "slaughter-pen," of prolonged "madness" beyond telling. The same nightmare repeated itself on the Somme, at Tarawa, on Okinawa's Shuri Castle line. "These were the red hours of conflict," Shelby Foote continues of the Bloody Angle, "hours no man who survived them would forget, even in his sleep, forever after." My mother's mother's father—how *wouldn't* consequences of such nightmares spiral on through time and generations?

When it was over, Daniel Clodfelter was one of very few men in the Second North Carolina still able to stand. For this luck, accomplishment, action of fate, or intervention of Divine Providence, he received a personal handshake from the man born at Stratford Hall. In a year's time from recruit into the ranks of the dead to wounded and disillusioned soldier to deserter to prisoner awaiting execution to survivor of humankind's worst nightmare to hero commended by the commander-in-chief himself. How could he tell himself that his fate was in the hands of either himself or a Christian God? Given his own immediate experiences, how could he maintain the war justifications of the Confederate States? How could he believe in anything beyond his own experiences?—even these not trustworthy. Not long after Spotsylvania, he dealt the killing that had been dealt to him: at Cold Harbor the Confederates killed or wounded seven thousand Yankees in less than hour. This young man from a North Carolina farm had experienced what Søren Kierkegaard had painstakingly described a few years earlier: modern absurdity, the absence of containing justifications for the individual and his actions. Young men are irrevocably changed by such events.

But his war was not over.

In Jubal Early's little army he marched Lee's last gamble, a bluff against Washington, D.C., which with Stonewall Jackson leading in 1862 had worked so well. In the brigade now reorganized again, Daniel marched west out of Richmond's fortifications to the Shenandoah Valley, then northeast to the Potomac, crossed into a fight at the Monocacy, then right down the Rockville Pike through Gaithersburg (within sight of where his granddaughter Elizabeth would live), Rockville, and up to the forts encircling Washington. He was within sight of where his last daughter, Dessie, would live in Takoma Park. He glimpsed the half-finished dome of the U.S. Capitol. Lincoln came out to see the Rebel army, which skirmished, made as if preparing an assault. But Lincoln and Grant, who used river steamers to reinforce Washington's forts, knew Early was too weak. For all their sore-footed marching, their good fight at the Monocacy, the Confederate bluff failed. Too few troops were pulled away from the Union's tightening hold on Richmond-Petersburg. Lee remained in Grant's trap. Early's Confederates turned on heel and began retracing their route. Now, though, they were pursued by large Union forces. At Winchester Sheridan beat them and Daniel's brigade was flanked, routed. At Fisher's Hill his thrice shredded brigade was surrounded by attacking Yankees and cut off. Many surrendered, including Daniel. After seeing Confederate prisons as a returned deserter, he now got to see Yankee prisons as a captured Confederate. He was taken first to the Old Capitol Prison (on the site of what is now the U.S. Supreme Court), then the worst of Yankee prisons, Elmira, New York. Lee's last gamble ended for Daniel when he became in actual fact the prisoner he had been since being drafted in 1862. He was relieved, I am sure, to be captured. But once at Elmira that healthy desire to be free of the killing was turned upside down. That Yankee fierce winter, cold and disease killed almost half of all Confederate prisoners.

He was released, if that is the appropriate word, at City Point, Virginia, and he walked a final 150 miles home to Davidson County. If there is a point in his life at which I might know his mind, it is here, on this journey through the devastated South of 1865. Towns dilapidated (or burned down), railroad rails torn up and heated and wrapped around big trees ("Sherman's neckties"), fields fallow, farmhouses abandoned with doors gaping open, manners dissolved into hunger, former slaves thronging roads with desire and panic. It was a landscape mirroring the devastation Daniel himself had suffered. All in 1861 that he had been certain of was in 1865 present only as loss. The gaping nihilism of Nietzsche expressed what many southerners had experienced: utter abjectness, a fundamental despair in any human endeavor.

Surviving the killing and death, knowing absurdity's grave-cold, Daniel had to turn his back on that gorgon's head. A necessity, otherwise putting one foot in front of the other would stop. But denying what he brought home from the Civil War made those losses the heavy legacy of his children (the generation of Faulkner's Mrs. Compson, of Daisy), his grandchildren (Faulkner, his Caddy and Quentin, my mother Elizabeth) and his great-grandchildren (me). Faulkner struggled with absence, alcoholism; Elizabeth struggled with the absence of her mother, with her alcoholic husband; I struggle here to live with the absence of a life of my own. Old shadows abide.

Arriving at his destination, Great-grandfather Daniel discovered that the little boy he had fathered in the sweet days before the war had died of diphtheria. The child he fathered while a deserter, Mary Alice, born while he was at Bloody Angle, had survived. Soon William McKay was born, 1866. He managed to keep his farm by selling off parcels of land. Three more children arrived: Nettie, 1869; John, 1871; Sallie, 1874. But death was never distant. Shortly after his return from the War, he carved his own tombstone of reddish sandstone, which I have seen at Pilgrim Lutheran Church, Davidson County. It was in the design of his German-Swiss ancestors. He kept his tombstone in the barn loft, with his death date blank.

In the winter of 1875, his wife, Mary Elizabeth, died a slow, lingering death of tuberculosis. His response reveals how the war had injured him. Except for the eldest, Mary Alice, who was old enough to do female chores, he gave away his girls. Nettie, age six, and Sallie, age one, went to other families. Both of the boys, William, age nine, and John, age four, he kept under his roof.

In short order he married Elesia Sowers, age twenty-two, sixteen years younger than his thirty-eight years. When Elesia saw her father off to the Confederate army in 1863, she was eight years old and he a middle-aged fellow, thirty-five, with prosperous farms along the Yadkin and a wife, Harriet, and he was father, too, of Tryphenia (Pheny) age two. Elesia brought a dowry of land.

✿

Mother of Daisy, Elesia also knew losses' anguish. Her father, Jacob, was in Lee's Army of Northern Virginia, Eighteenth Battalion, North Carolina Light Artillery. His war record, however, was an inglorious list of hospitals: Chimborazo Hospital #3, Richmond (diarrhea), August to September 1863; General Hospital #5, Wilmington, North Carolina (unspecified ailment), January to February 1864; Winder Hospital,

Richmond (unspecified ailment), April 30 to September 3, 1864. That day he received what he hoped for most, a passport home to North Carolina. But a few days later, as the fighting closed around Richmond-Petersburg that autumn, he reappears "sick" at General Hospital #9, Richmond. He was too sick to fight and too weak to get himself home.

In the slapped-together ward, among groans, cot creakings, and silences of the dying, Jacob watched autumn's dawns and dusks walk his ward. When sentient, he allowed that this was where he'd draw his last breath. Here under ill-nailed rafters, a sky of shingle nails in sunny morning, at dusk nail points fireflies, and at night distant and dim stars. Here in this revolving light and dark, on this mattress with its corn-shuck song. Now no prayers to hold Harriet; none for his sweet girls to gather around his knees once again when he sat down, on winter nights, their cheer gladdening his heart. In David's psalms no sought-for consolation; nor in Job's earth-shaking laments. Nor relief in the simple rush of memories, of dead weeds on a winter afternoon along a country lane, or lap and deep song of the spring-flooded Yadkin. These all remembered from a sweeter world, a place in his mind, like Eden, or Bethlehem, or Jerusalem. He would not ever again see his good wife, nor his girls (Elesia, little Tryphenia), nor his brother Philip, nor his home. Like rising morning mists in autumn along the Yadkin, a weight lifted. Here he was; he had prepared himself. Absent fear, an icy thrill went through his belly; contentment filled him. On his cot he died alone.

In spring 1865 Stoneman's Yankee cavalry swept through a token force of boys and old men with several antique artillery pieces and into Salisbury. The Yankees were mad as hell to get to the Salisbury prison, where thousands upon thousands of Federal soldiers had died of conditions as bad as Andersonville's. The Yankees rode south on Main Street and into hell on earth. The Rebs had transported the healthiest to keep them from being liberated by the Yankees. Only the walking dead and too-sick-to-stand remained. Stoneman's Yankee troopers found their sense of approaching victory turned upside down when, in the familiar music of cavalry jingle and clop, they trotted up to the main gate and saw with their own eyes those emaciated skeletons, their rags, the muddy filth in which they lived a Satan-nurtured inversion of life. They surely felt the slow-burning rage of U.S. troops (their grandsons) on entering Dachau and the

Japanese camps. How then did those same troopers want to punish southerners? At least, smash their gloved fists into the faces of every male they encountered on Salisbury's streets. How did they burn with rage at the pride and arrogance of women who scorned them on the streets and who—hypocrites! hypocrites!—could not have but known of Salisbury Prison, of human beings starving to death, dying of exposure, of wasting disease.

When Stoneman threw open the gates, those that could walk obeyed simple instinct. They started north along the railroad tracks, their hearts yearning for sanctuary. The next morning fifty skin-and-bones new dead were scattered along the railroad right-of-way. And Stoneman's cavalry, rage heaping on rage, went out in the spring morning with wagons, picked up the child-weight corpses. Not even Yankee cavalry troopers hardened by Georgia campaigning were unscathed after carrying the pitifully light bones of hopes come to naught. As the nation prepared to rise in salute to Sherman's and Grant's mighty armies, Stoneman's men were forced to witness hope's end. They ached for revenge against every southerner within a hundred miles of Salisbury Prison. (And Confederate troops, had they entered Elmira, New York, would have sought to exact no less.)

In early summer 1864 Harriet and the girls received news that Jacob would have a pass to come home September 3. They were elated. Then in mid-August 1864, they received news that he was too weak to come home. Sherman was knocking at the gates of Atlanta; Grant was strangling Lee at Richmond. And right here Jacob Sowers disappeared. No news, official or unofficial. In the cold spring of 1865, still nothing. A few veterans, hardly recognizable skeletons, drifted back, saying that Jacob had died in the hospital. No, they didn't know if he had received Christian burial; no, they didn't know where. (But in mind's eye they saw the muddy mass graves of the hospitals, white lye tossed over the dead from the previous night.) Reports of his death, but none exactly certain, not for sure. This for Harriet and the girls after a war full of weeding out futility, despair, and abject loss in order to nurture enough hope to go on living. Now eleven, Elesia was desperate for her father, in whom she had invested a war's worth of anxious love. But nothing, no definitive word, no grave. Pure absence, the worst wound inflicted on the human heart. Consider Tryphenia's (Aunt Pheny's) long lifetime of lashing out, of profound bitterness; consider her sister, Elesia, entering adolescence with an absent and unburied father. And Harriet married to widowhood—her angry shouts to silence hope, which came to her like the desire to sleep, that Jacob had not died in a Richmond hospital and, as she looked down the lane at twilight, would walk in his slow, ambling manner up to the house they had steadfastly kept for him.

The man's name is unknown. As the story came to me in whispers from Mother, in her last years, and Vada—both having heard it from their aunts Myrtle and Dessie (*not* a whisper from Daisy)—the man had no name. To be a "Yankee officer" as the story was first told in 1865 was to be outrage. For an officer in an invading and conquering army to have carnal knowledge of a Confederate war widow was terrible abomination, pure and simple. If some knew his name, it was quickly lost in adding-insult-to-injury rage. In a southern community possessing *only* pride, nothing so assaulted that last bastion more violently than the *very idea* of a Yankee officer exercising himself on a Confederate widow. His name, regiment, and home state were of no interest.

He had spent nearly a year galloping the back roads of the South with Stoneman, screening the flanks of Sherman, who was outfoxing Johnston and Hood. He had seen life's darkest side: Atlanta depopulated and burned; a thirty-mile-wide burned swath from there to Savannah, women and children left to starve. Horse sweat in his nostrils, galloping thunder in his ears, he rode the ill maps of dusty, muddy back roads. He condoned what his men did but didn't himself take silver, hams, watches. He did not himself throw flaming kerosene lanterns into houses and barns to set them into dry-timber infernos. He did not himself shoot the twelve-year-old boy charging around the corner of the house with an ancient fowling piece (his father's soft voice in his ears: "Take care of things, son, until I can get back. Will you do that for me?"), shot offhandedly by Sergeant Phipps smack in the middle of his chest, his innocent corn-blue eyes going through a lifetime in an instant as he was thrown backward by the big .44 slug—bloody splotch on his chest—and was dead before he hit spraddle-legged the hardpan of the yard, mother and sisters so shocked they did not scream. And Sergeant Phipps, before the war a decent-hearted farmer, already throwing his leg over the big buckskin he had taken off a farm last week. How damn ordinary to see that boy lying dead in the yard and the sky the clear blue of autumn.

Did not himself shoot the boy or burn the houses and barns but was not, for a tick of his father's watch, fooling himself about not being, absolutely, both complicit and responsible for the actions of his men in this U.S. Army. When they were halted he saw two or three ride off hell-for-leather, and on the fall wind he heard, words indistinguishable, their smirky yells and the girls screaming. He tried to remember his home, his wife and his girls, but it had been so long ago it seemed last night's dream he was attempting to remember. He had Phipps mount the troop, galloped them all so those screams would not reach his ears. (But he heard them; he heard them in his nightmares; he heard them in the crackle of a pine-chip fire.) And he was not a religious man, a whiskey Methodist instead, yet without trying he knew what they did was wrong. He knew that the most important thing he was doing in the war was to know how wrong this all was, what a violation of the heritage of his flesh and blood. But he was complicit in the destruction of the property of the innocent and defenseless; he understood punishing. He had done his share of killing Rebs.

She was a thirty-six-year-old recent widow with children who had anguished through the war over her sick husband off with Lee's army. Recently she had learned that he was probably tossed with other overnight dead into a mass Richmond grave. And he was a conscience-stricken cavalry officer weary of war, of too much cheap killing and blood-rousing destruction, who wore the Yankee blue-belly uniform, the hatred of which bound the Confederate nation more than any abstract principle, especially and particularly a Yankee in Sherman's army. (I hear Mother's vehement bitterness when, after seeing *Gone with the Wind* in 1946 at the conclusion of another war, she told me what Sherman had done in 1864–65. How cowardly to assault defenseless women and children! And I add now: How utterly defeated are southern men who cannot defend their own innocent children!)

So how did it happen that Harriet Sowers and the Yankee enemy found each other in 1865's abject springtime? What glint in her light blue eyes, what posture, or head tilt, or inflection of voice leapt—lightning's sizzle and sweet smell—through years of engendered hatred, death upon death, loss compounded and compounded again until nothing remained at all that in 1861 was certain. Forcing or rape was not mentioned, not even by faint innuendo. If they could have, they would have, to diminish the eye-lowering shame. I am quite sure Harriet told them no, that was not it, not it at all. And the family said among themselves: she should have at least the common decency to tell us the Yankee *forced himself* on her. If it was not true, she could have told us it was. Harriet could have reduced the family's shame. But no.

Harriet understood the crux of spring 1865.

My imagination, to which I have given free rein here, now balks. Harriet's dark, threadbare clothes and the Yankee's ill-fitting blue-belly uniform I see. A tattered quilt, a summer morning with a hint of cool and the haze lifting into a bright blue sky. He must have thought that Harriet any moment would haul out an ancient revolver, touch the cold muzzle to his bare chest, fire point-blank, a joke even he for a final instant could appreciate. But no, hands strong, eyes wide (as if she might miss some-thing), her direct, purposeful actions carried them along. And then his senses were spilling over with this good, strong woman, and he thought that if she shot him now, by god it would be worth it. Only later, when she would not answer his notes, did Harriet return to the mysteries of her sex.

And Harriet, she had seen to her girls, put them over at Uncle Philip's or at a friend's down the road. After suffering the war, her judgment was never better, nor ever further from the county's opinions. Jacob was gone, his bones moldering in Virginia dirt. She caught herself hoping otherwise, but no. No. The Yankee she had judged correctly, the sort of man he was—a family man, what he had seen of the war twisted in him, hard-pulled in knots, but his spirit burned still, a good bright flame. As sure as the ground under her feet, she knew the Yankee was honest. Although he overthought things (as she did), he was strong, had a spring in his step. War had stripped their lives like raging wood's fires, burned them down to black obsidian. So many dead men, women, and children. All that remains is warm sun on your face and love—even brief love, that surging, and the hope it brings that is most beautiful of all. Yes, sin; yes, wrong, evil; hide it from her girls. But all in this life a body can cleave to; all there is.

Before the first frost he was gone home to his wife and family. Her heart was strong. When she realized she carried another child, she scarcely could contain her joy. Her girls, of course, and all the devastated people she also loved: their boiling-over and bitter anger she had misjudged because she did not share it. Shaking her head, smiling at her hubris, Harriet had got that contrariwise—thought in the surging of her own heart, in the heady relief of having this monstrous war done with, that love with the hated Yankee enemy was better. And a beautiful baby, that gift like the Christ Child at Christmas. But no; on this her judgment had failed her.

I know the child, Mary, born in 1866, appears on the 1870 census in Harriet Sowers's household. The scandal whispered *sotto voce* to me over a century later was the result of both the existence of an illegitimate child by a Yankee officer, this baby Mary, and from Harriet's shameless refusal to hide the sign of her terrible sin against God, her neighbors, and the South. What moral strength did Harriet find in herself in those grim postwar years sufficient to stand against the *only thing* southern people could cling to, their unvanquished pride? How endure scorn, year after year, from virtually every man, woman, and child in the South? Little Mary on her hip, then toddling at her side, Harriet was the moral descendant of Hester. But she had to contend also with the intensifying complication of a destroyed society trying to salvage a speck or two of human dignity from the ashes of abject defeat. The existence of little Mary was a reproach, a living sign of the community's shame. And Harriet refused to send her away, out of sight, as a decent woman would have done. Mary's half sister was the infamous Aunt Pheny. Here was another cause of her life-hating. Here, too, roots of her other half sister's, Elesia's, insistence on extremes of Victorian propriety that became in Daisy rage at any departure from the ideal of a southern Christian lady.

✡

Aunt Mary was beautiful, with blonde curls and a calm, self-possessed manner. The year her mother died (1889), she married a Southern RR clerk who took her to live up in Washington, D.C. The family was relieved to have her out of sight at last. But the damage had already been inflicted. (Mother's and Aunt Vada's voices contained relief when they told me of Mary's departure for Washington, which of course was long before either was born.) It was a blessing, the family thought, that Mary remained childless. Her shame would not be perpetuated by hard-to-explain cousins. They could have forgotten her, almost, or at least put her out of mind, had she not regularly returned to North Carolina for Christmas.

Sometimes her husband, also a quiet person, came with her. She was welcomed at Uncle Philip's, although she was no blood kin. As girls, Mother and Vada saw her there. "She was beautiful all right," Mother said. "She looked like a little doll. She was nice, too, but Mama told us not to bother with her." Her husband died young. With his pension she lived alone in Washington for thirty-five years. Mother with Aunt Dessie (who was Mary's niece) went to visit her a few times in her little row house off Sixteenth Street. Great-aunt Mary intrigued Mother, especially in Mother's young and rebellious first years in Washington. She liked her dark, family-rattling story. But Aunt Dessie, generous and forgiving and the opposite of Daisy, still could not bring herself to have much to do with this blood kin living so close by. It was Mary's living in Washington that made that city a Gomorrah, site of profoundest sin, and Yankee capital to boot. No wonder Daisy's heart was hard when she forbade her flesh-and-blood daughter, hardly sixteen, to venture into that evil place.

As Mary was about to die in 1936, she looked toward home. She wished to be buried not with her husband in Washington but in North Carolina with the mother whose strong heart and passion had given Mary life. Her grave is beside Harriet's in the Concord Church cemetery in Davie County, North Carolina. It gladdened my heart to find her grave and, in the muggy Carolina summer, to stand quietly beside it.

✿

For Mary's half sister Elesia, age twenty-two in 1876, Daniel Clodfelter represented her lost father returned at last from Virginia. He was a widower sixteen years older, wounded in Lee's Lost Cause, survivor of Elmira prison. Marrying her brave veteran, Elesia hoped to purify herself of terrible family shame. Her own mother had betrayed all with a Yankee officer and borne the monster's child. Elesia was desperate to leave forever her warm-cheeked shame at her own mother's sinning so openly against God, the South, and her father's heroic memory. Sinned, in fact, with the vileness of her body and with her *father's enemy!* Married to her veteran, she would at last be a head-held-high wife and mother. Harriet and ten-year-old Mary were not invited to the wedding. Elesia's heart shut them out.

Her killing stress on being a lady, a proper southern Christian one, chilled her daughter's heart. Embracing so fiercely loss's promised compensations, Elesia made those losses permanent inheritance of her children (Daisy), grandchildren (Elizabeth), and great-grandchildren (me). Although Daniel promised to restore Elesia's worst losses, he became instead daily and living reminder of her lost father, her lost family honor, and her own mother lost to sin and dishonor. The more vigorous the assertion of the contrary, the darker and more driving the loss.

On his young wife Clodfelter begat nine children to add to the five by his first wife. Unfortunately for this second family, only two of nine were of the gender Daniel had *not* given away when his first wife died. And one of the boys, Okra, died at age eleven, in 1898. (His ghost my mother distinctly saw with other family members on a mist-rising summer evening out at the Clodfelter homeplace.) So only one son, Oliver, survived to adulthood. All remaining children of Daniel and Elesia were females: Eula, Willie, Callie, Daisy, Cora, Winnie, and Dessie.

In 1885, when Daisy was born on the Clodfelter farm in Davidson County, she was the fourth child and fourth female born in six years to Daniel and Elesia. He was forty-seven years old, already the father of eight living children. To baby Daisy he was as remote as Cathay (or the Bloody Angle). To death's veteran, Daisy was another daughter, another appurtenance to the family he surrounded himself with. Baby Daisy had no recourse but to find her life within the great, shadowed absences spinning through generations of her family.

Clodfelter begat children on his young wife into his late fifties. Then his old friend showed up. In 1910 his Elesia died, she then fifty-six and he seventy-two, leaving the old veteran with teenage daughters, Winnie and Dessie. Shortly thereafter, Clodfelter decided to sign over his house and farm to a son-in-law. In exchange the son-in-law pledged to care for the old man and his daughters. Like Lear, Clodfelter was blinded by his years and a good-enough life. He may have been irascible, again like Lear, and struck out at his son-in-law and married daughter, they now living under what he would always consider to be his roof (where he was born, his father, where his first wife and children had died). But the story, true to that time, is sentimental and melodramatic. The son-in-law, Simon Legree, drove the poor Lee veteran out into the cold. He slammed the door on the old fellow and his last two daughters, including Aunt Dessie. They had no home, no place to live.

In September 1912 he put himself into the Confederate Veterans Home in Raleigh, North Carolina. He had joined the army in Raleigh in 1862, exactly a half century earlier. Now he returned to the war he had never left or forgotten. And the men, now old, who had also charged, whooping, at blazing musket volleys and grapeshotted artillery, and who still did not comprehend, as he did not, even after fifty years, why it was that they had survived and so many others were killed. (And for what? What exactly was it all for?) He got a simple bed in a barrackslike room beside a wild old fellow who wanted to tell the world something he had personally witnessed with Genr'l Jackson. But he never got to the main point of his story; maybe he had forgotten it. Pretty girls and sweet-smelling women came to the Confederate Home, doted on him, took him to church, invited him for Sunday dinners. He had nothing, but he was happy enough.

But not his teenage daughters. He did with them in 1912 when Elesia died what he had done with his other daughters in 1870 when Margaret died. He let them out to families who needed help caring for children, teaching ABCs, doing housekeeping. After all, he had been left an old widower and swindled out of house and farm. What else could he do? (Forged in abandonment, no wonder Aunt Dessie's love of others was so profound!)

Daisy's father's troubles came to a head just as Elizabeth was born in 1912. Seventy-two years old, her daddy had been betrayed by his own daughter (and her sister!), driven out of the family's homeplace, and forced to live with nasty old men at the Confederate Home in Raleigh. And the girls, her poor baby sisters Winnie and Dessie, cast out in the cold to work for room and board. Idealizing her father, seeing his generosity treacherously used, Daisy was heartsick, despondent. When baby Elizabeth was born, she was distracted. Her sensitivity to family shame and hot concern for female propriety are not surprising. Nor is Elizabeth's desire to flee such an oppressive atmosphere for the indulgences of Aunt Myrtle and Grandmaw. In spite of herself, Daisy had indulgent love to give too, but it went to her little bulldog.

Death came for him at age eighty, in 1918. His tombstone was hauled down from the barn loft (a magnanimous gesture by the son-in-law, who wanted it known that, technically, he owned the tombstone, too). It got cut with the old man's death date, July 3, the fifty-fifth anniversary of Gettysburg, and went to mark his country grave at Pilgrim Lutheran Church. A few months later, his only surviving son, Oliver, marched off to the trenches of World War I. (He was gassed, never fully recovered. His terrible hawking cough I can still hear.)

✫

So Elesia's daughter Daisy was no villainess. She was as damaged as the rest of us. Her daughter Elizabeth rebelled against what Daisy valued most, the sacred ideals of a southern and Christian lady. And did so by running off to Gomorrah, where the family shame, Mary, resided! As death drew near, Daisy held to what she had. If she forgave Elizabeth, she would have profoundly denied herself. Elizabeth had slipped loose from exactly what bound Daisy so tightly all of her forty-six years. On her deathbed, that would be hardest of all to forgive.

The consequences of what happened there, in 1931 in that downstairs back bedroom in East Spencer, North Carolina, I carry as heritage because Mother did. Elizabeth struggled with her mother's obsession with being a proper southern lady. She was and was not that lady (and bottomless shadows accompanying that figure). In 1938, struggling to be both mother and independent modern woman, Mother fell back into those deepest shadows. As she was dying in 1982, however, she looked calmly into death's terrible absence as she told me of her lifelong fight. She began the cure I attempt to complete here.

Now something unexpected happens. This world of wounded family that I have constructed out of remnants of the past suddenly turns outside in. What I have built is, in mirror and shadow, what I am at this moment, sightings in a vast inner night that I possess more truly than I possess anything. I inherit this with my life. It is a dark sun and one source of every thought, word, and deed I have ever had or ever will have—this giant absence, my inheritance. It belongs to me, and I, who have thought I belong to nothing, belong to it.

Abiding Figures

In 1987, at age fifty-one, I went home to the city of my birth.

The morning I left Oklahoma, ice storms hard-glazed the roads, cars had spun out. My belly expected, any instant, a fishtail's icy sick. Crept along, windshield fogged, sleet singing with the shush of tires. Up near the Missouri line, bright sunlight broke through. Rolling down the window, I gulped cold air. In the ice-dazzle, road signs were glazed, barns and farm houses slid by in their universes of sparkling ice—all blazing, so alive my eyes stung. I wanted to stop, get out, kneel to pray thanks.

At Saint Louis, slow rain. Ticking off landmarks: the site of the house where I had lived the summer of 1958, and crossing Lindbergh Boulevard, down through Webster Groves, the location above the south shoulder where we had lived in 1964 when I discovered how starved I was for words. Windshield wipers slapped dirty spray thrown by passing cars. By Forest Park, where the 1904 World's Fair was, where in 1922 a sixteen-year-old Oklahoma runaway had stolen apples, and where in 1963 I had parked for the downtown bus to my job. Then the castlelike Union Station, where we had changed trains when returning from Oklahoma in 1945. On the same highway, going the opposite way, I came through here in 1982 with new hopes, heading back to a new life in Oklahoma. Then I remembered, but I did not understand; then my new hopes were simple ciphers of despair.

✫

A week before Christmas I rented a Capitol Hill apartment. The weather outside was bitterly cold, but dazzling and warm sunlight moved through the living room. Two blocks away, my life had been conceived in 1935. It was an old apartment house on Massachusetts Avenue next to Union Station plaza. Down the street was the Supreme Court, site of Old Capitol Prison, where Mother's grandfather (Daisy's father) was briefly imprisoned in September 1864. He was captured as the Confederacy's hopes died.

At Woodward and Lothrop there were marble floors I recognized from childhood; this was the first escalator I had ridden. Her hand holding mine, Mother had whispered cheery assurances.

At the nearby Library of Congress a librarian brought me some of Jefferson's original letters. Reading his 1788 account of riding over Jenkins Hill to inspect the new Capitol's site, I had the delicious sensation of being exactly there. On another cold day I walked Henry James's footsteps of 1904 while reading his description of the Jefferson Building, Library of Congress. My joy was in the exuberance he scolded. Standing at the south window of my apartment in warm sunlight, looking down on East Capitol Street, I guessed Walt Whitman ambled right by here on his walks out to visit outlying hospitals. Revisiting the Capitol I had known as a child, I remembered Whitman's splendiferous descriptions of these hallway murals and mosaics. Seeing mosaic floors at the Old Patent Office, I recollected Whitman seeing this same floor with pushed-back exhibit cases and war wounded lying on bloody cots.

Our World War II house in Takoma Park was unchanged, except for big, dark shrubbery. Our unhappy house in Bethesda, where we lived when the Korean War started, had gone classy, but a front-yard cherry tree I recognized. Now filling the rooms of both were lives bearing other burdens of family, history, and time.

My heart brimmed with Washington's pearly light and cloud and shadows with softened edges and the luminous glow of December sunsets on high old trees. My belly lifted at the site of the Smithsonian Castle, the brave proclamation of the lighted Capitol dome, the scar mark at the height of the Washington Monument during the Civil War (grounds then used for cattle, slaughtering), and at the solemn quiet of the Lincoln Memorial—*presences* sharing this December cold.

I recognized porches of row houses, gliders under tarps, on streets with remaining elms intertangled, bare-leafed, tossing with winter wind. I recognized marble curbs and old police call boxes and light poles with ornate and pointed lids recalling kaiser helmets. Everywhere in D.C., too, pressure of the half-remembered: running across Pennsylvania Avenue at the old FBI, a car I never saw almost hitting me; at Union Station, crowding memories of leave-taking, of soldiers returning to tearful hugs; at Woodward and Lothrop's Christmas display windows, galled expectations I had tried to shake by looking hard at the gingerbread house that trapped Hansel and Gretel. Seeing each presence, here (as I am), not locked between my ears, but existing still.

✡

Along Sligo Creek I walked steep, wooded hills dusted with snow. Myrtle, green in winter, I remembered, and particular oaks and poplars that were still here. Self-conscious, lips tingling, I walked up to one, put my hand on its corrugated trunk, and said, "Hello, old fellow. I'll bet you remember me."

Fresh sights were forty-year-old memories too: here we played war, there a pool beneath big rocks where we held our breath underwater, and here a stretch for fast ice skating, and further on huge, half-buried boulders where robbers must have buried gold. Leaping sensations when I recalled that right here on a summer afternoon Dad killed the copperhead. Exactly here the spot on the woods trail where Dad found me oblivious to suppertime.

Sligo Creek, twisting, tree-shaded course of huge rocks, pools, stretches over pebbles—nothing so life-restoring—had been torn up end to end for a sewer line. (In the sixties, a neighbor friend told Mother.) Only the huge boulders remained; the creek now looked more ditch than living stream. But memories of summer afternoons came, of playing war (during World War II), of springtime's rushing cold current when, for the first time that year, I put my pale bare feet into glorious, living water.

Up on a wooded hillside I found what I had almost forgotten. Through the heart of what was now a large oak was a rusty strand of barbed wire; it came out on both sides. I remembered it from 1941 when we had first moved from the center of Takoma Park (across from Aunt Dessie) to

Hillwood, this new development. Then the strand of barbed wire was just under the bark, but it was still a mystery to me. It was October, leaves down, bare limbs up in chilly sky. Too young for first grade, I wandered afternoons in the leaf-crunching woods. A few days later, abrupting along here, I scared up cows that trotted and crashed away from me. Cows from Powell's farm on the other side of our housing development. Oh, I thought then, these woods and the land where Hillwood was, all once Powell's farm too. That barbed wire was from old times when Powell's farm came down over what was our little neighborhood of new houses and into these woods above Sligo Creek. That strand was from an old fence when this was a farm. The depth of what my five-year-old self saw, with the fact that *I knew something my mother and dad did not know,* glittered like quicksilver.

After that first discovery I often visited the oak with the barbed wire through it. As its leaves opened yellow-green, fell bronze, acorns green and then dirt-brown, the oak laid wood rings over barbed wire. The tree, and my knowledge of it, was a treasure to hold in my heart. It was as rich as the rock-tumbling music of the creek itself at the bottom of that slope.

When we moved from that neighborhood, I missed friends lost, but losing the creek, the woods, that oak tree—these left aching absence. We moved away to Bethesda (1948) and to Baltimore (1951), and I went out into adult life (1958). The oak was forgotten, or almost so, but it grew no less, season after season; with its vigor, and the fundamental mystery back of that vigor, it overcame the rusty thorns of barbed wire (as Daisy's toy bulldogs in the dream did not overcome the tightly bound cords).

Now, 1987, not looking for it, not consciously, I had found the oak again, big now, wire still there. While I had lived nearly fifty years— raged at Dad that Christmas, rushed to get married, fought despair and passion, watched Mother die—this oak had grown, not dissolving with wood rings what was nailed into it, but growing still. What I had found in 1941, that first sharp thrill, had now become profound mystery of great extent in time, of bottomless substance. The oak's beautiful story had become mine.

In snowy woods, awe blossomed like wild dogwood in springtime.

✿

Shortly after returning to Washington, I came up out of the Metro's dark rushing into bright downtown sunlight. In that cold air, straight across the street, I saw a neon tube sign in red, slanting, 1940s-style lettering: 11TH AND F HATS. I stopped; the crowd passed around me.

Stirrings, sad and resigned, joyful too. That sign, so clear in my memory, was right here in this bright December afternoon.

The big bus, lumbering downtown on Saturday afternoons in springtime, pulling to a stop. Out my window, seeing 11TH AND F HATS. "Look for the sign," Mother had said, grinning at me. "It says exactly what you want to know—Eleventh and F, that's where you get off." She was delighted at the coincidence; I was amazed at her command of the universe. My stop. I got up quickly, clambered off. Two blocks down F Street, two blocks up Thirteenth, and I was at Mrs. Neese's for my Saturday art lesson.

An apartment on the second floor, furniture removed, redolent of oils, of turpentine, brimming with full late-afternoon light glowing rose. Sensations so full I thought that if Mother knew, I would be punished. Just being there was getting away with something.

Mrs. Neese was a big, lively woman with strong hands and wrists. Her gray hair tumbled out of the hairpinned bun at the back of her head; she always was trying to tuck up stray strands with a clean finger. Sometimes she had pigtails. Her eyes, also gray like spring sky, changed constantly. She talked to me bluntly. The tip of her brush, where it touched was magic. When she liked something I had painted, her eyes filled with light and for a moment she stopped biting the corner of her lip, smiled big enough to warm the room, grasped my arm, squeezed it hard, and said, "That's it, Clay. Right there."

She always knew where I had enjoyed myself (secretly I thought) and those patches she praised. She also got me interested in doing increasingly difficult homework exercises in perspective. She took me to sketch the big church up on New York Avenue, and Mercury in the rotunda of the new National Gallery of Art, and a little park of summertime elms with shadows of cobalt blue. When I took a picture home, I did not mention how much pleasure I had making it. Mother said my pictures were excellent, but she was leery, too. She began to shrug off what I brought home. "Uh-huh," she said, not even turning from the sink to look.

Mrs. Neese lived in a garden apartment built along the other side of Sligo Creek. It was an apartment that faced north into the dark green of the creek gorge. Summers she painted, did not give lessons. But she asked if I would like to come to her apartment for a lesson once every two weeks; I was flattered, said sure. Her apartment, which was dark, messy, and musty-smelling, I did not like, but I did like her, and I loved (almost as much as baseball) art. My baby sister at home fussed all the time; Dad was working hard on moving us all to New Orleans, where he thought he could start up his own X-ray distributorship. My older friends were getting interested in girls.

When I asked about summer art lessons, Mother said no.

"How come?"

"Your father's money doesn't grow on trees."

I overheard her tell Dad that Mrs. Neese needed cash for the summer. This hurt, but I did not mention it. The next Saturday, I told Mrs. Neese I could not do it. Her gray eyes, which were flecked with rust, flared—me falling into them. I told her we could not afford it.

"You want to, Clay?"

"Yes, ma'am. I want to paint the creek." This blurted out.

She took my head between the palms of her strong hands, which smelled of linseed oil, and smiled, room getting warm—that good heat in my chest all afternoon. "Let's just do it for fun."

When I told Mother, she said, "Well, we don't want to be beholden to Mrs. Neese and I don't want you—under such circumstances—going over there to her apartment by yourself."

I argued.

Mother allowed me to go one time. The note from her said this was the first and last time. Mrs. Neese and I crashed down into the woods along the creek, to the spot I had chosen, and she collected her skirt around her knees, sitting in the sun on a rock at the edge of the creek while I struggled to paint what I saw. I got angry, scribbled up the canvas board. The sunlight and dappling shadows on her wide shoulders I could see; and her pig-tailed gray hair, arms bare, grasping her knees.

When Mrs. Neese realized I had wrecked a canvas, she got up, dusted twigs off the seat of her skirt, went up to her apartment, and returned with another prepared canvas. But the aching remained, mixed now with belly-churning anger. I threw raw color; I screwed up the perspective. And the creek I loved (and dreaded losing if we moved), now in late afternoon shadows, and Mrs. Neese with her back to me, down on the big rock across from where Dad killed the copperhead, I could not get it down. Light was too dark, all dissolving into black.

"Mrs. Neese," I called nice and loud. "Let's go, okay?"

When I got home, Mother gave me a lecture, "in no uncertain terms," about this being the last time I would see her this summer. (Her vehemence I understood, but not its source.) She did not care if we had been down at the creek, I was not going again.

After this, Mother's attention warmed. She told me she had thought a great deal about the matter and had concluded that I was better off enjoying boy things, baseball, "running in the woods," not taking up art lessons in the fall with Mrs. Neese. A knot of anger sat in my belly.

"You're all boy, Clay. You really want to take art lessons?"

A week or so later, I told Mother I did not. She said she would be delighted to call Mrs. Neese, thank her for what she'd done, and tell her I would not return. The next day she said Mrs. Neese had been very nice on the phone.

I never saw Mrs. Neese again.

✳

I waited for the return bus at O'Donnell's on E Street between Twelfth and Thirteenth. "Straight down Thirteenth to E, then left and look for O'Donnell's window. That's where you catch the bus." She knew O'Donnell's window fascinated me. It was crushed pure ice, even in summer, and arcs of scattered crabs and bilaterally arranged lobsters (antennae twitching), oysters (under gray, spitlike glop, pearls I was certain), and clams opened to the pink flesh, others closed on beautifully ringed shells. Tossed raw shrimp, gleaming. And fish sleekly silver, always seeming in motion. Big, shockingly pinkish red ones, others black as the ocean's depths, and others—big flat jobs—as coal-soot black on one side as sky white on the other. Into the lucidly clear eyes of the fish I stared: black pupils, a startled gaze. What had they seen in the ocean's depths? How was it wriggling in nets they could not escape, and being coal-shoveled into stinking holds of fishing boats. Seeing a gill twitch, looking into the clear unblinking dot-black eyes, I knew some were still alive, that they saw what was me on the other side of the glass, and I wished for their misery and suffering to end.

These thoughts were silent.

But while downtown on my own, I took sweet comfort from Mother's presence in the sign at 11TH AND F HATS and in the window at O'Donnell's Seafood. "You show me a boy," she said "who wouldn't love to feast his eyes on that. And when you're looking at that mess of fish, lobsters, you are exactly where you should be to catch your bus home." She loved her story, smiling, that beautiful gap between her front teeth. And she was right. Her story I did love, and on every single downtown trip, its sweet comfort protected me. Forsaking it, I would be alone.

Coming up out of the Metro that December morning and seeing 11TH AND F HATS, I was once again within her marvelous sphere—forty years and that boy again. In the next instant, lost forever. Standing on Eleventh Street in bright sunshine, I felt the gaping hole of Mother's death. My own stories, tangled-up darknesses, did not do what hers had done.

The hat store was vacant. A few days later I took pictures of that sign with its distinct 1940s-style lettering, and others of the elegant little building with its windows empty. As I expected, a few months later the sign that had been my comfort and guide forty-one years earlier was taken down, hauled off. The store now is JUDY'S BEAUTY AND HAIR SUPPLY, letters as abstract as computer print.

✡

When family came to sightsee, we sometimes took them to the Shrine of the Immaculate Conception, the spires and great vaults of which could be seen from a nearby hilltop where I galloped horses. Inside the monumental spaces of the shrine I was bored; but below, in dark tunnels exactly like Rome's catacombs (Christians hiding out to escape being slaughtered, even burying their dead there in little niches), there was the turmoil of a powerful story. The gift shop had a crucifix for sale. It was wood, and Jesus was real-looking, a crown of thorns. It was both strange and beautiful. With saved-up lawn-cutting money, I bought the crucifix and hung it by a nail driven into the wall above my bed. My friends, all Protestants, were curious, teased me. But my heart was stirred. Johnny Hill, however, goaded me with talk of graven images, the golden calf, sinfulness. I told him he was lying. We got into a fist-throwing fight and, headlocking him, I shoved his face into scratchy shrubs until he yelled "I give!" At night I lay in bed feeling Jesus' suffering up there from nails driven straight into the open palms of his hands, into his bare feet crossed over. I did not tell Mother.

Mrs. Denny, the mother of the boys who, later, gave me my bloody Sunday initiation, invited me to go with them to their Trinity Episcopal Church up in Takoma Park. I was nervous about it until Mother said, "Oh, why don't you go. It might be fun."

It was not. All the kneeling, standing, and sitting was confusing. But that stone-laid church, with its colored-window stories of Jonah, of Jesus listening to children, burned hot in me. Those blues, reds, purples touched my hands, shimmered with outside wind-stirred leaves. And the prayer book's rolling cadences, half the words unintelligible (to me), were music—not flat, staccato, punched up as in the Baptist church, but intricate, rising and falling like breathing. When I got home I told them I liked it. My heart was beating fast in the fullness of what had happened.

I started going regularly, although soon I was dismissed to Sunday school in the parish house basement. To my great amazement, Mother and Dad started going to Trinity Episcopal. They got confirmed there.

Although it was the beauty that stirred me, that still sings in my chest, I must admit that I was deathly afraid of Baptist baptisms since first witnessing one at age five. From under the stage a big tank was rolled out. If my head was put back like that, put under, I would be drowned. Nobody did I trust enough to let them do that to me.

From a little font, in a niche of the church with more beautiful story-windows (I remember the lambs, Jesus), I received the wet mark of a cross on my forehead—only that. God was not raving, teaching hopeless guilt, terror; God might be gentle, be stirred by beauty as I was.

✳

If Whitman's years in Washington were commemorated, I might have understood sooner that war is hospitals as well as heroic battlefields. From his digs in a cheap rooming house at the foot of Capitol Hill on Pennsylvania Avenue (now that triangular block once swarming with life is a flat green park), Whitman, dressed and scented, "pleased" with himself, set out to care for the wounded, the sick, the near dead. Over Tiber Creek, then an open sewer, he ambled. He crossed what is now the mall to the military hospital where the Air and Space Museum now stands. In huge wards the casualties of Fredericksburg, of Chancellorsville, of dreary winter camps, lay stinking, dying, and alone. (At Chimborazo in Richmond, Jacob Sowers was the same.) Whitman gave to the men little cakes, tobacco, and writing paper (often writing their letters for them), but it was his strength—rooted in the wood's earth of exuberant life (that is, in death too)—that Whitman gave to their suffering and despair. What courage sustained him day after day, month after month, year after year? Whitman reversed what I had always believed. I was his brother George, the soldier fighting battles, wounded, captured by the enemy.

Nothing marks where Whitman lived at the foot of Capitol Hill, or where he dressed wounds, or the place at Vermont Avenue and L Street where, in summer twilight, he saw Lincoln himself making his way in a carriage escorted by a troop of cavalry up to the higher ground at Soldiers' Home, where he might sleep better in Washington's muggy summer. What is not commemorated, in public as in personal life, is as significant as what is commemorated: General Logan, General McPherson, Uncle Billy Sherman, not the gift of Walt Whitman to American life.

He is one of my three self-catechized fathers. In the explosion of up-state New York springtime, I found him, an answer at last to all my fighting and military yearnings. William Faulkner is another. In the Webster Groves rented house I found him in 1964, two years after his death, the year when black people would no longer be absent in America. In Faulkner's best he speaks the terrible news that we have human courage enough to face the emptiness within ourselves. Where Faulkner lived and wrote, Rowan Oak, was just across a steep, darkly wooded ravine from the house off Lamar Street where he had lived as a child and fallen from innocence into first grief. The Mississippi he wrote was the Mississippi of my father's family from 1811 to 1903. Their woods and dirt fields I had walked. Faulkner seized on the inter-generational passage of loss (as it had seized upon him). He comprehended from within what is still not acknowledged in American life.

The third is Henry David Thoreau, whose sun-flecked pond was the redemptive reverse of Faulkner's dark woods and roaring-hot cotton fields and gutter-busted, decaying monuments to the vanity of human desire ("mausoleum[s] of all human hope"). I first read Thoreau on an island,

Isle au Haut, at the entrance to Penobscot Bay in Maine. He had passed here, I did not then know, on his trip to the Maine wilderness. Nearby was an island where there was a "house-dent," stacked rock walls running through 150-year-old second-growth timber, a beach of almost-singing pebbles. The site spoke of the hope of redemption by nature. My life then was a recent second marriage, a new job and life in Oklahoma, a great second chance in full swing. Despairing that my second chance was also empty, simply another version of my terrible abjectness, I seized on Thoreau. Back in Oklahoma this second chance shattered, and I descended to worst's worst. When I next visited Walden Pond in 1987, I understood that when I first looked into *Walden* I had really seen only my callowness and fear. Instead Thoreau, sentence after sentence, shows us that despair is not to be ignored or fled from but instead taken to Walden Pond. Only then can one's heart be eased.

That night in 1987, a cold one, I stood on the bridge over the Concord River as the moon rose over the hills to the east. I walked on across the bridge to the minuteman statue. It was above me, and all around it a profusion of stars. Thoreau's grave, a simple stone ("David") in the family plot of his father, was on that dark hump of a hill above which the moon was rising. Faulkner's grave was at the bottom of the cemetery slope down in Oxford, Mississippi—red clay silting out onto FAULKNER on the flat stone. And Whitman's remains lay with an uncarved boulder down in Camden, New Jersey. With fathers such as these, one may discover his own capacities. One can with them struggle despair into hope; inheritance into true choice, freedom; loss into restitution of love.

✳

Living in Washington, I was my father's father. We had dinner together every Sunday. We spoke of Mother, his boyhood in Oklahoma, the army, and our shared past. My memory included much that he had forgotten. We watched baseball games on TV. One included a recruiting commercial for the U.S. Army. A young soldier just out of recruit training is returning home to his father, who had disapproved of his enlistment. A brother meets him at the train station. Nearing their home, the young soldier becomes apprehensive. He goes up on the porch, enters the front door. He is greeted by his father's back, but then the man turns, grins, holds open his arms in welcome. Father and son embrace.

Quietly my father said, "I wish they had welcomed me."

He meant his 1930 return to Oklahoma, when he had wanted to go to college and had found his family living in dire circumstances. Almost every week, he brought up his lack of a college education. This wound he had carried in memory fifty years. Regret is in every life, I tell him. He was a great provider; we got good educations. And his grandchildren got good educations, one a lawyer, another preparing to teach U.S. history at a university. He nods.

Springtime and another visit, forsythia exploding in the cold, bright afternoon, lilacs—flower of memory—so pungently sweet, as I wheel him on the grounds of the nursing home. He leans forward in his wheelchair, though wind is in our faces. We cross the earthen dam of a pond; wind sweeps riffling sheets across the water, stinging cold.

"You cold, Dad?"

"Naw."

"You're a tough old guy."

He grins. His eyes are teary from the wind. "Tough enough," he says, smiling a little.

The wind strips apple blossoms in swirling pink clouds, but we go on, chins down, talking of his hard times. When I tell him of my plans to remain in Washington, he says, "Now you're talking, son!"

A few weeks later, when I tell him I have gotten a pretty good job, he says, *"Well by damn you got that job! You got that job, did you?"* He's happy; his emotions are direct.

"Yeah Dad," and tears are in my eyes.

Without work in which to lose himself, without vodka, he felt what most of a lifetime he had tried to forget. He was resigned, inarticulately sadder than I had ever seen him, but uncomplaining. He also took heightened pleasure in things: fried chicken, crab cakes, butter he spooned, news of his grandchildren, visits from my sister. He relished remembering the details of the stone house he had built for us in Baltimore (1951); he talked with warmth about the big garden he enjoyed tending at that house, a garden we did not have. I was glad to tell him a young family, with little children, now lived there. In almost every visit he told me that Mr. James Picker, who owned and was president of the X-ray company Dad worked for, had been a better father to him than his own Oklahoma father. He was right.

But always he spiraled back to those couple of days in Colera, summer of 1930, and further than that to 1922, his father suffering his mother's tirades of almost-consuming envy of her sisters and rage at him, E. R., for not giving her the life she thought she deserved. From Dad's bed upstairs at the back of the house, he heard the yelling down in the kitchen half the night.

Then one night Dad told me that Wilson, his older brother, a bully nearly twice his size, tried to sodomize him.

"What?"

"I never told anybody."

"Did he?" Dad meant something akin to male rape.

"No. But I wasn't sure I could keep him away. We shared a room. He was a big guy."

"This was when you ran away?"

"Yes."

"Why didn't you . . . ?" But no. In his shoes I would not have asked my folks for help. Wilson was the favored son, their Abel, their Jacob, and Dad was their Cain, their Esau.

"That's awful, Dad."

"As far as I'm concerned, I came out all right," he said. "I ain't complaining." He laughed at his slang.

And back still further, 1911 or 1912, to his earliest memory. He had malaria, bad fever, slept around the clock. When he woke up, he called out, but there was no answer in the empty house. Famished, he managed to get downstairs. On a high shelf he spotted a mixing bowl, crawled up on a chair, got it—fried chicken. He ate it all, became violently ill, vomited blood. He almost died. (Raw appetite, alone, no self-control; chicken or vodka, it was the same.) But now, dried out, he told me with the tone of his voice how he felt. That emptiness, and out of it, his strength, resolve, and intelligence rising up. Now he was back to losses that were his life's engine.

I felt contact with him.

✡

I helped him change sopped diaperlike pads, wet trousers; our good humor, a southern resource, did not desert us. When I put my arm around his shoulders, he grinned; the hard strength of him was now gone. My napkin I touched to stray food on his lip; he thanked me. When he ate with his fingers, I fought back revulsion at his ignoring the manners he helped to teach me. He kept a paper napkin, smeared with spittle and food, tucked between the buttons of his sweater. He resisted my attempts to replace the napkin with a clean one. From the dining room he filched napkins, which he stashed away in a dresser drawer. (Through most of his adult life he had picked up restaurant sugar and catsup packets, napkins, plastic forks, which he kept in a kitchen drawer. In this, scars of his past.) With the skill he had taught me, I tied his necktie.

At my house for Christmas or Easter, he was congenial. He pretended to hear when he could not. He used silverware, but often short-circuited with his fingers. He dropped food in his lap, what he used to do when drunk, but now we pretended we did not notice. Children were annoying to him: "Oh brother," he said of their small demands or protests, forcing a laugh. But from his heart he thanked us, looking straight into my eyes. And when I left him back in his nursing-home room, he said cheerfully, "Take it easy, son."

My heart filled with love for his rebellious spirit, for his toughness, for the dignity with which he sustained his life in a wheelchair.

After visits with him, driving home on dark country roads, I sang "Red River Valley," where he was born, "Mine Eyes Have Seen the Glory," and "Amazing Grace," songs I had sung in the misery of Oklahoma—weeping as I rocked my little daughter to sleep—now sung in good times, in my birthplace, on a road much like old Ballas Road in Saint Louis.

At a dinner with cousins, he announced, "I didn't know Clay until now. We've gotten to know each other."

That is the truth; he was eighty-two and I, fifty-two.

✡

Once I saw my father as he is to himself. In the suburban town house, Mother was upstairs dying of cancer and we, her returned family, lived in that slow time. Dad had been out for two hours, so we knew he would return drunk. Out the front window I watched him park, one wheel up on the curb. For a long while he just sat there. Then he slowly got out, closed the door. Bracing himself against the side of the car, he again waited. Then summoning his energies, he straightened up, started across the lawn toward the house. He began staggering, going faster—this heartrending, pathetic, hilarious. Then he swung a wide out-of-balance arc across in front of the window and, miraculously, did not crash into the wall of the garage but hit the door, went inside out of sight. Even closed the door behind him. He would be rooting out one of his vodka bottles stashed in his golf bag or in an old paint can. The air was stingingly cold. When I got out there, closing the door behind me, he was bracing himself over a trash can, hands on the round lid, head down. Panting breaths, vapor. In dimness I smelled dripped car oil, Mother's turpentine, the vodka on him.

"Dad, you okay?"

"Yeah."

And his hands still braced on that round lid, he rolled his face around and up toward me, some light from the dirty garage window catching on it. He had always been a sloppy drunk, but his blue eyes flashed wild with grief and his violent conviction that he should trust only himself—as drunk as he was, this not stilled.

"She's dying," he said. "She's lying up there in that bed and dying."

"Yeah, Dad."

"Goddammit to hell, I love her."

In him life burned.

✡

After my return to Washington, Dad asked to visit our Hillwood house in Takoma Park. Living here from 1941 to 1948, I was a kid, Mother trying to maneuver tending to me around her downtown job, and he an ambitious X-ray equipment salesman. As we turned off New Hampshire Avenue, started up the steep hill, he recognized our little brick two-bedroom house: "That's my house."

It was the first house he owned. Although at times his memory stumbled, he identified many nearby houses with neighbors from those years. He remembered Sligo Creek, so important to me, but to him it was, summer and winter, where I could be found. Driving through newer houses (built in the boom after World War II), I said, "Here's where we used to cut our Christmas tree when this was all woods and pines. We used to find flint arrowheads here too." He did not understand; I had crossed over into my memories.

Up in Takoma Park, he remembered the location in a row of stores where he got his haircuts at Nick's every other Saturday. It was now a Pizza Express. Two doors down had been Woolworth's—just a gap, must have burned out—where an older second cousin got me to steal a black click-click gun and then told the family. It marked my initiation into a world of right and wrong. This I did not mention. On Second Street was the bungalow we had rented in 1940–41 across the street from Aunt Dessie. He did not remember the house at all.

We drove by the prim Takoma Public Library, where we had gone on Tuesday nights without fail, all three of us; by the Takoma Park swimming pool; by the Takoma Park movie theater; and by Trinity Episcopal Church, which we had all joined. Except for the library, he did not recognize these as part of our public life.

"Dad, I'm going to take you to a place you probably won't recognize." His competitive spirit stirred.

We crossed into the District of Columbia. Recently I had noted the Kennedy Street address on my birth certificate. These two-story apartment buildings across from the Kennedy Theater were where we had lived on August 4, 1936. This was my first home.

Only once did Mother mention living on Kennedy Street. One winter Sunday afternoon (about 1946) when we emerged from the Kennedy Theater into eye-blinking bright, Mother had said, "We lived right there when you were born."

It had startled me. Often we had gone to the Kennedy. Why hadn't she ever mentioned this?

Pleas for more details brought her to say, "There's no more to tell," voice turtle-stubborn. As usual Dad hurried away from us toward our Dodge; he never uttered a word about Kennedy Street. But forty-some years later, we were on the other side of the street, in front of that little apartment. Instead of a pleasant neighborhood, Kennedy Street was now mean-looking, dirty, grim. Retail stores had barred windows, heavy iron-mesh gates for doors.

"I remember this place," Dad said to my surprise. "It was an efficiency.

We had a bed that pulled down out of the wall. Betty was supporting us when we lived here."

"You didn't have a job, Dad? You weren't working?"

"Oh, I was working all right, but Betty was making the money. We couldn't live on my salary. We couldn't eat without her check."

"And this is where we lived when I was born?"

"That's right."

Now 1936, the beginning of sensation.

✿

For the years from their marriage in 1931 to my birth in August 1936 and my memory's awakening in 1940–41, Mother had spun up a nice story. "We were young," she told me. "We were footloose and fancy free." At the drop of a hat, they moved from one apartment or rental house to another. This confection, which owes something to films of that era seen at the Kennedy Theater, did not completely hide the life-and-death struggles of those years.

Mother had mentioned that Dad, in those years, drank too much. Once at a party she had discovered him down in the basement in his white suit, "drunk as a skunk," wallowing around in a coal bin where he had fallen. Aunts and uncles from both sides of the family told me that they had never seen two people fight as meanly as Mother and Dad did in those years. "I wouldn't have bet they'd last 'til winter," Uncle Gat told me, shaking his head. All was not sunny skies or pennies from heaven for a couple of carefree kids making their happy-go-lucky way in the world.

Now I saw, clearly, what then I had only glimpsed.

Mother's confection reversed the true story. To marry Elizabeth, Dad had to give up his commission in the army. What he had gained, bootstrapping, was not status enough for her. (Here she was Daisy's daughter.) And while she found successes in the heady excitement of Roosevelt's New Deal, in the office of Harry Hopkins himself, Al faltered, backslid. He worked at low-paying jobs as a medical technician in hospitals where blood tests and X-rays reminded him of the education he did not have.

He drank hard on Saturday nights. He insisted on his sports. He asserted other white southern male prerogatives. But, clear-eyed about himself, he knew his lousy job was going nowhere. Snapshots from these early married years show Dad swaggering, a cocky tilt to his snap-brim hat, a cigarette in hand.

From small-town southern traditional lives, they both were unmoored. Their jumping from apartment to apartment was unrequited yearning. Al was desperate for satisfaction of his own loss-fired ambitions. Elizabeth had a desirable job, that flash of prestige and money; but she also had her own loss-fired and unrequited desire. She wanted to have children, be a mother—not like her own, Daisy, but in repudiation of her. To be her Aunt Myrtle and Grandmaw Kenerly. The absolute last thing Al wanted was a child. It's no wonder he remembered, in his eighty-second year, the exact apartment building on Massachusetts Avenue where I was conceived fifty-one years earlier. And nine months later on Kennedy Street, there I was, jaundiced, ugly, "like a little old man." Mother's romantic longings hit hard up against the cruel necessities of life in August 1936.

Al's pride required that he earn the money. His family he had fled, and now he had his own family to support. But no. He was not man enough to do it. His wife was the main breadwinner. His Oklahoma family's view of him as a no-account son, a black-sheep failure, was turning out to be all too true. Supported by his wife, all Al had was his male posturing. My birth in 1936 threw him back into the dark of 1930 and, further, to his folks' turning him out in 1922. As a baby he had not been welcomed, either.

My birth did the same to Elizabeth. Her own mother had turned away from this baby girl with Robert's fierce character. Then in 1931, Daisy's death-bed scorn of Elizabeth's rebellion was fierce, unrelenting. Now, five years after that, Elizabeth herself was about to become a mother. Motherhood she wanted, but she no less desired the independence that she had established as the basis of her considerable pride. As my birth approached, she could not see Daisy's shadow on all of her desires.

The plan seemed easy. First she and Al moved from the Massachusetts Avenue apartment to Kennedy Street, to be much nearer Aunt Dessie. Every day she would drop me off at Aunt Dessie's, then bus back downtown to the excitement of her job and the paycheck they needed. But a month after I was born, Aunt Dessie determined that I needed my mother. She loved having a baby to care for, but she told Elizabeth it plain was not right to deprive that baby of its natural mother. She told Elizabeth that she would just have to quit her job to take care of her little boy. Remnants of this struggle (which repeated the terms of Elizabeth's struggle for independence from her natural mother) occurred whenever Mother and Aunt Dessie discussed childrearing. With her fierce independence, Mother decided to thumb her nose at Aunt Dessie.

She arranged for a maid to take care of me, a country woman from North Carolina. (She wanted somebody like Aunt Myrtle or Grandmaw.) But of course the first of these women could not do things correctly, as specified in the latest theories, and she did not even understand how to buy groceries at the DGS. Mother fired and hired several of these country women, although each time she fired one she created a problem that required speedy solution. (When my sister was born twelve years later, Mother did the same. She hired unsophisticated women like Aunt Myrtle and Grandmaw whom the Daisy in Mother could not abide.) To fill in gaps in the care of the baby, Mother pressed Aunt Dessie for help or, anger rising and shading into despair, she herself took off from work to stay home with him.

As Washington's elms mottled yellow-brown, Elizabeth stayed with her job in FDR's administration, Al dragged himself down to his technician's job at D.C. General Hospital, and Clay stayed in the efficiency with a string of country women brought up from North Carolina.

"It didn't work," Al said that cold afternoon in the parked car.

In winter 1936–37 Elizabeth resigned her job, though they could not afford it. She had lost her modern woman's belief in her independence. That dream's reverse (the shadow of her mother) once more eclipsed Elizabeth.

Although my articulate memory did not exist, my life still stands on this hard-fought ground. After stowing the Murphy bed, with what prospect did Elizabeth regard the hours of the day? What spirit moved her hands, breath, the syntax of touch and action which the child learned? When she told me I slept best outside in a buggy, bundled in the cold, she also mentioned that the neighbors looked askance at her when she left, went inside, and went about her business. To check me, she looked out the front window.

"Your cry could wake the dead."

And it had awakened Daisy. (And no less the cold abandonment of Al's Oklahoma family.) In her prideful independence, how Elizabeth must have yearned for someone to help her. How as her independence (so connected with her work life) collapsed, must Elizabeth have yearned with choking grief for the excitement of her Harry Hopkins New Deal job. And heaped scorn on herself for believing she could have a baby and work. While out the front windows the marquee across the street at the Kennedy Theater mocked her with the names of glamorous Hollywood stars and movie titles pulsing with romance and adventure and pure escape. As winter days tolled through the little apartment, the baby crying hard, Elizabeth lost her bearings in that excruciating and abject mix of guilt, self-pity, rage, and abiding despair. It is my belief that forty-seven years later, in 1983, when Mother herself died, my little daughter was born, and I nearly lost my job, I felt as she had. And this affliction may persist, too, in the lives of my children.

About to lose everything, Al put aside his fierce male pride and independence. Rummaging in the corners of the family that had rejected him, he found his mother's uncle, who was then a U.S. senator from Mississippi. He went up to Capitol Hill to see Senator Patterson and to ask for a job at the Glendale TB sanatorium, which was to open soon for federal employees. The senator called a few people, and Al got the job heading the lab and the X-ray facility. From the dark terrors of Kennedy Street they moved way out to Glendale. Mother thought she did not need Aunt Dessie at all. Cut loose from family ties, even to Aunt Dessie and other relations in Washington, they were free of dependencies, independent, but therefore falling.

✶

Out on a lonely country road near Glendale, the little shingle house had no neighbors. Elizabeth was home all day with me while Al was away all day with the car. Her old job now was the afterimage of a romantic novel read long ago. Her family, even Aunt Dessie (now three bus rides away), considered her strange for moving so far away and to a remote house. Within the dreary walls of the rented house, baby crying, country silence tolling in her ears, Elizabeth's spirit collapsed. At night when she ought to be sleeping, she read Edgar Allen Poe.

"The well ran dry," she had told me.

She feared for her mind.

She feared she could not take care of the boy.

Al told her she had to get hold of herself.

Mother left, taking me, and went home to North Carolina to her father and stepmother, Mama Mae, who was a nurturing woman like Aunt Dessie. Flying off to independence in Washington had again circled back to North Carolina, but this time it was likely permanent. How did she face the scathing and cracker-funny humor of her father? How did she face her traditional sister, Vada, married to the town druggist? And how her traditional married friends to whom Washington was the moon? The damage to her pride, her most precious possession, was huge and the equal of Al's when he could not support the three of us at my birth.

"Insult was added to injury," she told me. In October a letter arrived from a gossipy acquaintance back in Glendale. Taking one look at the envelope, its fussy handwriting, Elizabeth immediately knew what news it contained. In the house built by her mother's great-uncle in love and obligation to his brother lost as the Confederacy fell, Elizabeth went quietly into the parlor, which, her mother then long dead, was little used. She closed the door behind her. She sat in her mother's platform rocker.

"Damn you, Albert," I think she said. "Just damn you."

She could not tell her father or Mama Mae.

That night after a dinner she could not eat, she took the boy out on the back porch, drew a basin of water, had him sit in a chair, and lathered his feet. The little bones—so intricate, fragile. He was quiet, as if he understood her. Bitter tears stung her nose. She was about to sob.

Roughly she dried his feet with a towel hung on the nail.

Going back through the kitchen, she saw her father reading, as usual, the Salisbury paper spread out on the oilcloth of the table. She saw the shouting headlines. She wished the news weren't *always* so bad from Europe, this Hitler.

Their room upstairs was the one she had shared with Vada. As Clay's solemn eyes watched her, she lit the wick of the kerosene lamp. She got him over the slop jar, that light ringing, then put the lid on—heard chinking die into stir of early evening noises outside. She wondered if next door Aunt Pheny, awful old thing, who had smelled scandal the second Elizabeth arrived, would now catch a stronger scent.

"Stay, Mom."

"You're not afraid, are you?"

"Stay?"

"All right."

She kissed him, sat down in a squeaky cane-bottom rocker. Still unusually quiet, the boy watched his mother rock, that song in twilight, until his eyes floated closed. Then in Elizabeth's eyes tears welled up, ran down her cheeks. In this room she had hatched so many of her daring plans—dodging her mother's scrutiny to fly with devil-may-care barnstormers, steeling her nerve to actually go up to Washington. No more. At the end of her rope. That was it, plain and simple.

When she told Aunt Myrtle about Al, that country woman had hard-headed advice: "It don't matter, sweetheart, what Al's done, or didn't do. That's his business. You know your place and your baby's place is with your husband. There ain't any other way to figure it."

In Aunt Myrtle's furniture-cluttered parlor Elizabeth struck the tough bargains she kept to her last breath.

"More than for myself, Clay, I went back for you," she told me on that trip to Stafford. "I didn't blame him. He thought I was gone for good."

Swallowing all that remained of her pride, tasting bitter broken dreams, Mother determined to return to Washington and Al. With iron will she would endure shame, but life's bright, sweet promise would be hers no more.

She and I returned on the Southern. Maybe Dad arranged his golf or work to meet her and the boy at Union Station. Within a month, to escape the terrors of the little Glendale house and some of the shame of Al's infidelity, we moved to Greenbelt, a brand new federal community and an FDR hope-building project for the struggling lower middle class. Elizabeth got neighbors, new friends.

✡

On our trip down to Stafford Hall, Mother left out a detail about her return to Washington with me in 1939. She could not bring herself to add this. On the last night of our last visit, she fixed my favorites for dinner: cheese grits, homemade slaw, green beans cooked with ham hock. As everybody drifted away from the table, she began to talk urgently to me in her darting, upcountry-South way: "Now you be sure and take that painting of the little boy and wagon. I want you to have that."

It was a dreamscape, blues of El Greco, with a crying boy in bib overalls, a busted wagon.

She would live ten more years, I was certain.

There was no transition. "You remember what I told you about the well running dry."

"Yes," I said, looking up into her brown eyes, which caught the lighted candles.

"Well, the nurse your father was running around with was Georgia, of Vince and Georgia."

"Georgia? Naw——."

"Yes, it was. Listen to me." Anger flashed in her eyes.

"You said the woman wasn't married."

"She wasn't when she and your father had their to-do. She met Vince after that."

Georgia, of Vince and Georgia, with whom Mother and Dad had played bridge for nearly forty years! As a child, once a month on Friday night I was hauled out to Cheverly, Maryland, where they lived, and put to bed under a blanket on top of Georgia and Vince's bed. I thought I would never get to sleep, their voices mumbling downstairs, occasional shouts of excitement, and then Dad, being gruff but gentle, was lifting me in his strong arms. As he carried me downstairs, Georgia, who remained without children, smiled brightly up at me. Mother, happy to see me, asked if I would like some of Georgia's wonderful cake before we went home.

Too sleepy, I usually said no.

One other Friday night a month Vince and Georgia would come to play bridge at our house in Takoma Park.

When Georgia inserted clamps in my scalp that bloody Sunday, 1945, I was blind to that moment's moral complexity. My first fall into vulnerability was linked through Georgia to Mother's final fall, what set her adult course. How could Mother possibly be bridge-playing friends for forty years with the woman who committed adultery with her husband? How could her fiery southern pride and hot temper, her lashing out at women

(Mrs. Parker, Mrs. Neese), possibly accommodate remaining friends with the woman who had shamed and humiliated her?

But I do understand now.

For Mother's ways I now recognize in myself. Elizabeth continued to socialize with Georgia in order to perpetuate self-mortification and to show Al that she would not forget, even for a split instant, both what had happened and what, at her father's house and at Aunt Myrtle's, she had determined with fierce willfulness to do about it. She reminded Al and herself of that pride-annihilating wound on Friday nights for forty years. She kept it center stage. She asserted her mastery of adultery, her strength of mind, her self-denying devotion to me the child, whenever they met for bridge. It cost her, the festering of that wound, but for her grief she gained control of Al and Georgia. Vince, I think, was innocent of the whole business.

The crux of Mother's strong character, its terrific, reason-defying reversals, is here. After we returned from North Carolina and were living in Greenbelt, she wrote a novel, which she called *Marriage Bliss and Blisters*. Her first attempt to gain mastery of this terrible thing that had happened in her life, the novel contained a good bit of Dad's indiscretion with Georgia. When he discovered and read it, he burned every page in an incinerator. (When Mother told me this with Dad present, she attempted to make it a funny story. I was shocked. Dad did not utter a single word of apology.) It was after he destroyed her novel that Mother's genius made this exquisite substitute which, twice a month, proved her steely resolve.

About 1975, long before I knew about Georgia and Dad, I asked Mother why she did not anymore mention Georgia and Vince, who I knew had retired and kept a place at Nags Head, North Carolina. Mother said, "I guess you'd say we've had a falling out."

"Meaning?"

She bristled: "Meaning just that, a falling out."

Something of the delicate counterpoises Mother maintained with her strong intellect had slipped with the years. If not this, then Georgia, also in her late sixties, thought to unburden herself to Vince about that little indiscretion with Al in 1939 when she was a single nurse at Glendale. Vince, from Brooklyn, a navy officer in WWII, had a bully's easily wounded pride.

✶

Here a wider prospect opens. Mother allowed to stand in her life the exact sin, adultery, that her grandmother (Elesia) attempted to annihilate by marrying one of Lee's honored Lost Cause veterans. Elesia was fleeing her mother's, Harriet's, adultery and its living consequence, blonde, curly-headed little Mary and the ear-burning shame of her. That Harriet was not at the time married, her husband dead in Virginia, mattered not one iota. In the South in 1865 it was *terrible adultery* for a Confederate widow to have intimate relations with anybody—but with a blue-belly Yankee officer, my lord in heaven! And besides, that Yankee was married. So Elesia, never truly free of her mother's shame, taught all of her daughters, very much including Daisy, passionate revulsion of flesh in all its manifestations. That is, Elesia taught Daisy the offices of a southern lady, a Christian one. And this compelled Daisy both toward vigorous Robert, on one hand, and on the other toward Tennysonian seclusion, her poetry, and her damn toy bulldog (which will not absent himself from my dreams). And Daisy did unto her daughters as had been done unto her. She instructed Elizabeth in the same office, in the same passionate revulsion of the flesh. And the lesson took, for Elizabeth, although rebellious, feared physical activity and in vigorous Al sought compensation for this denial. But Daisy's lesson to Elizabeth also *did not take*. For Elizabeth allowed adultery, sin of sins, to stand in her life, exactly as her mother and grandmother were in unceasing flight from it. None committed that sin. But Elizabeth for a lifetime accepted the shame of its being committed against her and publicly broadcast, I am sure, by the gossip who wrote to inform her. Her mother's obverse she reversed.

To reject Harriet's adultery bound it more tightly into the fabric of their lives and thus into the legacy they passed to their children. Elizabeth, accepting that sin, violated in an outrageous way the code her dead mother had lived by. She most assuredly was *not* entirely her mother's daughter. And there may have been another small gain. Perhaps Elizabeth did not just seek to cancel her mother's strictures as much as she sought to align herself with her great-grandmother Harriet, that larger-than-life woman, who, newly widowed, in the aftermath of, let us hope, the worst killing and most devastating war ever on the North American continent, found in her heart love, still, of the enterprise of life. Yes, at nerve-root of it all, love and love's loss.

✡

With the fierceness of her damaged heart, Mother loved me. And who among us does not have a damaged heart? My existence reminded her of loss and of loss's bitter compensations. These weaves and counterweaves, obverse and reverse, come down through generations to me. Their persistence is the strongest testament I know of to love's persistence, even when that persistence is itself denial. The beauty of this inheritance is almost sufficient compensation for its inclusion of a dark hating of life. Mother loved me and she taught me to walk straight into life's roaring fire. Life without passion I cannot comprehend.

Finding the impress of inheritance, the exact figure of despair and hard yearning that comes down to you through the workings of time, history, and family, is to find one's self. To begin to find true freedom.

To flee despair and light out for the territories loses the moral universe and thus makes us atoms of self, prisoners of inheritance, not free at all. (It also loses the courage in one's inheritance.) Stand, I tell myself, do not allow fear to sit in your stead, look straight at griefs, huge losses, terrifying absence. Consider the workings of intergenerational symmetries and there discover the greatest testament on this earth to the unfailing power of love and the prospect of human glory. Tonight, in moonless dark, I discern the abiding figure of my life, that mottle of lament with joyful noise.

Love is deeper, broader and stronger, than we have thought; it is time's mighty river.

Last Glimpses

At Greenbelt, Maryland, 1939, memory begins.

I am on our old brown mohair couch. Mother grasps my head in her hands. She tries to hold it still as I thrash, and Dad, blocking my arms with his body, pries open my jaws with his strong fingers. His other hand rams a tart, alcoholy swab right to the gag at the back of my throat. "It's for your own good, son," he says, voice tight with our struggle. "It's what the doctor ordered." Mother's hands tighten; it is going to happen *again*. They are stronger, and I cannot twist away. I fight anyway, thrashing, gritting my teeth until forced open. But in my vision is not his face, nor mother's inverted face above me. My eyes have moved to my right, out over the hump of the mohair couch, through the window, and up to tall pine trees in gray winter sky. In what fills my eyes is anchoring calm. Within the gag, within the fright of perfect weakness, I make this calm.

✿

Another early memory took place in Greenbelt. This occurred, if I'm figuring correctly, the following summer, 1940. My four-year-old self is running across streets, and the sun's warm presence is spread across my back. Urgency, the rush of disobeying. At the bottom of the hill is the grocery store. Through the delicious feeling of doing the forbidden rise desperation and panic. Approaching the store, I see several women, grinning, pointing at me, and I realize suddenly that my mother is not there.

Immediate crying because, although I have been running away from her, it devastates me to reach a place where she is not. Within a few minutes Mother comes to get me. She, amused by all this (perhaps then, certainly in subsequent years), told me I ran away constantly. She said I was a difficult child.

✡

Greenbelt is in a third memory from the summer of 1940, as Hitler's Panzers rolled through Europe and the British evacuated Dunkirk, as my father worked at his medical-technician job at the Glendale TB sanatorium. Because this memory lacks the pure sensation of those recollected above, and because in it there are unaccountable memory gaps along with a definite moral tone, I conclude that I am beginning to become human, with a moral sense.

The event itself, as opposed to its aftermath, I have no direct memory of. That day was hot, and memory begins as I walk out from the apartment's cool into the warm afternoon. Mother has seized my hand and marches me along. In the square behind the buildings there are sandy dirt, scraggly patches of grass, and tall pines (scaly-barked) that rise into the needled tops up in the hot white sky. Across the way from us, there is a sandbox. In stippled amber shade, mothers' heads lift, look, stare—then the kids. I am embarrassed to be in a just-ironed playsuit Mother has put on me, but I also understand it is not the playsuit they stare at. A mother and a girl come toward us, also remaining on the sidewalk. We meet. The mother's voice I hear but not her words. The little girl's voice, too. Her face is lowered.

"Say you're fine, Clay," Mother's extremely pleasant voice says. "Accept her apology."

My sentient life begins here. With a bursting sensation I realize that what Mother told me to do in the sanctum of her bedroom, shades drawn for summer coolness, is exactly what now I should do. She had dressed me in this starched playsuit. It startles me that *then* is related to *now*. At that instant I know, suddenly, that my eye hurts, that on my right eyelid and temple rides a white blob of bandage, that under it my eye stings and is swollen. (I can't explain why I was not, until then, aware of this. I can't account for why I didn't and don't then or now remember in any way the injury itself.)

I hesitate. I know the sting and throb of my eye is the truth. I know everybody can see the big bandage.

I mumble something. I have not made Mother glad, but I have not, either, made her mad. She is all I aim to please.

And as Mother chats nervously with the other mother, I look to my right, past that woman—this vivid, not adult retrospect—to the wall of a nearby apartment building, screens darkening the interiors (making them seem sweet) and the white-painted brick is gauzy with sunlight and faint blue pine shadow. I have a sensation of waking. A voice in my mind says, "Oh, this is how it is."

Eye throbbing, confused by the moral complexity into which I have blundered, I grasp loss for the first time, grief (a death has occurred) and, also for the first time, surging wonder at the discovery, at last, of the world—at what I would call, today, its presence. The self I am began in that moment.

My mother enjoyed telling and retelling the story of Clay, out at Greenbelt, getting pushed into a garbage can by a little girl. That I am at fault for allowing this to occur I continue to feel. When I look in the mirror at my sixty-year-old face, I see that scar on my right eyelid and I have a twinge of shame. But I have no memory of how I stupidly allowed this to occur. Or memory of the incident itself. Or memory of the little girl other than an impression of sulkiness.

✼

There is one other memory from Greenbelt. They told how I painted my Uncle Rob's black car with white paint; and how I escaped the house to play naked in the front yard with the hose, dousing anyone, including Mother, who came to take it away from me; and my uncles, aunts, and older cousins say that I as a small child was a terror and fearless. But these incidents I do not remember.

It is, instead, a moment when I stood in front of our old, beat-up vegetable bin, a green tin thing which sat at the top of the cellar steps, on a landing, just outside the cellar door. It smells musty, of potatoes and onions. I am staring at it.

For years I wondered why the sight of this insignificant object should be one of my earliest memories. Late in my thirties, as my own children entered high school, I read Nabokov's great autobiography, *Speak, Memory*.

He recounts his entry into time. It is an elegant moment in the family's summer-home garden, his birthday, strolling hand in hand with his father, his mother.

And casting back into my earliest memories for an equivalent moment, I recalled the vegetable bin at the top of the cellar stairs. With a refreshing jolt I recollected not only that vegetable bin but the rattly sound of the house's rooms, the empty of pots and pans kitchen cabinet where I had played, the couch-place empty but for wooly-bears. This vegetable bin, with earthy aroma of potatoes, I thought *eternal, always and forever exactly here*. But now, no. It is changing with us to our new house across the street from Aunt Dessie.

That autumn of 1940 I entered time, change, and thus first glimpsed my own death which is now, as I write, much nearer.

✿

It is then the bungalow across from Aunt Dessie's in Takoma Park. I stand on the wooden kitchen steps. Dusk is lavender and the hedged-in backyard slopes steeply away. Inside the dark sheen of the screen door is the kitchen. To have sugar bread for dessert, Mother said, I had to stand out on the back steps.

The screen door latch clicks. Out comes Mother's hand with the bread glop-smeared with butter and sprinkled with sugar. I take it, take a big bite. Sweet rushes with shivers, mixes with cooling summer dusk, bluing shadows, and the remaining light in the sky. Split with happiness, rush of pure sensation. As I eat the delicious bread, sugar sprinkles off onto my bare feet and grits the step. Then my face, my mouth, I press against the tang of screen door. The hedges drop into pure dark; light inside the kitchen remains cheerful. The screen latch clicks, out comes Mother's hand with another sugar bread. I take it. As I bite gooey sweet, the screen latch clicks back. I am anxious in the dark outside. In this moment of summer, 1941, I have discovered pleasure, beauty, and its accompanying sadness.

✿

On a Sunday morning that autumn, 1941, my memory tells me I discovered what is just as essential. It is blustery as Mother angrily jerks me out onto the front porch of the Takoma Park bungalow. Dad, down the sidewalk at the curb, dressed up too, looks at me, snaps at Mother.

He says in my overcoat I'll burn up.

She says it is cold, that I'll freeze, but jerks me around, back through the door—its glass rattling—into the house, where, roughly, she strips off the coat.

Just as roughly she hauls me back out on the porch where, seeing me, Dad's eyes flare angrily.

I do not know if it is cold or hot. I do not know if I want to wear a coat. I do not know what to think. Then a voice inside my head says, "I don't want to be here. I don't want to be here." My voice—that of my self-consciousness—announces its view of the situation.

We were going to Petworth Baptist Church. That Sunday morning a knotted historical legacy came to me. They did not understand this then, nor did I later understand when I performed the same office with my children.

✿

Now I live in a little white clapboard house, a proper colonial revival of the 1930s sitting up high on its lot. It has a sitting porch off the living room, with a swing, and two stories above, an attic dormer window on our double-hip roof. My house is inside the District of Columbia by a few blocks, in the same belt of near-in neighborhoods as Kennedy Street and Takoma Park. Just a couple of miles from here is the Bethesda house that remains my imagination's home. The year after my house was built, Mother and Dad married. Courting, taking drives in Dad's Chevy, they may have happened down this one-block street or by it on nearby River Road—the oldest road in this region, used by Indians, colonials, Washington and Jefferson, and Union Civil War regiments. A block from my house is a small park, Fort Bayard in 1862–65, where gun emplacements remain visible on the crown of a sharp little hill.

In 1990 the woman from Chicago and I got married here in Washington, where we both work. My job is not unlike Whitman's clerking. As dawn rises, as light changes subtly through the day, as spring and autumn explode, my heart revolves also. This is solace to the frantic pace, the compulsions, the horns blowing the instant stoplights change.

In 1992, February, we had a baby, my fourth child. She is named Elizabeth after Mother. Although I worry about death taking me before Elizabeth gets set up in life, she is minute by minute a source of true joy and hope, a blessing of my days. First seeing her face as the light-glossed placenta was stripped away, I noticed the intensity in her eyes, her little being, and confirmed what I had suspected, that character is inherited. She is an exuberant child.

After work I take her to the nearby park. She loves the swing, tall slide, trucks and buses noisily passing. At the end of the day, we are alone, shadows rising up. Behind the ill-kept, fenced-in play yard is the fort's steep hill, darkening too, that goes up to a sharp crest. There are shagbark hickories in a grove silhouetted by embering sunset. Their leaves, mottles of oxblood and burnished gold, catch the sunset. And their glow in gathering dark does satisfy the heart's terrible yearning. Then the western sky is suddenly plum, and the hickories at the crest, which I associate with Mother and hickory switches, become for a moment incandescent, fill the rising dark of the city with their brilliance. Light up my face, open mouth with wonder, and Elizabeth's. Then gone, dark rising out of the earth's shadows, up through the trees, deepening the bruise-blue of the sky.

Beautiful, says my heart.

Then the pale scythe blade of a new moon rides the darkening sky to the south, and, hugging my treasure close to my chest, I think that life is wonderful. Yes, this is plenty.

The woman from Chicago and I have found happiness. In my bones I hear my life's woeful song—burden and sorrow of many failings. But in it, too, not to be missed, is the bright, swift melody of my days, of rising hope; I think I heard it first by the soft tumblings of Sligo Creek.

Elizabeth's name is from her grandmother, dead almost ten years before she was born, and from (with Daisy's assent) her grandmother's paternal grandmother, Elizabeth Earnhardt Kenerly, who as a little girl saw the killing of war, brothers lost, and, in 1865, her daddy lost to absence, which is worse than death. It is joy, thwarted, that gives heavy sorrow to our losses.

I point up at the new moon riding above the darkening shadows of hickories.

"Sweetheart, see the moon?"

She looks up, eyes full of the sky's remaining light, and I see her smile. "Touch?" she asks. "Touch moon?"